Critical Acclaim for *Red Wine*

"Forget what you think about wine books, that they're stuffy or snobby or will put you to sleep faster than drinking a bottle. *Red Wine* isn't a book made to collect dust on your shelf, it's a book made to be used. . . . Quick references make the book super user-friendly and a must-check before running out to the wine store. . . . I'm seriously hoping these guys are plotting a follow-up on white wine. Unlike so many other wine books that do just sit on my shelves, this book has been commuting from my coffee table to my dining table and back, being absorbed bit by bit. While I'm learning a lot about these globe-trotting grapes as I go, it doesn't feel like an effort, it feels like the enjoyment of drinking red wine."　　　　**—Huffington Post**

"This new, definitive resource . . . [is] perfect for wine newbies and experts alike."

—Marie Claire

"With eye-catching photography and engaging anecdotes from winemakers the world over, *Red Wine* is . . . a great, easy-to-read resource with tasting notes, food pairings, and more for every major red wine grape. . . . A great gift for the novice and geek alike."

—Wine Enthusiast

"Fantastic . . . my copy has grown dog-eared and wine-stained from regular use."　**—Forbes**

"User-friendly. . . . The combined expertise of the three wine minds behind this guide is equal to almost a century's worth of wine education and experience."　　　　**—Forbes.com**

"It's a great introductory book for a new wine lover—the chapters are short and punchy but thorough—and also a very solid reference text for true experts as well. *Red Wine* is their most ambitious, interesting, downright-useful effort yet . . . a great addition to your wine library, whether as the first entry in your collection or the 100th."

—Santa Barbara Independent

"The book's superb format deftly presents what otherwise might be an overwhelming cache of useful and intriguing information. In fact, the authors recommend dipping into and out of the volume over time while drinking examples of each of the red wines covered. Can't argue with that sound advice."　　　　**—Dave's Wine Cellar**

"It's easy to read and gets right to the heart of the matter with engaging and in-depth details. The authors recommend reading up on the grape varieties before, during, or after drinking a bottle of red wine. Now doesn't that sound like fun?!"　　　　**—The Wine Chef**

"Simply stated, an exceptional book."　　　　**—Wineormous**

WHITE WINE

The Comprehensive Guide to the
50 Essential Varieties & Styles

Mike DeSimone & Jeff Jenssen

FOREWORD BY **Rob Mondavi Jr.**

Countryman Press

An Imprint of W. W. Norton & Company
Celebrating a Century of Independent Publishing

For information about permission to reproduce selections from this book, write to
Permissions, Countryman Press, 500 Fifth Avenue, New York, NY 10110

For information about special discounts for bulk purchases, please contact
W. W. Norton Special Sales at specialsales@wwnorton.com or 800-233-4830

Manufacturing by Toppan Leefung Pte. Ltd.
Book design by Chrissy Kurpeski
Production manager: Devon Zahn

Countryman Press
www.countrymanpress.com

An imprint of W. W. Norton & Company, Inc.
500 Fifth Avenue, New York, NY 10110
www.wwnorton.com

978-1-68268-784-0

10 9 8 7 6 5 4 3 2 1

To our friends in the world of wine who always
have welcomed us with open arms and open bottles.
Thank you from the bottom of our hearts
and the bottom of our wineglasses!

CONTENTS

FOREWORD

ONE OF THE FIRST TIMES that Mike, Jeff, and I enjoyed a glass of wine together took place at Auction Napa Valley on a sunny, beautiful, warm day. Vineyards growing grapes for Napa's iconic reds surrounded us, but we chose to drink a crisp, slippery, succulent To Kalon Sauvignon Blanc—and not only because of the heat of the day. We chose this delicious white wine because of its allure as well as its bracing minerality and stony complexity, with full-on flavors of white peach and lime. I remember that day and wine vividly because of the visceral pleasure of enjoying both with great friends.

Many people assume that I, a fourth-generation winemaker and grandson of the man who created Fumé Blanc, have a fairly balanced passion and understanding of both red and white wines. But the truth is, until just a few years ago, my tasting habits gravitated strongly toward red wines. The robust scents of grapevine-grilled lamb, succulent stocks bubbling on the stove, and the aromas of both red and white wines that I was "in charge" of opening for family gatherings and events imbue the memories of my youth. During this time, red wines played center stage, but the first wines I recall enjoying weren't red. They were white wines, a dry Chenin Blanc and the tasty treasure of a sticky, late-harvest Sauvignon Blanc.

Our business, vineyards, and guest tastings focus on Cabernet Sauvignon, so I eagerly devoured Mike and Jeff's previous book, *Red Wine*, which expanded my knowledge of that variety and other reds not grown in Napa Valley. When they asked me to write the foreword to this book,

their heartwarming invitation reignited my deep passion for white wine, and it's my hope that it will inspire you as well. Just as my family proved key to my understanding of wine, so I hope that this book will act as your cipher to unlocking some of its many mysteries.

White wines require ferocious attention to detail in the vineyards and in the cellar to achieve greatness. They demand an astute yet gentle-handed winemaker to showcase the vines and varietal character and display the soul of the grape within the glass. This book shares those nuances, those wine-expert pearls, and Mike and Jeff's personal perspectives of the regions and cultures add tremendous color, making this book rich in detail and a page-turning joy. The challenge with great authors, such as Mike and Jeff, is pinpointing similar distilled, descriptive details of their work. It seems unfair to the breadth of their delicious content. As wine lovers and professionals, they have mastered being approachable and engaging, and their inspired content calls me to continue the exploration of white wines both in the glass and via travel.

This book truly inspires me, and it's an honor to share these few, heartfelt remarks about how special I feel to write their foreword and how meaningful their work is in the world of wine. As their friend, I can tell you that their voice and heart infuse each page of the book, giving it life, texture, truth, and relevance. I hope you use it both as a proper reference guide and also to inspire your senses.

Warmest regards,
Rob Mondavi Jr.

INTRODUCTION

ARCHAEOLOGICAL EVIDENCE TELLS US that we humans have been drinking white wine for many thousands of years. The quality of today's wines no doubt improves on what people drank in antiquity, but the residue of white wine found in amphorae in the tombs of the pharaohs speaks volumes about the historical importance of the paler fruit of the vine.

Several countries advance competing claims as the "birthplace" of wine, but archaeological and documentary evidence points to the Middle East, eastern Asia, and the Mediterranean basin. Stone crush pads and potsherds highlight the importance of wine at religious festivals and at the tables of royals and commoners alike. Unearthed in Georgia (country), sarcophagi bearing images of wine pitchers and drinking vessels bear witness to winemaking there occurring at least 7,000 years ago. Scientists have carbon dated fossilized grape seeds from Macedonia to 4000 BCE.

Ancient poetry from the Babylonians and Phoenicians also mention wine. At that time, merchants shipped clay amphorae containing numerous liquids, including wine, throughout the Mediterranean. We have ample evidence of winemaking taking place on Crete and other Greek islands as well as in what today are Moldova, Türkiye, Armenia, Lebanon, Israel, and China, among other locations.

The Homeric tradition sang of the "wine-dark sea," clearly alluding to red wine, but the Greeks of old drank wine made from white grapes shipped across the Aegean Sea in clay amphorae sealed with pine resin. This Retsina style survives today, and you can learn more about it in the chapter on Assyrtiko (page 10), a grape that hails from Santorini. In ancient Thrace, the cult of Dionysus celebrated the fruit of the vine with wine made from wild grapes, sweetened with honey and blended with water. From that period, about 90 percent of drinking vessels

LEFT *The Happy Violinist with a Glass of Wine* (c. 1624) by Gerrit van Honthorst

relate somehow to wine. A Cypriot chalice that survives from the 500s BCE features the inscription "Be happy and drink well."

No matter where it started or who did it first, ancient winemaking was a relatively simple process with minimal intervention. This is the secret formula to wine and all other alcoholic beverages:

Sugar + yeast = alcohol + carbon dioxide

It's that simple! Farmers grew grapes, harvested them, crushed them, and allowed them to ferment using the yeast occurring naturally on their skins. The resulting wine went into clay vessels for storage, and the producer usually mixed it with water when serving it.

Any history of wine, however brief, must touch on the writings of Pliny the Elder, a Roman statesman, soldier, and scholar who died in Pompeii during the eruption of Mt. Vesuvius in 79 CE. Prior to his time, religious and legal texts often mentioned wine, but Pliny wrote about the qualities of the wines themselves and their potential health benefits. He mentioned the famous Falernian wine, a high-alcohol white from Campania probably made from Greco (page 82). He also wrote about Picinum, an ancient version of Prosecco (page 214), as well as a still, Roman-era forerunner of Franciacorta (page 216). More than 2,000 years later, Italians and people across the globe still enjoy these wines.

By the Middle Ages, winemaking centered in Europe, where the process retained its relative simplicity. Priests and monks made it for religious purposes, with the Benedictine and Cistercian orders as two of the largest producers in today's France and Germany. Around this time, winemakers recorded differences in wines made from grapes grown in different areas or soils. So began the process of charting and naming vineyard blocks.

Winemaking moved from Europe to the New World in a variety of ways, though mostly with ties, direct or indirect, to the Catholic Church. In South Africa and

Australia, Protestants played an important role in the development of viable winemaking industries in those countries, while in South America and New Zealand, missionaries planted the earliest grapes for sacramental purposes as well as table wine. Winemaking in California began as missionaries moved from Chile, Argentina, and Mexico northward.

The past 40 years have seen explosive changes in how people around the world enjoy wine. We have more choices now than anyone even a few decades ago would have thought possible, and winemakers the world over have learned different techniques and styles by traveling to the opposite north–south hemisphere to work an "off-season" harvest with their counterparts in different regions.

The basic wine equation given earlier may look disarmingly simple, but winemaking today relies on a lot of hard science, including weather stations, soil analysis, DNA testing, onsite laboratories, and temperature-controlled fermentation. But despite all the technology available to

agronomists, viticulturists, and oenologists, winemaking still remains an art. Decisions about when to harvest, which yeast to use, and whether to use tanks or barrels all involve instinct, skill, and the subjective senses of smell and taste. From its simple beginning as fruit on a vine to its honored position in the glass you raise to your mouth, always remember that wine is a living, breathing liquid.

Some people drink only red wine or consider red wine more valuable and therefore more serious than white. We invite them to dive into the rich worlds of white Burgundy (page 20) or German Riesling (page 128). White wine can serve as an easy-drinking, warm-weather libation, true, but critics, collectors, and everyday drinkers alike prize many exquisite, expensive examples of whites. Champagne (page 192), Condrieu (page 220), and Tokaji Azsú (page 244) all stand tall as some of the finest wines in the world.

For a multitude of reasons, white wine has grown in popularity in recent years. Many people are eating lighter, and white wine tends to match lighter fare better.

Laboratory wine analysis at Adega de Monção in Portugal

Younger drinkers are gravitating toward lower-alcohol wines as well, a category into which many white wines easily fall. Aromatic varieties, such as Albariño, Assyrtiko, Gewürztraminer, Grüner Veltliner, and Riesling, offer a sensory celebration in a glass and, as such, have captured the attention of international markets. White wines somehow have more cachet with many wine drinkers. Not convinced? Try to think of an "indigenous" red grape that doesn't hail from France, Italy, or Spain that has caught on outside its birth country. (We'll crack open a bottle of Riesling while you ponder.) Chardonnay, Pinot Grigio, and Sauvignon Blanc now grow around the globe. Such varieties as Chasselas and Furmint haven't traveled much beyond their home countries other than in bottles, but many sommeliers and beverage directors have fallen in love with some of these more esoteric varieties and are spreading the love by adding them to wine lists and pairing menus.

Many wine books start with geography, but we decided to tell the story of white wine through the grapes and styles themselves. You may wonder why we didn't include a certain variety, perhaps thinking that we covered grapes too obscure or hard to find. Some varieties rarely leave their places of origin. Wine trends always run slightly ahead of what anyone is writing. Every book has space constraints. We want to give you in-depth information and recommendations for single-varietal and regional blends or styles that you can go find right now in a good wine shop or restaurant. Obscurity may suit more academic texts, but we want you to put this book into action.

You can read this book in long stretches, as you would a novel, but we suggest that you pick it up and then put it down again so that you can pick up a bottle or glass and transform knowledge into experience. No one knows more than we do that drinking wine is far more enjoyable than reading about it. Increasing your knowledge should make for a gratifying experience, but reading a book of this nature straight through would be like drinking a whole cellar of wine. You would develop palate fatigue and quickly lose interest.

Near the back of the book, you'll find a checklist to help you track the wines that you try. Use it and the rest of the book as you would a travel guide. When traveling, you don't visit *every* church, museum, restaurant, and ruin—just the ones that appeal to you. The same goes for wine. Some of us like cheap and cheerful Sauvignon Blancs. Others are looking for the ultimate expression of buttery Chardonnay. A select few are keeping an eye out for the next big thing. If a variety or style sounds good to you, buy a glass or a bottle, give it a go, and check it off the list. Worst-case scenario, you've spent a few dollars on something not to your liking that you don't have to buy again. On the other hand, you could open a door to a whole new world of wine.

We invite you to use this book as a tool for learning and discovery. Read up on a few varieties or styles before *and* while enjoying them to be able to make sense of what you're reading and drinking. Host a tasting for friends or other loved ones featuring Sauvignon Blancs or Chardonnays from around the world or comparing four different Grecos or Carricantes to determine what they have in common and what sets them apart. You don't have to be an expert to open a few bottles and talk about what you smell and taste, what you like and dislike.

If you live in or near a large city, attend tastings and dinners featuring different wine styles. Even if you live in a more remote area, online tastings that come with wine deliveries have become commonplace. Wine doesn't exist in a vacuum. It drinks best alongside food, friends, and loved ones. Wine writing doesn't exist in a vacuum, either. Pick up your glass as readily as you pick up this book. We want you to enjoy this fresh take on one of the world's oldest beverages, always remembering to have a good time.

As wine educators, we love to share our knowledge, and there's always work to be done. Type "what grape" into an internet search bar, and see what autosuggestions appear. Possibilities include: "is Chardonnay," "is Sancerre," "is Chablis." If you don't know the answer to those questions, this book gives you the perfect place to start. If you do, stop rolling your eyes and flip ahead to a variety or style you don't already know, such as Pošip or Catarratto. But first, pour yourself a glass of white wine.

Cheers!

TASTING WINE

WINE HAS FOUR SENSORY COMPONENTS: color, aroma, taste, and flavor, the last one serving as the union of the previous two.

COLOR

Throughout this book, you'll see the following color scale, which gives the range typical for the given variety or style. Remember, however, that every wine looks different at different times, and what you pour might not match our color designations perfectly. Unless there's something truly wrong with the wine, that's OK!

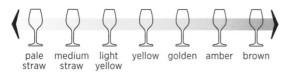

pale straw · medium straw · light yellow · yellow · golden · amber · brown

AROMA

Smell represents one of the most primal, important senses. The scent of smoke or coffee, for example, can rouse you from even a deep sleep. Your nose has a membrane called the olfactory epithelium, which contains special receptors. Odor particles pass over this membrane, bind to those receptors, and trigger an electrical signal. Your brain processes that signal, compares it to known smells, and maybe triggers a particular feeling or emotion. Does it smell nice or dangerous? Is it a gardenia or a pear? Does it make you hungry? You can tell a lot about something by how the smell of it makes you feel. The human nose can differentiate more than 200 scents in wine, and all of them should make you feel good!

TASTE

On your tongue and elsewhere in your mouth, you have roughly 7,500 taste buds, but we humans can detect just five basic tastes: bitter, salty, savory, sour, and sweet. Your sense of smell represents about 80 percent of what we commonly describe as how something tastes. Don't believe us? Hold your nose shut, take a bite of your favorite dessert, and swallow. Tastes like bland mush, doesn't it?

FLAVOR

This is where the magic happens. Flavor combines the almost countless number of aromas that you can detect, pairs them with the five basic tastes, and creates an incredible sensory experience. A lot of people find tasting notes for wine perplexing and occasionally overdone. But the art of making wine uses different kinds of yeast to transform different kinds of grapes into a whole universe of possibilities. Plus, smell and taste are subjective. If a glass of wine just tastes like "wine" to you, that's OK. If someone drinking the same wine detects notes of grapefruit, herbs, and minerals, think about each of those items as you sniff and sip. The more you smell and the more you taste, the more these tasting notes will make sense. We've compiled the tasting notes from the book into this handy table, which we offer here as a tool to help you think about what you encounter in the glass.

HOW TO TASTE WINE IN SIX EASY STEPS

We all grow up eating and drinking, but few of us learn how to catalog what we consume and appreciate it accordingly. Here's an easy way to enjoy wine while taking note of what you're drinking. We call these the six Ss of tasting wine:

SEE

Pick up the glass of wine by the stem (not the bowl) and hold it against a neutral white background. White wines range from pale straw to brown, depending on variety and style, and they gain color as they age. Whatever the tone, the wine should appear clear and clean, not cloudy.

SWIRL

Carefully swirl the wine in the glass to aerate it, which releases its symphony of aromas. If this step makes you nervous about spilling, put your other hand over the mouth of the glass as you swirl it or set the glass on a flat surface and move it gently in a circle.

SMELL

Put your nose into the glass and inhale deeply. What do you smell? If you're not sure, look at the aroma and flavor table (page xvi) for possibilities.

SIP

Tip the glass into your mouth and take just a sip of the wine. Let it linger in your mouth for a few moments. Draw some air over the top of it to release more aromas. What do you taste? Is it sweet or acidic? What fruits do you taste? Do you like it?

SWALLOW

As you swallow, note if you detect different aromas, which the act of swallowing can reveal. Does the wine have a pleasant aftertaste?

SAVOR

The elements of white wine consist of acidity, sweetness, fruit, and alcohol. Some wines have more of one element than another or one that lasts longer than the others. A good wine maintains a balance of all these elements equally, and great wine maintains that balance for a long time. Close your eyes and focus on them at intervals of 15, 30, and 60 seconds. Now talk to your friends or loved ones. What did you taste? What did they taste? Wine is a contemplative and communal experience.

ABOVE Ready for wine tasting at Sella & Mosca in Sardinia

White Wine Aromas & Flavors

FRUITY		FLORAL	VEGETAL		SPICY		MINERAL
TROPICAL	Banana	Acacia	**FRESH HERBS**	Cut grass	**SWEET**	Baking spices	Flint
	Cantaloupe	Citrus blossom		Eucalyptus		Cinnamon	Gravel
	Gooseberry	Clover		Green herbs		Clove	River rocks
	Guava	Geranium		Mint		Nutmeg	Oyster shell
	Honeydew	Elderflower		Oregano		Vanilla	Salt
	Lychee	Freesia		Sage	**PUNGENT**	Anise	Seashell
	Mango	Hawthorn		Thyme		Black pepper	Slate
	Papaya	Honeysuckle	**DRIED HERBS**	Hay		Ginger	Stone
	Passion fruit	Jasmine		Tobacco		Licorice	
	Pineapple	Lavender		Tomato leaf		White pepper	
CITRUS	Grapefruit	Lemon blossom	**VEGETABLES**	Asparagus			
	Lemon	Lilac		Bell pepper			
	Lime	Lily		Fennel			
	Orange	Orange blossom		Green pepper			
ORCHARD FRUIT	Apple	Petunia		Jalapeño pepper			
	Apricot	Plum tree blossom					
	Fig	Rose					
	Nectarine	Verbena					
	Peach	Violet					
	Pear	White flower					
RED FRUIT	Red currant	Zinnia					
DRIED FRUIT	Candied fruit						
	Date						
	Prune						
	Raisin						

CARAMELIZED	NUTTY	WOODY		BIOLOGICAL		DAIRY	CHEMICAL
Beeswax	Almond	Oak		ANIMAL	Cat pee	Butter	Petroleum
Caramel	Hazelnut	Pine			Lanolin	Cream	
Chocolate	Marzipan	Resin		EARTHY	Forest floor		
Honey	Nuts	SMOKY	Coffee		Mushroom		
Honeycomb	Walnut		Leather		Truffle		
Toffee			Smoke	YEASTY	Biscuit		
			Toast		Bread		
					Brioche		
					Yeast		

Slate soils at Clean Slate in Germany

ABBREVIATIONS

Throughout this book, you'll find many abbreviations for designations of origin. They vary from country to country, but all of them guarantee the place of origin and a certain level of quality control. Not all designations cover the same aspects, however. Spain's DO specifies aging requirements, but the AOC regulations of France don't.

ABV Alcohol by volume.

AOC Appellation d'Origine Contrôlée, name of controlled origin, France.

AOP Appellation d'Origine Protégée, name of protected origin. Under new EU laws, France is replacing AOC with AOP.

AVA American Viticultural Area, USA.

DAC Districtus Austriae Controllatus, controlled district of Austria.

DO Denominación de Origen, name of origin, Spain.

DOC Denominazione di Origine Controllata, name of controlled origin, Italy; Denominação de Origem Controlada, Portugal.

DOCa/DOQ Denominación de Origen Calificada/Qualificada, name of qualified origin. Rioja and Priorat have stricter standards than other regions in Spain.

DOCG Denominazione di Origine Controllata e Garantita, name of controlled and guaranteed origin, a designation for wines made in a more specialized region or with a stricter standards than DOC wines, Italy.

IGT Indicazione Geografica Tipica, typical geographical indication, denoting wines from a particular area that don't follow the stricter rules of a DOC or DOCG but have a higher quality than wine labeled "VdT" (*vino da tavola*, table wine), Italy.

PGI Protected Geographical Indication, EU.

PRICE GUIDE

BARGAIN	up to $20
VALUE	$21 to $40
SPECIAL OCCASION	$41 to $99
SPLURGE	$100 or more

DIFFERENT PEOPLE HAVE different budgets and financial parameters for buying wine. Defining agreeable boundaries is harder than it sounds. It's nearly impossible to find a bottle that costs $1, but plenty of people regularly drink $5 wine. The bargain category highlights wines that punch higher than their weight, meaning they have an excellent price-to-quality ratio. We considered capping the category at $15, but a lot of very good wines cost just a little bit more than that. Value wines offer solid alignment between quality and price. You get what you pay for: a good or excellent bottle for a fair price. Special occasion and splurge wines fall beyond the reach of the average consumer on a regular basis. You certainly can enjoy one of them with an ordinary weeknight meal, but the act of opening one of these higher-priced bottles instantly turns that meal into a special occasion.

For these categories, we relied on producer's suggested retail price, which can vary slightly from region to region. When that approach wasn't possible, we used the average price as listed on popular websites, such as Wine-Searcher.com, Wine.com, and other pages.

GRAPE
VARIETIES

ALBARIÑO

(ahl-bah-REEN-yo)

IN THE GLASS

⟨ 🍷 ⟩

SMALL BORDEAUX GLASS, PALE STRAW TO MEDIUM STRAW IN COLOR

TASTING PROFILE

ACIDITY

BODY

SWEETNESS

LOW   MEDIUM   HIGH

TASTING NOTES

GRAPEFRUIT   LIME   WHITE PEACH

Wines made from Albariño grapes usually feature high acidity. They have aromas of citrus blossoms, grape-fruit pith, and honeysuckle and flavors of white peach, apricot, lemon-lime, and lemon rind with a zesty, crisp, clean finish.

YOU SHOULD KNOW

In Spain, it's called Albariño. It's Alvarinho in Portugal, where many still and sparkling wines made from this variety (sometimes blended with other white grapes) may be labeled "Vinho Verde," the name for the Portuguese wine region where the wines are made (see page 248.)

FOOD PAIRINGS

FISH   SUSHI   PAELLA

Albariño pairs perfectly with fresh seafood, including oysters, clams, and sushi. It also makes a great match with fish tacos, steamed mussels, seafood risotto, and ceviche. Try it with grilled fish, calamari, and octopus or a pasta dish that incorporates different types of seafood.

RECOMMENDED WINES: SPAIN

BARGAIN

Bodegas Terras Gauda Abadia de San Campio Albariño

Ethero Albariño

Licia Albariño

Marqués de Cáceres Deusa Nai Albariño

Martin Códax Albariño

Nora Albariño

Pulpo Albariño

VALUE

Fillaboa Albariño

Granbazán Etiqueta Verde Albariño

Lagar de Cervera Albariño

Paco & Lola Albariño →

Serra da Estrela Albariño

SPECIAL OCCASION

Bodegas Gerardo Mendez Albariño Do Ferreiro
   Cepas Vellas

Bodegas y Vinedos Attis Mar Albariño

Bodegas Zarate El Palomar Albariño

Pazo Barrantes Albariño

ALBARIÑO IS INDIGENOUS to the border between western Spain and northern Portugal, and it's the most widely planted grape in the region. *Alba* in Latin means "white" or "whitish." The *-riño* ending purportedly derives from the Rhine River in Germany, with the idea that Cistercian monks carried these vines with them to Spain while caring for the footpaths and vineyards of the Camino de Santiago.

Spain has more than 13,000 acres of Albariño, and Portugal, almost 6,000. It's the most widely planted grape in Galicia, and it grows most commonly in the Rías Baixas DO (meaning "lower rivers," referring to the region's brackish estuaries). Growers often cultivate it near the sea or those estuaries, and many wine experts, alluding to this terroir, describe its taste as savory or salty. This part of Spain also produces some of the world's best mussels, clams, oysters, and other seafood.

Rías Baixas consists of five subregions: Val do Salnés, O Rosal, Soutomaior, Ribeira do Ulla, and Condado do Tea. Val do Salnés, the wettest and coldest subregion, lies on Spain's Atlantic coast. Wines made from grapes grown here have an intense salinity. O Rosal is a bit warmer, with vines planted on the slopes of the Miño River. Many wine lovers prefer this subregion because the wines made here tend to have more complexity and flavors of white and yellow peach. Soutomaior, a tiny subregion, has only a few small wineries that make Albariños with more minerality and flavors of graphite, chalk, and river rocks. A relatively new growing area, Ribeira do Ulla has plantings on both sides of the Ulla River, and its wines taste a bit fruitier. Condado do Tea lies farther inland, and its Albariños have more florality. Other Spanish regions that grow Albariño include Ribeiro, Ribeira Sacra, and Monterrei.

Albariño vineyard at Scheid in Monterey, California

Rías Baixas lies in "green Spain," meaning the part of the kingdom with high rainfall, which facilitates plant growth. Grapevines don't always prefer these climates and can succumb to diseases such as rot and mildew. Albariño is a relatively thick-skinned variety, however, and winemakers use elevated pergola systems to increase air circulation to keep those diseases at bay.

Many winemakers ferment and vinify the grapes in large stainless-steel vats. Some prefer concrete tanks, and others let the wines sit on the lees to create creamier textures. Most Albariños don't age in wooden barrels, although some winemakers have been doing so for decades, producing wines with more complexity and body than their stainless-steel counterparts. Barrel aging creates more complex flavors and increases food pairing options. Most Albariños are designed to be drunk young while still vibrant, fresh, and fruity.

Other countries with Albariño vines include New Zealand, Australia, Britain, and America. In California, producers in San Luis Obispo, Napa Valley, and Santa Ynez are making quality wines from the variety. Winemakers in Oregon and New York are beginning to work with it as well. Washington's 2020 harvest brought in 182 tons of the variety, so watch out for Evergreen State Albariños in the future.

RECOMMENDED WINES: PORTUGAL & USA

BARGAIN

Idilico Albariño, USA: Washington

Soalheiro Alvarinho Granit, Portugal

VALUE

Artesa Napa Valley Albariño, USA: California

Barnard Griffin Albariño, USA: Washington

Billsboro Albariño, USA: New York

Casa do Valle Grande Escolha Alvarinho, Portugal

Scheid Vineyards Albariño, USA: California

Soalheiro Alvarinho Classico, Portugal

Vara Albariño, USA: California

Alvarinho vineyard at Soalheiro in Portugal

WINEMAKER WISDOM

"The two biggest Alvarinho regions in the world are neighbors: Galicia in Spain and Monção and Melgaço in Portugal. Val do Salnés has a big Atlantic influence, and our region is surrounded by mountains. The aromatic intensity and acidity are more pronounced in Monção and Melgaço because we rarely do malolactic fermentation. In warmer regions, it will have more ripe fruits, and in colder regions it will be more citric."

—Luís Cerdeira, winemaker, Soalheiro

"Albariño from California's Central Coast has flavors of white and yellow freestone peaches with hints of bitter almonds and citrus notes. Great wines made from great grapes can be found all over the world. In California Albariño, you typically get more weight on the palate due to the sunshine. Spanish Albariño wines can be more austere and flinty."

—Louisa Sawyer Lindquist, winemaker, Vara

"Albariño is one of the most exciting alternatives to Chardonnay. It has a unique flavor profile that's very consistent each year. It's a complex, aromatic variety without being too floral or spicy but very distinctive with a minerality that I really enjoy. My favorite Albariño wines come from Spain, but many enjoyable wines are being made domestically as well as in South America and New Zealand."

—David Nagengast, VP of winemaking, Scheid Family Wines

ALIGOTÉ

(AHL-ee-go-TAY)

IN THE GLASS

⟨ 🍷 ⟩ ▬▬▬▬▬▬▬

BURGUNDY GLASS, PALE STRAW TO MEDIUM STRAW
IN COLOR

TASTING PROFILE

ACIDITY ▬▬▬▬▬▬▬▬
BODY ▬▬▬▬▬▬
SWEETNESS ▬▬

LOW   MEDIUM   HIGH

TASTING NOTES

ORANGE BLOSSOMS   GREEN APPLE   RIVER ROCKS

This delicate, light, dry wine has aromas of white peach, freshly cut herbs, white flowers, and river rocks. In the mouth, it features excellent minerality with flavors of green apple, citrus, and white peach.

YOU SHOULD KNOW

Aligoté may be Chardonnay's less attractive stepsibling in Burgundy, but it has its own international association of fans. Formed in 2018, Les Aligoteurs aim to popularize the variety in the American and British markets.

FOOD PAIRINGS

SHRIMP   CRAB   FRENCH FRIES

The variety's bracing minerality fits naturally with all types of seafood, especially shrimp, crab, and oysters, and it stands up to even the briniest of shellfish. Its high acidity means that it pairs well with fried foods, such as French fries, fried calamari, or fried chicken. In France, try it with escargot.

RECOMMENDED WINES: FRANCE

BARGAIN

Albert Bichot Bourgogne Aligoté
Domaine Marc Colin et Fils Bourgogne Aligoté
Domaine Roux Père et Fils Bourgogne Aligoté
Louis Latour Bourgogne Aligoté

VALUE

Calera Mt. Harlan Aligoté, USA: California
Defaix Frères Aligoté
Domaine Denis Bachelet Bourgogne Aligoté
Domaine Fernand et Laurent Pillot Aligoté
Maison Chanzy Bouzeron Aligoté
Petit-Roy Bourgogne Aligoté
Thibault Liger-Belair Bourgogne Aligoté Clos de Perrières
   la Combe

SPECIAL OCCASION

Domaine Marquis d'Angerville Bourgogne Aligoté
Domaine Sylvain Pataille Bourgogne Aligoté Les Champ Forey
Philippe Pacalet Bourgogne Aligoté

SPLURGE

Domaine Ponsot Clos des Monts Luisants

Most wine drinkers know that Chardonnay and Pinot Noir come from Burgundy, but many people haven't met Aligoté, the region's third grape. Perhaps you have encountered it but didn't realize. The Kir cocktail contains crème de cassis (blackcurrant liqueur) and white wine, originally Aligoté. Recent DNA testing has identified the variety, indigenous to the Burgundy region, as a cross between Pinot Noir and Gouais Blanc.

One of the more versatile grapes grown in the region, Aligoté is sturdier than Chardonnay, ripens earlier, is more resistant to frost, and generally has higher acidity.

It grows nicely in Burgundy's chalky soils to produce delicate wines, but it grows equally well in the sandier soils of the Rhône Valley, where it produces more full-bodied wines, particularly from the Châtillon en Diois AOC. Some of the best expressions come from Bouzeron in the Bouzeron-Aligoté appellation, and you can find good examples from the Bourgogne Aligoté AOC as well. It also goes into Crémant de Bourgogne (page 199). In contrast to Chardonnay, the wines rarely age in barrels.

Aligoté is a popular grape in Romania and Bulgaria. Eastern European winemakers often use it as a blending grape because of its high acidity, and it's worth noting that northern Romania lies at the same latitude as northern Burgundy, thus providing similar (but not exactly the same) growing conditions. Smaller plantings also grow in Ukraine, Russia, and Moldova. Winemakers in California, Oregon, and Washington have experimented with the variety as well. Calera in Hollister, California, produces Calera Mt. Harlan Aligoté, which often sells out on release. Château de Charmes in Niagara-on-the-Lake, Ontario, has one of the largest plantations of Aligoté in North America with about five acres of vines, many planted in the early 1990s.

Aligoté grapes at Domaine Fernand et Laurent Pillot in Burgundy, France

WINEMAKER WISDOM

"The freshness of this variety is always great, whatever the vintage. Aligoté is a very good tool for the expression of the soil. I love seafood and asparagus with this wine, also a good Bresse chicken with cream."

—*Thibault Liger-Belair, owner,*
Domaine Thibault Liger-Belair

"Aligoté is a rare grape in Chassagne-Montrachet, with big aromatic potential. It could go from white flowers to butter, always with a fresh touch and some tension."

—*Adrien Pillot, winemaker,*
Domaine Fernand et Laurent Pillot

ARNEIS

(ahr-NAYZ)

IN THE GLASS

AROMATIC GLASS, MEDIUM STRAW TO LIGHT YELLOW IN COLOR

TASTING PROFILE

	LOW	MEDIUM	HIGH
ACIDITY			
BODY			
SWEETNESS			

TASTING NOTES

GREEN APPLE   NUTS   PEACH

This variety has ethereal aromas of clover honey, white peach, white flowers, apple, and almonds. Flavors include Honeycrisp apple, white peach, and a touch of baking spices before the soft, fruit-filled finish.

YOU SHOULD KNOW

Most Arneis are made to drink young, within three years of bottling. Most are never fermented or aged in oak. A few winemakers use oak discerningly, however, to create very interesting fuller-bodied wines that can age for up to 10 years in the bottle.

RIGHT Arneis vineyard at Michele Chiarlo in Piedmont, Italy

FOOD PAIRINGS

BEEF   SALAMI   CHEESE

Local Roero specialties pair best with Arneis, such as vitello tonnato (sliced veal in a tuna sauce), bagna cauda (vegetables dressed with olive oil, anchovies, and garlic sauce), smoked meats, beef carpaccio, prosciutto, hard cheeses, and salami.

RECOMMENDED WINES: ITALY

BARGAIN

Angelo Negro Serra Lupini Roero Arneis

Beni di Batasiolo Roero Arneis

Brandini Le Margherite Arneis Langhe

Cornarea Roero Arneis

Fontanafredda Pradalupo Roero Arneis

Langhe Arneis Langhe

Malabaila di Canale Roero Arneis

Marco Porello Roero Arneis

Michele Chiarlo Le Madri Roero Arneis

Roberto Sarotto Runchneuv Arneis Langhe

Tibaldi Roero Arneis

VALUE

Bruno Giacosa Roero Arneis

Cascina Val del Prete Bizzarro Roero Arneis

First Drop Vivo Arneis, Australia

Giacomo Fenocchio Roero Arneis

Giovanni Almondo Bricco delle Ciliegie Roero Arneis

Pio Cesare Arneis Langhe

Seghesio Family Vineyards Arneis, USA: California

Vietti Roero Arneis

I N THE LAST 70 YEARS, Arneis has come a long way. Piedmontese growers used to plant it alongside cherished Nebbiolo vines in the hope that birds would eat the more fragrant white grapes, leaving the red grapes alone. In 1960, fewer than 10 acres of Arneis remained in the region, but today it has more than 1,800 acres under vine, largely a result of the Vietti family, who have championed the grape for decades, and consumers' growing desire for delicious, aromatic white wines.

Most of Piedmont's Arneis grows in Roero, which takes its name from the influential banking family who controlled much of this territory in the Middle Ages. If you visit the region, go to Monticello d'Alba (between Bra and Asti) and see the castle built by the Roero family in 1376. Today the town has only 3,000 residents, but the best Arneis originates from Roero—millions of years ago, an inland sea—because the sandy soils, limestone deposits, and fossilized marine creatures help create wines with superior minerality.

The small Roero region lies on the north bank of the Tanaro River. It runs about 16 miles in length but has 23 villages, Canale being the largest. The area received DOC status in 1985, upgraded to DOCG in 2005, and became a UNESCO World Heritage Site in 2014. Winemakers here also produce a Roero Arneis spumante (sparkling) and Roero Arneis Riserva. To qualify for the DOCG label, bottles must contain at least 95 percent Arneis, and Roero Arneis Riserva DOCG wines must contain 100 percent of the variety.

Arneis also grows in the Langhe and Liguria regions of Italy as well as in small quantities in New Zealand, Australia, Oregon, and California. Examples from New Zealand in particular taste amazing.

WINEMAKER WISDOM

"Due to its local origins, we are very attached to this wine. On the nose, Arneis is intense, with balanced fruity notes of peach, apricot, and floral hints of acacia and glycine flowers. On the palate, it's fragrant and fresh, thanks to a good sapidity and minerality that enhance the citrus character and give the wine length and a persistent tenacity."

—*Bruno Giacosa, owner, and Giuseppe Tartaglino, oenologist, Bruno Giacosa S.A.S.*

ASSYRTIKO

(ah-SEER-tee-ko)

IN THE GLASS

SMALL BORDEAUX GLASS, PALE STRAW TO MEDIUM STRAW IN COLOR

TASTING PROFILE

	LOW	MEDIUM	HIGH
ACIDITY			
BODY			
SWEETNESS			

TASTING NOTES

GRAPEFRUIT   APPLE   SALT

Aromas of citrus fruits and salt air conjure summer days at the beach. Strong scents include zesty lemon, and flavors summon grapefruit and green apple. It has a bold, pleasant acidity on first sip.

YOU SHOULD KNOW

Assyrtiko generally ages in stainless steel, so it maintains a crisp, clean character, but a few winemakers on Santorini are aging it in oak barrels. The resulting wine has more body and roundness, which makes it more interesting for food pairings.

FOOD PAIRINGS

OYSTERS   SUSHI   CURRY

Crisp and clean, with high minerality, it pairs perfectly with shellfish, such as raw oysters and clams, as well as with sushi and sashimi. It also stands up to high spice and heat in Thai or Indian curries.

RECOMMENDED WINES: GREECE

VALUE

Jim Barry Assyrtiko, Australia
Santo Wines Assyrtiko
Tselepos Canava Chrissou Laoudia Assyrtiko
Venetsanos Winery Assyrtiko

SPECIAL OCCASION

Boutari Santorini Assyrtiko
Domaine Sigalas Santorini Assyrtiko
Estate Argyros Assyrtiko
Gaia Assyrtiko Wild Ferment
Hatzidakis Nikteri
Mikra Thira Terrasea Assyrtiko
Pure Santorini Assyrtiko

SPLURGE

Domaine Sigalas Kavalieros Assyrtiko
Gaia Thalassitis Submerged Assyrtiko
Hatzidakis Assyrtiko de Mylos Vieilles Vignes
T-Oinos Clos Stegasta Rare Assyrtiko

RIGHT Assyrtiko grapes in *ampele* at Estate Argyros in Santorini

ON THE GREEK ISLAND OF SANTORINI, what look like large green wreaths grow on the black volcanic soil. Most winemakers here train their Assyrtiko vines into circles called *ampele*, reportedly from Ampelos, a Greek satyr transformed after death into a grape vine. Growers position the vine circles in shallow, saucer-shaped holes in the soil. This ancient technique keeps the vines safe from the wind while maintaining constant moisture (from rain, fog, maritime humidity) due to contact with the volcanic soil. The leaves shade the grapes from the harsh and constant sun.

Harvesting grapes from ampeles is much more back-breaking than from traditional trellises. The shape and position of the vines make it nearly impossible to use mechanized harvesting methods. Under the hot sun, harvesters must remain bent over all day while working on sun-scorched earth. As a result, many winemakers here pick their grapes at night, which allows the fruit to maintain its acidity, producing zesty, bone-dry wines with amazing minerality.

In the last two decades, winemakers have been planting Assyrtiko on mainland Greece, and many of them are using different growing and trellising techniques, which yield wines with differing levels of acidity, minerality, and aromatics. Some vintners combine Assyrtiko with other grapes, such as Athiri and Aidani, to make interesting, consumer-friendly blends.

Assyrtiko also features in Retsina, a Greek wine style that incorporates pine resin. In antiquity, merchants transported wine in clay amphorae sealed with pine sap.

Many ancient Greeks thus associated the flavor of pine with quality wine. This trend continues today with older consumers demanding the taste of pine and modern producers adding just a touch of pine to crisp white wines that appeal to younger palates. Winemakers also use the variety to create sweet, nutty, dessert wines called Vinsanto. Producers dry the grapes to concentrate the sugars and make sweet wines from the raisinated fruit. Some controversy surrounds the name "Vinsanto." Many Santorini residents claim it means "wine from Santo(rini)" while others elsewhere hold that the name means "holy wine."

The grape is indigenous to Santorini, but it also grows on a few other Aegean islands, including Paros. Many of the Santorini vines are more than 75 years old, many of them nongrafted. Jim Barry Wines in South Australia and others in Lodi, California, grow it, but the majority of available wines come from Greece.

ABOVE Assyrtiko vineyard at Estate Argyros in Santorini
RIGHT Plowing Assyrtiko vineyards at Estate Argyros

AUXERROIS BLANC

(ohx-ehr-WAH BLAHNK)

IN THE GLASS

SMALL BORDEAUX GLASS, MEDIUM STRAW IN COLOR

TASTING PROFILE

	LOW	MEDIUM	HIGH
ACIDITY			
BODY			
SWEETNESS			

TASTING NOTES

APPLE　　　WHITE FLOWERS　　　SLATE

This light wine has aromas of Granny Smith apple, citrus blossom, and white peach. On the palate come flavors of citrus, pear, and white stone fruits with good minerality. It has low acid levels, so it usually has a softer finish.

YOU SHOULD KNOW

People often mistake this grape for Auxerrois Gris, more commonly called Pinot Gris, and confuse it with Auxerroir Noir, which most wine drinkers know as Malbec.

FOOD PAIRINGS

FISH　　　OCTOPUS　　　CHEESE

It pairs beautifully with Dover sole, flounder, and salmon, with or without cream sauce. It makes a great match for grilled seafood, such as octopus or calamari, and soft cheeses, such as Camembert, Brie, and even stinky cheeses, such as Époisses or Limberger.

RECOMMENDED WINES: AROUND THE WORLD

BARGAIN

Cave Gales Remich Hopertsbour Grand Premier Cru Auxerrois, Luxembourg

Domaine Clos des Rochers Grand Premier Cru Grevenmacher Auxerrois, Luxembourg

Domaine Fernand Engel Auxerrois Vieilles Vignes, France

Elemental Cellars Zenith Vineyard Auxerrois, USA: Oregon

Weingut Heitlinger Auxerrois, Germany

VALUE

Albert Mann Auxerrois Vieilles Vignes, France

Domaine Mathis Bastian Auxerrois Remich Goldberg, Luxembourg

Domaine Thill Château de Schengen Auxerrois, Luxembourg

Domaine Trapet Auxerrois Ox, France

Laurent Bannwarth Auxerrois Qvevri, France

Raptor Ridge Zenith Vineyard Auxerrois, USA: Oregon

Rolly Gassmann Auxerrois Rotleibel de Rorschwihr, France

Swick Wines Auxerrois, USA: Oregon

Weingut Odinstal 350 NN Auxerrois, Germany

Weingut Odinstal Basalt Auxerrois, Germany

Zenith Vineyard Estate Auxerrois, USA: Oregon

AUXERROIS BLANC AND CHARDONNAY are siblings, but Auxerrois Blanc is the less famous of the two, a little like Olivia de Havilland and Joan Fontaine; Liza Minelli and Lorna Luft; or Phylicia Rashad and Debbie Allen. Auxerrois Blanc comes from Gouais Blanc and the Pinot family, as does Chardonnay, which in some areas led to mislabeling in favor of the more popular name.

In the Lorraine region of France, where it's indigenous, vintners use it in wines labeled either "Auxerrois Blanc" or "Pinot Blanc." In Germany and Luxembourg, producers often make it into single-varietal wines called either Auxerrois or Auxerrois Blanc. It often grows on limestone-rich hillsides—producing wines with great complexity, lower acidity, and substantial minerality—predominantly along the banks of the Mosel(le) River. As it crosses borders, the river changes names or just spellings, really. In France and Luxembourg, it's Moselle, and Mosel in Germany. Grapes and good wine know no borders. The town of Schengen lies at the intersection of these three countries, famous for the agreement signed nearby, in the middle of the river, in 1985. The Schengen Agreement abolished border checkpoints and today remains central to the EU economy, affecting 26 signatory countries and more than 400 million people.

Many of the wonderful, smaller-production wines of Luxembourg don't make it to the American or British markets, which gives any lover of white wine a compelling reason to plan a trip here. Winemakers in France's Alsace region also grow it, as do some British producers, who often blend it with other varieties. Canada has a few vineyards in the Okanagan wine region, with vines planted as early as the 1970s, and on Vancouver Island, also in British Columbia. You can find a few plantations in the Willamette Valley in Oregon as well.

Domaine Mathis Bastian in Luxembourg

WINEMAKER WISDOM

"It is a pleasurable wine that can be served both as an aperitif and with a meal. It's less acidic and can be kept for several years if stored well."

—Frank Keyser, managing director, Domaine Keyser-Kohll by Kohll-Reuland

"I particularly appreciate Auxerrois Blanc's perfect harmony, balanced freshness, and high aging potential. It can be enjoyed with Asian cuisine as well as with starters, such as salad bowls and soups."

—Anouk Bastian, coproprietor, Domaine Mathis Bastian

CARRICANTE

(kah-ree-KAHN-tay)

IN THE GLASS

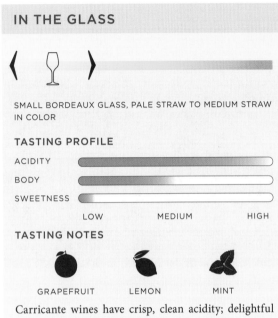

SMALL BORDEAUX GLASS, PALE STRAW TO MEDIUM STRAW IN COLOR

TASTING PROFILE

	LOW	MEDIUM	HIGH
ACIDITY			
BODY			
SWEETNESS			

TASTING NOTES

GRAPEFRUIT   LEMON   MINT

Carricante wines have crisp, clean acidity; delightful citrus aromas of mandarin orange, lemon-lime, and lemon blossom; and flavors of lemon peel, lemon curd, and green apple. Volcanic soils give them a strong mineral backbone and a touch of salinity in the finish.

YOU SHOULD KNOW

If picked too early, Carricante grapes create highly acidic wines. Many winemakers pick later in the season and allow their wines to undergo malolactic fermentation to counteract the acidity.

FOOD PAIRINGS

SUSHI   FISH   OCTOPUS

It pairs amazingly with sushi, sashimi, and other raw seafood. Its high acidity offers the perfect foil for lime juice in fish tacos and ceviche, and it makes a great match with grilled seafood especially calamari, octopus, and swordfish steaks.

RECOMMENDED WINES: SICILY

BARGAIN

Cantine Nicosia Contrada Monte San Nicolò Etna Bianco

Pietradolce Etna Bianco

Tasca d'Almerita Tenuta Tascante Etna Bianco

Torre Mora Scalunera Etna Bianco

VALUE

Cusumano Alta Mora Etna Bianco

Donnafugata Sul Vulcano Etna Bianco

Federico Curtaz Gamma Etna Bianco

Graci Etna Bianco

I Vigneri I Custodi delle Vigne dell'Etna Bianco

Planeta Etna Bianco

Tornatore Etna Bianco

SPECIAL OCCASION

Benanti Contrada Cavaliere Etna Bianco

Benanti Pietra Marina Etna Bianco Superiore

Girolamo Russo San Lorenzo Etna Bianco

Planeta Eruzione 1614 Carricante →

SPLURGE

Pietradolce Sant'Andrea

I F YOU LIKE A LITTLE ADVENTURE in your wine, try one made from grapes grown on an active volcano. Mt. Etna lies on the eastern side of Sicily, and locals tell us, "She can be very moody." Confirmed by NASA, Mt. Etna erupts around 200 times per year. The first-recorded eruption took place in 1500 BCE, but some of the volcano's most significant changes occurred in 2021, when the National Institute for Geophysics and Vulcanology reported that the Mt. Etna had an explosive growth spurt, gaining 100 feet in height over just six months.

Winemakers have to worry about sunshine, rain, mold, fungus, mildew, frost, hail, and other meteorological crises, but the brave producers who grow grapes on Mt. Etna also must keep an eye on the volcano's daily "moods." They benefit, however, from volcanic soils rich with copper, iron, and magnesium that help produce some of the world's most interesting white wines from Carricante grapes. Most experts agree that Carricante is indigenous to this area of Sicily and has grown on Mt. Etna for more than 1,000 years.

The Etna DOC consists of vineyards on the north, south, and east slopes of the volcano. Vineyard altitudes vary from 1,300 feet in Viagrande to 3,600 feet in Milo. The grapes consequently receive excellent sunlight, and nighttime breezes at altitude cool them and allow them to rest. Wines authorized by the Etna DOC as Etna Bianco must contain at least 60 percent Carricante, and Etna Bianco Superiore must have at least 80 percent. Many quality producers use 100 percent Carricante grapes for their Etna Bianco and Etna Bianco Superiore wines. Only wines grown in Milo can use the title Etna Bianco Superiore.

WINEMAKER WISDOM

"Our family's Mt. Etna wine journey began in 1865, when my forefathers made wine on the northern slopes of Etna. In the 1970s, my father began purchasing land for vineyards, focusing on indigenous grapes, including Carricante. We love this indigenous variety as a distinctly Etna grape with the capacity to age."

—Francesco Tornatore, proprietor,
Azienda Agricola Tornatore

BELOW Planeta Carricante vineyard on Mount Etna in Sicily

CATARRATTO

(KAH-tah-RAH-toh)

IN THE GLASS

⟨ 🍷 ⟩

SMALL BORDEAUX GLASS, PALE STRAW TO MEDIUM STRAW IN COLOR

TASTING PROFILE

ACIDITY			
BODY			
SWEETNESS			
	LOW	MEDIUM	HIGH

TASTING NOTES

LEMON BLOSSOM   CITRUS   GREEN APPLE

Aromas and flavors include lemon blossom, citrus peel, and green apple. The wines generally have low body, making them perfect to enjoy on their own on the beach.

YOU SHOULD KNOW

For generations, many producers of Marsala (page 210) have used Grillo (page 86) and Inzolia, but some have replanted with Catarratto because of the variety's higher yields. The name hasn't changed officially yet, but the Sicilian DOC Consorzio encourages calling the variety Lucido.

FOOD PAIRINGS

FISH   BOUILLABAISSE   PAD THAI

Catarratto with good acidity pairs nicely with briny seafood and grilled fish. Oven-baked, salt-encrusted branzino makes a perfect pairing, as does a seafood stew, such as cioppino or bouillabaisse. Producers usually make Catarratto wines in a light, simple style that matches nicely with Asian noodle dishes, such as pad thai or chow fun.

RECOMMENDED WINES: SICILY

BARGAIN

Castellucci Miano Catarratto

Diversi dal Solito Catarratto

Donnafugata Anthilia Catarratto →

Feudo Disisa Lu Bancu Catarratto Sicilia

Feudo Montoni Vigna del Masso Catarratto

Iniceri Abisso Catarratto

Tifosi Catarratto

Valdibella Isolano Catarratto

VALUE

Abbazia San Giorgio Lustro Catarratto

Aldo Viola Krimiso Catarratto

Baglio Antico Catarratto

Barraco Catarratto

Bosco Falconeria Falco Peregrino

Caruso Minini Naturalmente Bio Catarratto

Feudo Montoni Catarratto del Masso

Porta del Vento Saray Catarratto

SPECIAL OCCASION

Sergio Drago Macerato

OST OF THE CATARRATTO IN ITALY grows on Sicily—primarily in the western provinces of Agrigento, Palermo, and Trapani—but it still remains one of Italy's most widely planted varieties. Generations of winemakers here have used this grape to make well-priced, easy-quaffing, white wines equally at home on the island's beautiful beaches or waterfront cafés. Historically, many smaller growers sold their grapes to the island's larger producers and cooperatives that made passable, low-cost wines. Thankfully that trend is changing as younger producers talk their fathers and grandfathers out of selling grapes and into letting a new generation make quality wines.

Because of their history, Catarratto vines have the unfortunate reputation of yielding large amounts of low-acid grapes that make uninteresting wines. Younger winemakers have changed vineyard techniques, including trellising and later picking, to make wines with much better profiles. They also have implemented pruning to reduce yields and increase quality. Modern winemakers have coaxed higher acidity from the grapes along with citrus and herbal characteristics that make for intriguing fresh white wines that appeal to younger wine drinkers.

History aficionados, take note that Sicily boasts some of the world's most impressive and well-preserved Greek ruins. Trapani is home to Selinunte, Europe's largest archaeological park (650 acres), which boasts the ruins of a 7th-century BCE settlement built for Mediterranean trade, which of course included wine. On Acropolis Beach, nature worshippers will love the golden sand and views of the sun setting behind Selinunte's temples. If you visit, also make time for the Civic Museum of Castelvetrano.

Catarrato harvest in Contessa Entellina vineyard at Donnafugata in Sicily

WINEMAKER WISDOM

"Lucido, now the official name for Catarratto, is an interesting, flexible grape, capable of responding to climate change and drought, thanks to its inner resilience toward water stress. At the same time, it makes highly contemporary wines that are fresh and aromatic, with low to moderate alcohol, appealing mostly to younger generations. A juicy minerality and prolonged aftertaste come with the best terroirs."

—*Antonio Rallo, CEO and winemaker, Donnafugata*

CHARDONNAY

(shar-dohn-AY)

IN THE GLASS

SMALL BORDEAUX GLASS, PALE STRAW TO YELLOW IN COLOR

TASTING PROFILE

	LOW	MEDIUM	HIGH
ACIDITY			
BODY			
SWEETNESS			

TASTING NOTES

APPLE   LEMON   RIVER ROCKS

Chardonnay can run the gamut from light and citrusy to bold and buttery with notes of toast and spice. In unoaked, cool-climate versions, expect aromas of Granny Smith apple, lemon, and river rocks or oyster shell. In wines that have undergone malolactic fermentation and barrel aging, you'll sense vanilla, baking spices, and toffee. Flavors include Bartlett pear, green apple, pineapple, and lemon in wines produced entirely in stainless steel or concrete. Maturation in oak gives notes of butterscotch, caramel, and clove.

YOU SHOULD KNOW

Almost a blank canvas, Chardonnay, like all grapes, reacts to terroir, but the winemaker's hand has a lot to do with the final profile. Overoaked, buttery Chardonnays flooded the market a few years ago, but winemakers have followed consumer tastes toward lighter, fresher wines with just a touch of oak or none at all. If you belong to the ABC crowd—"anything but Chardonnay!"—give it another chance and look for a cool-climate, unoaked bottle.

FOOD PAIRINGS

OYSTERS   EGGS   PASTA

Because of its variety of styles, Chardonnay pairs with just about anything. Whether from Chablis, Chile, or Sonoma, cool-climate Chardonnay goes perfectly with oysters or your favorite raw bar selections. Try more buttery, oaked versions with egg dishes at brunch, especially omelets, tortilla española, or eggs Florentine. Creamy Chardonnays pair with white pasta dishes, such as fettuccine Alfredo or spaghetti carbonara.

RECOMMENDED WINES

See regional recommendations throughout the chapter.

SOMETIME IN THE 1990S, too many Chardonnays underwent malolactic fermentation and matured too long in new oak barrels, creating, as a friend called it, wine that tasted like "a two-by-four with a slab of butter on it." The backlash came swiftly, and that past reputation unfairly lingers. As consumer tastes have changed, winemakers worldwide have forsaken their oak regimes, crafting light, fresh Chardonnays. You still can find plenty of buttery versions, if that's how you like them, but if not, you don't have to head for the hills when you spot a bottle of the number one white grape grown in the world.

Chardonnay takes its name from a village in the Mâconnais region of Burgundy, the grape's birthplace and spiritual home. The offspring of Pinot Noir and Gouais Blanc, a lesser-known but prolific grape, Chardonnay has close botanical relationships to Aligoté (page 6) and Pinot Blanc (page 110), which often grow near it in Burgundy. As a result, growers there frequently confused the varieties. Over the years, the French have spelled it Chardenay, Chardonet, and Chardonnet, among other variations. They also called it Chardonnet Pinot Blanc as well as Beaunois, meaning "from Beaune," a term they also applied to Aligoté—none of which helped clear any confusion prior to DNA testing.

French labeling conventions for wine privilege appellations, or geographic names, rather than varietal names, so for years many consumers didn't realize that the luscious white wines from Burgundy consisted of Chardonnay. Bourgogne blanc, Chablis, Meursault, Puligny-Montrachet—it's all Chardonnay! A few years ago, members of the BIVB, Burgundy's regional board, asked what they could do to improve the sales of their wine in America. "Put the variety on the label," we said. "Americans love Chardonnay and Pinot Noir, but they have no idea that those are the grapes

inside your bottles." Much disagreement and shaking of heads ensued, but many entry-level white Burgundies now include "Chardonnay" on their labels.

Farmers have grown grapes in Burgundy since Roman times, but modern winemaking in Burgundy began during the Middle Ages, when religious orders gained importance and influence. Noble families granted the Cistercians and Benedictines tracts of land, in which they planted vineyards. The Cistercians centered on the Abbaye de Cîteaux, founded in 1098, and had land holdings mainly in the Côte de Beaune and Côte de Nuits, with smaller plots in Chablis and the Côte Chalonnaise. Headquartered in the Abbaye de Cluny, the Cluniacs, a branch of the Benedictines, held vineyards mainly in the Côte Chalonnaise and the Mâconnais, with smaller holdings farther north. By the 1400s, the wines of both orders had become famous throughout France and the rest of Europe. These orders critically developed the concept of terroir, breaking it down even further into the concept of *climat*, a precise plot of land that offers specific growing characteristics for grapevines. Burgundian monks also introduced the term *clos*, meaning a single vineyard enclosed by a wall.

Today, Burgundy has 84 AOCs, which includes regional appellations; village appellations, such as Meursault or Puligny-Montrachet; and Grand Cru appellations, such as Bâtard-Montrachet or Corton Charlemagne. Puligny-Montrachet, for example, divides further into 43 *climats* at the Village, Premier Cru (sometimes abbreviated "1er Cru") and Grand Cru levels, such as Puligny-Montrachet Premier Cru Les Perrières and Puligny-Montrachet Les Pucelles. If this system seems confusing, remember two easy pieces of information. White Burgundy is Chardonnay unless it says Aligoté on the label, and the more words the label has, the more site-specific and most likely higher quality it is.

Chardonnay grows widely throughout France—in the south, labeled "Pays d'Oc" or "Appellation France"—but you can find 60 percent of the total in Burgundy and Champagne. Of those two regions, Champagne grows more of it than Burgundy, which makes sense when you note that it's the only white grape allowed for France's most famous bubbly. Across the Channel, English vintners also use it to produce still and sparkling wines.

BURGUNDY

CHABLIS

Wine drinkers of a certain age may recall when any dry white wine, regardless of the grapes used, went by the name Chablis. EU law now protects the name of this wine region southwest of Paris, so wine labeled "Chablis" can come only from here and consist of 100 percent Chardonnay, the only grape allowed in the appellation. Area soils, running along the Serein River, consist of clay, limestone, and fossilized oyster shells, which we mention for two reasons: first to remind you that oysters and Chablis make a sublime pairing and, second, to touch on minerality in wine. Fossilized oyster shells contain calcium, which, when combined with limestone, creates the mineral component variously described as river rocks, flint, and slate alongside the traditional green apple and citrus flavors from the grapes. These 150-million-year-old soils once lay at the bottom of a vast ocean, and in this cold-weather region, the oyster shells absorb daytime heat that, at night, rises toward the vines, keeping the fruit at temperatures suitable for ripening.

Chablis has a crisp, clean style. Bottles labeled "Petit Chablis" almost always ferment in 100 percent stainless steel, while Chablis, Chablis Premier Cru, and Chablis Grand Cru can rest in previously used or lightly toasted barrels, which imparts softer flavors and characteristics, for a short period of time. Wines labeled "Chablis" or "Chablis Villages" can come from one of 20 village appellations. Within those nest 40 Premier Cru climats, or named vineyard plots, so a label may read "Chablis Premier Cru" or it can have name the climat after that. At the apex of the Chablis pyramid sits Chablis Grand Cru, the finest expression of Chardonnay from the region's best sites. The seven Chablis Grand Cru climats are Blanchot, Bougrot, Les Clos, Grenouilles, Preuses, Valmur, and Vaudésir. Reportedly the first Chardonnay planted in Chablis grew in what is now the Les Clos Grand Cru site.

Premier Cru and Grand Cru Chablis nicely contradict the misplaced belief that white wines are best when consumed young. Even village-level Chablis will evolve in the bottle for three to five years, and the higher-quality levels can age gracefully for a decade or more.

WINEMAKER WISDOM

"The lifeline of our Chardonnay is good energy and acidity. They balance a nice complexity and the opulence of our great terroirs."

—*Fréderic Barnier, technical director,*
Louis Jadot

"My objective is to reveal with each new vintage the richness and complexity of our incredible terroir. At J. Moreau & Fils, we prefer lees instead of sulfur, and *bâtonnage* (stirring) isn't a dirty word. Lees are the best natural protection for wine. With long aging on lees and regular bâtonnage, we can have minimum level of sulfites. In the cellars, I like to give time to time. A day in the cellar is as important as a day in the vineyards."

—*Lucie Depuydt, winemaker, J. Moreau Fils*

RECOMMENDED WINES: CHABLIS

BARGAIN

La Chablisienne Petit Chablis Dame Nature

Domaine Bachelier Chablis

Domaine Félix Petit Chablis

Domaine Millet Petit Chablis

VALUE

Domaine Jean-Marc Brocard Sainte Claire Chablis

Domaine Laroche Chablis Saint Martin

Domaine Louis Moreau Chablis

William Fèvre Champs Royaux Chablis

SPECIAL OCCASION

Domaine Louis Moreau Chablis Premier Cru Vaillons

J. Moreau & Fils Chablis Grand Cru Les Clos

Joseph Drouhin Drouhin-Vaudon Chablis Premier Cru
Montmains

Louis Jadot Chablis

Thomas Labille Chablis Premier Cru Mont de Milieu

SPLURGE

Domaine Christian Moreau Père & Fils Chablis
Grand Cru Les Clos "Clos des Hospices"

Domaine François Raveneau Chablis Premier Cru
Monts Mains

J. Moreau & Fils Chablis Grand Cru Valmur →

René et Vincent Dauvissat-Camus Chablis Grand
Cru Les Preuses

CÔTE D'OR

South of Chablis and the city of Dijon lies the Côte d'Or, the premier region for white and red Burgundy. About 30 miles long, it divides into two distinct regions, the Côte de Nuits and Côte de Beaune. Mainly red wine territory, the Côte de Nuits, the northern half of the Côte d'Or, makes some of the world's finest Pinot Noir. Only 5 percent of the wine made here is white. A small amount of wine from the Hautes Côtes de Nuits, the higher slopes to the west of the main production area, is white. The best whites of the region come from Vougeot Premier Cru and Musigny Grand Cru.

Moving south through Burgundy brings us to the small city of Beaune and the surrounding Côte de Beaune, one of the world's finest regions for white wine and red. A 15-mile length of vineyards holds 18 village and eight Grand Cru appellations. From north to south, the main white wine appellations are Corton-Charlemagne, Meursault, Puligny-Montrachet, Chassagne-Montrachet, and Saint-Aubin. Wines from Grand Cru and Premier Cru sites will

age for up to 20 years, taking on an amber tone and generous secondary characteristics atop the standard apple and citrus flavors and strong minerality.

About 20 percent of Beaune wine is white; the same percentage of white wine comes from Hautes Côtes de Beaune, the hills above the Côtes de Beaune. Saint-Romain and Auxey-Duresses have good reputations for making quality white wines as well; the former's vineyards divide evenly between Chardonnay and Pinot Noir, while the production of the latter is about one-third white wine. Savigny-lès-Beaune and Monthélie also produce small amounts of white.

People around the globe covet Corton-Charlemagne wines. This Grand Cru appellation on the Corton hill in the north of the Côte de Beaune spreads across three villages: Aloxe-Corton, Pernand-Vergelesses, and Ladoix-Serrigny. The story goes that, in the late 700s, Emperor Charlemagne ordered white grapes to be planted on the hill after his wife complained that red wine stained his beard. Corton-Charlemagne features perfumed aromas, full body, and flavors of apple pie, lemon zest, and shale. Both Pernand-Vergellesses and Aloxe-Corton produce a significant amount of white wine outside the Corton-Charlemagne appellation. Ladoix-Serrigny produces smaller amounts. Pernand-Vergelesses has three white-wine-only Premier Cru sites: Sous Fretilles, Clos du Village, and Clos Berthet.

South of Beaune and north of Puligny-Montrachet, Meursault has 19 Premier Cru sites, the best known being: Meursault Charmes, Meursault Perrières, and Meursault Genevrières. These sites—known for the fullest, richest expressions of Meursault, with flavors of lemon, butter, and flint—abut the vineyards of Puligny-Montrachet.

It's no exaggeration to say that the Grand Cru Montrachet vineyard, first planted in the Middle Ages, yields the best dry white wine on the planet. Nineteenth-century French novelist Alexandre Dumas père advised drinking the wines of Montrachet "on bended knee, with head bared." That's fine for the first sip, but we prefer to enjoy its flavors of green apple and lemongrass with elegant touches of river rock and oyster shell while sitting at a table with good friends and food.

At just under 20 acres, Le Montrachet sits on the hill above the villages of Puligny and Chassagne, each of which, since the end of the 19th century, appended its name with "-Montrachet." It divides almost evenly between the two communes, bordered by four other Grand Cru vineyards which also bear the world-famous moniker: Chevalier-Montrachet, Bâtard-Montrachet, Bienvenue-Bâtard-Montrachet, and Criots-Bâtard-Montrachet.

West of Le Montrachet, Saint-Aubin consists of 415 acres, of which 340 produce white wine. Don't get too excited, Burgundy prices being what they are, but if there's a "bargain" in the region, you *might* find it here. Far less famous than its neighbors to the east and north, Saint-Aubin vintners create a fresher style, with flavors of white peach, lime, and a dusting of chalk.

RECOMMENDED WINES: CÔTE D'OR

VALUE

Château de Santenay Bourgogne Chardonnay Vieilles Vignes

Domaine Justin Girardin Bourgogne Chardonnay

Domaine Matrot Bourgogne Chardonnay

Domaine Thevenot-Le-Brun & Fils Bourgogne Haute Côtes de Nuit Blanc

Edouard Delaunay Bourgogne Septembre Blanc

SPECIAL OCCASION

Alain Gras Saint-Romain Blanc

Bouchard Aîné & Fils Chassagne-Montrachet Premier Cru

Domaine Coffinet-Duvernay Chassagne-Montrachet Premier Cru Les Caillerets

Domaine Matrot Meursault

Jean-Claude Boisset Haute Côtes de Nuit

Joseph Drouhin Puligny-Montrachet

Louis Jadot Meursault

SPLURGE

Albert Bichot Meursault

Bouchard Aîné & Fils Meursault Premier Cru Le Porusot

Bouchard Aîné & Fils Meursault Premier Cru Les Perrières

Domaine Antonin Guyon Corton-Charlemagne Grand Cru

Domaine Bertagna Vougeot Blanc Premier Cru Les Cras

Domaine Michelot Meursault Premier Cru Genevrières

Domaine Parent Corton Grand Cru Blanc

Jean-Claude Boisset Corton-Charlemagne Grand Cru →

LEFT Joseph Drouhin Chardonnay vineyard in Chablis

WINEMAKER WISDOM

"In the winery, our objectives are to respect and extract as much as possible of the fruit, the aromas, and the purity of the grapes on receiving the harvest. As with the great whites of the Côte de Beaune, Chardonnay grapes are pressed in whole bunches and left to settle for about 48 hours; then the must is fermented, first in stainless-steel tanks, then in barrels. Close partnerships with coopers allow us to work with different types of toasting. I use 50 percent new barrels for this wine, with an aging period of about 15 months before bottling. In keeping with Burgundy tradition and the maison's style, the wine is *bâtonné* for two months, which means the lees are put back into suspension to give it more body and roundness."

—*Laurent Mairet, winemaker, Bouchard Aîné & Fils*

"We are in favor of long aging, most of the time 18 months, in 450-liter barrels with a large quantity of lees to protect the wines from oxidation. It ferments with indigenous yeasts in these large barrels to balance the oakiness of the wine and underscore its tension and length. Corton-Charlemagne Grand Cru is the only white Grand Cru in our cellar. We particularly cherish it. From the Pernand side, it always shows a powerful structure and great finesse combined with a mineral flavor, the profile you expect from a Grand Cru white Burgundy."

—*Grégory Patriat and Laure Guilloteau, winemakers, Jean-Claude Boisset*

"Chardonnay adapts so well to different soils and can be found all over the world but always in harmony with the terroir. I have enjoyed many different Chardonnays from around the world: South Africa, America, Italy, Spain, and Eastern Europe. Acidity, skin thickness, minerality, and much more differ in each place, and the style of winemaking makes every Chardonnay unique."

—*Eva Reh, winemaker, Domaine Bertagna*

RIGHT Barrel cellar at Joseph Drouhin in Burgundy, France

CÔTE CHALONNAISE

Named for the town of Chalon-sur-Sâone on the River Sâone, the Côte Chalonaise runs 15 miles long, directly south of the Côte de Beaune. Its two most important white-wine communes are Rully, which has 23 Premier Cru appellations and makes twice as much white wine as red (including sparkling Crémant de Bourgogne), and Montagny, which produces only white wine among 49 Premier Cru sites. These fresh, lively wines with bright acidity and strong minerality drink perfectly right away or age for three to eight years.

BELOW Chardonnay during winemaking process at Joseph Drouhin

MÂCONNAIS

Farthest south in Burgundy, the Mâconnais occupies a 21-mile-long strip of land just north of Beaujolais. The Abbey of Cluny stands here as a reminder of this region's importance to Burgundy's winemaking history. The village of Chardonnay, purportedly the source of the variety's name, lies in this region as well. Of the grapes grown here, 80 percent are Chardonnay, interspersed with small plantings mainly of Gamay. The Mâconnais has five village appellations: Pouilly-Fuissé, Pouilly-Loché, Pouilly-Vinzelles, Saint-Veran, and Viré-Clessé. Of these, the most well-known is Pouilly-Fuissé, which has opulent texture and flavors of peach, grapefruit, and pineapple with strong minerality. (Don't confuse it with Pouilly-Fumé, made from Sauvignon Blanc, which hails from the Loire Valley.)

Depending on quality, the wines will feature increasingly specific regional distinctions: Mâcon, Mâcon-Villages, Mâcon plus the name of the village and/or a vineyard name or designation. Some 27 villages may appear on labels; the most common is Mâcon-Lugny. Drinkable on release, Mâconnais wines have flavors of lemon, grapefruit, and acacia blossom and will benefit from an additional three to five years of aging.

RECOMMENDED WINES: MÂCONNAIS

BARGAIN

Albert Bichot Mâcon Lugny Les Charmes

Domaine des Terres Gentilles Mâcon Lugny

Joseph Drouhin Mâcon Lugny Les Crays

Louis Jadot Mâcon-Villages

VALUE

Bouchard Père & Fils Mâcon Lugny Saint-Pierre

Château de Messey Mâcon Chardonnay Les Crêts

Louis Jadot Pouilly-Fuissé

Réserve des Rochers Mâcon-Chaintré

SPECIAL OCCASION

Château de la Chaize Pouilly-Fuissé

Château Fuissé Pouilly-Fuissé Le Clos Monopole

Domaine Jules Desjourneys Pouilly-Fuissé Vignes de la Côte

Domaine Thibert Pouilly-Fuissé Vignes Blanches

OTHER NOTABLE COUNTRIES

ARGENTINA

Chardonnay grows widely in Argentina, with high concentrations of plantings in Mendoza, especially in the high-altitude vineyards of Luján de Cuyo, Maipú, Uco Valley, and Tupungato. Argentina's appellation system will never reach the complexity of Burgundy's, but people are talking about the Chardonnay from Tupungato's Gualtallary subzone and the Tunuyán subregion in Uco Valley. These Mendoza vineyards stand at altitudes between 2,300 and 3,280 feet, offering hot days with maximum sun exposure and cool nights to help preserve freshness and acidity.

Growers also cultivate Chardonnay at extreme altitudes in Calchaquí Valley, the country's northernmost wine region. Vineyard heights range between 5,600 and 9,842 feet, offering challenging conditions that produce stellar examples of the variety. In the far south of the country, Patagonian vineyards stand closer to sea level and closer to Antarctica, providing a cold climate that the grapes enjoy. Chardonnay thrives in every region between these two extremes, and winemakers create crisp, steel-fermented versions and full-bodied, well-oaked styles.

WINEMAKER WISDOM

"If I had to define the Uco Valley in a single word, I would say: diversity. We cultivate our vineyards at different elevations, with different solar exposures and most importantly with a great diversity of alluvial soils originating from the Andes Mountains. The grapes offer different expressions for these variants. Chardonnay from the lower part of the valley has a more tropical character, and as we ascend, more citrus and mineral characteristics appear, along with spice notes that make them unique."

—*Jose Galante, chief winemaker, Bodegas Salentein*

RECOMMENDED WINES: ARGENTINA

BARGAIN

Bodega Norton Reserva Chardonnay →
Familia Zuccardi Q Chardonnay
Salentein Reserve Chardonnay
Santa Julia Made with Organic Grapes Chardonnay

VALUE

Catena Zapata Catena Alta Chardonnay
Luigi Bosca Chardonnay
Susana Balbo Dominio de Plato Signature
   Barrel Fermented Chardonnay
Trapiche Terroir Series Finca Las Piedras
   Chardonnay

SPECIAL OCCASION

Bodega Chacra Mainque Chardonnay
Casa Yagüe Chardonnay, Valle de Trevelin,
   Chubut
Michelini i Mufatto Convicciones Chardonnay
Viña Cobos Bramare Chardonnay

SPLURGE

Bodega Chacra Chardonnay
Catena Zapata Adrianna Vineyard White Bones Chardonnay

AUSTRALIA

In 1832, James Busby brought Chardonnay here as part of his vine collection, but it took about 140 years before the grape made any impact. Left to its own devices, Australian Chardonnay—the nation's second most widely grown grape—will showcase flavors of green apple, peach, and citrus fruit, while barrel aging will add notes of buttered toast, vanilla, and soft spice. Expressions from inland areas, such as Riverina, Riverland, and Murray Darling, will have round tropical fruit flavors, while crisp lemon and lime notes stand out in cooler-climate versions from Adelaide Hills, Mornington Peninsula, and Tasmania. For sophisticated, barrel-aged Chardonnay, look for bottles from Margaret River, Coonawarra, Yarra Valley, Geelong, and Hunter Valley.

WINEMAKER WISDOM

"The Yarra Valley is a cool climate for Chardonnay in Australia. We often see characteristics of lemons, citrus peel, white stone fruit, and pear with floral notes of white flowers and fresh ginger. On the palate, these bright fruit flavours often balance with savoury and complex notes, such as shortbread and roasted nuts. At Giant Steps, our best Yarra Valley Chardonnays have a beautiful tension and fruit purity, as well great complexity, texture, and body. I love the simplicity of our Chardonnay with a beautiful hunk of cheese (preferably Gruyère) and sourdough bread. Is shrimp on the barbie a cliché here? It might be, but it totally works with Chardonnay!"

—*Melanie Chester, winemaker, Giant Steps*

RECOMMENDED WINES: AUSTRALIA

BARGAIN

McGuigan The Plan Chardonnay →
Penfolds Koonunga Hill Chardonnay
Tyrrell's Old Winery Chardonnay
Yalumba Y Series Unwooded Chardonnay
Zilzie Chardonnay

VALUE

Devil's Corner Chardonnay
Giant Steps Yarra Valley Chardonnay
Robert Oatley Chardonnay
Snake & Herring Tough Love Chardonnay
Vasse Felix Filius Chardonnay

SPECIAL OCCASION

By Farr Chardonnay
Leeuwin Estate Art Series Chardonnay
Mac Forbes Chardonnay
Shaw + Smith M3 Chardonnay
Vasse Felix Premier Chardonnay

SPLURGE

Cloudburst Chardonnay
Mount Mary Vineyard Chardonnay
Penfolds Yattarna Bin 144 Chardonnay

CHILE

Chardonnay grows extensively throughout Chilean wine country, although in recent years it has lost ground to Sauvignon Blanc as Chile's most popular white grape. It does especially well in the cool-climate regions of San Antonio, Casablanca, Aconcagua Coast, and Limari, which offer lean, mineral-driven versions made completely in stainless steel or with minimal time in oak. A lot of Chilean Chardonnay drinks easy at approachable prices, but vineyard expansion into the far north and south of the country and changes in winemaking styles have contributed to increased quality.

RECOMMENDED WINES: CHILE

BARGAIN

Concha y Toro Marqués de Casa Concha Chardonnay
Domaines Barons de Rothschild Los Vascos Chardonnay
Montes Classic Chardonnay
Santa Rita Medalla Real Gran Reserva Chardonnay
Tabali Talinay Chardonnay

VALUE

Casa Lapostolle Cuvée Alexandre Chardonnay
Clos d'Angel Cellar Selection Chardonnay
Miguel Torres Cordillera de Los Andes Chardonnay
Montes Alpha Chardonnay
Viña Leyda Chardonnay

SPECIAL OCCASION

Concha y Toro Amelia Chardonnay Las Petras
Errazuriz Aconcagua Costa Las Pizarras Chardonnay
Ritual Chardonnay

WINEMAKER WISDOM

"Chardonnay has more body than Sauvignon Blanc but is less aromatic. In the mouth, it has structure, and the range of styles can be very wide. In warm areas, we find more tropical notes than in cooler areas, where we find notes of asparagus and citrus fruits. If Chardonnay is planted in calcareous and clay soils, you get elegant, complex, structured wines that offer different layers. It also has a good aging potential. I like them when the notes aren't so pronounced and are more elegant: notes of gunpowder, slightly reduced, citrus aromas, white flowers. In the mouth, I like to find a natural acidity, silky tannins, and a saline touch. I like to enjoy Chardonnay with fatty fishes from deep sea, such as salmon, tuna, halibut, hake, and Chilean sea bass, also with rice (paellas) and goat cheese."

—*Eduardo Jordan, chief winemaker, Sociedad Vinícola Miguel Torres Chile*

"Chilean Chardonnays have a lot of mid-palate body and consistency, making them wonderful wines to pair with food. Numerous flavors—apricot, hints of banana, a bit of vanilla from oak aging, and some subtle notes from malolactic fermentation—all this makes the wine very complex, which I love."

—*Aurelio Montes Jr., chief winemaker, Montes*

WINEMAKER WISDOM

"I am looking for freshness, saltiness, and sapidity. I do tend to prefer white wines with structure and those that have a long finish. I cannot resist aged white wines, either! You commonly will find rich aromas of dried mango, lemon pie, clove, buttered toast, and burnt caramel. I enjoy Chardonnay with raw fish and shellfish dishes, but it also makes an exceptional pairing with white-meat dishes."

—*Laura Bianchi, winemaker, Castello di Monsanto*

"Chardonnay adapts to each terroir and soil where it grows in a very particular way, becoming almost an indigenous grape variety in each region. In Barolo and Barbaresco, Chardonnay made its first appearance only in the 1980s, and my father, Pio Boffa, was among the pioneers. We planted it in 1981 and released Piodilei Chardonnay in 1985. My father decided to dedicate Piodilei (meaning "Pio for her") to the ladies of our family because of the great similarities between them: long aging potential, elegance, and finesse. I love Piodilei with risotto alla parmigiana with white truffles, fried eggs with fondue on top, a good plate of pasta with meat sauce, or even fish with an intense butter sauce."

—*Federica Boffa Pio, proprietor, Pio Cesare*

NEXT PAGE Chardonnay vineyard at Fabrizio Bianchi in Italy

ITALY

As elsewhere, Italian growers often confused Chardonnay with Pinot Blanc. It grows mainly in the north of the country, both in Trentino–Alto Adige and Friuli–Venezia Giulia, where fruit-forward versions, unoaked or lightly oaked, prove popular. Piedmont and Tuscany also cultivated, as do Puglia and Sicily in the far south. Italy takes great pride in its native varieties, so it's astounding to see how much Chardonnay the country produces. At the beginning of the century, it was the fourth most widely planted white grape in the country.

RECOMMENDED WINES: ITALY

BARGAIN
Alois Lageder Chardonnay
Cantina Terlan Chardonnay
Caparzo Chardonnay
Kurtatsch Caliz Chardonnay
Tormaresca Chardonnay

VALUE
Castello di Monsanto Fabrizio Bianchi Chardonnay
Fabrizio Bianchi Chardonnay →
Gradis'ciutta Collio Chardonnay
Massolino Langhe Chardonnay
Pio Cesare Chardonnay

SPECIAL OCCASION
Castello Banfi Fontanelle Chardonnay
Jermann Dreams Chardonnay
Pio Cesare Piodilei Chardonnay
Planeta Chardonnay
Tenute del Cabreo La Pietra Chardonnay

SPLURGE
Ca' del Bosco Curtefranca Chardonnay
Damilano G.D. Chardonnay
Gaja Gaia & Rey Chardonnay

NEW ZEALAND

Chardonnay first came to New Zealand in the 1830s, dying off due to phylloxera but returning in the 1970s at the advent of the country's modern wine industry. Perhaps surprisingly, Chardonnay ranked as New Zealand's most widely planted grape until 2002, when Sauvignon Blanc bested it. Around 40 percent grows in Gisborne, 30 percent in Marlborough, and a quarter in Hawke's Bay. Winemakers vinify two-thirds of the country's harvest into still wine and the balance into sparkling. The nation's cold climate perfectly coaxes out Chardonnay's apple and citrus flavors, while judicious use of oak brings out a more sophisticated, complex style.

RECOMMENDED WINES: NEW ZEALAND

BARGAIN

Babich Wines Unoaked Chardonnay

Kim Crawford Unoaked Chardonnay

Nobilo Chardonnay

Oyster Bay Chardonnay

VALUE

Craggy Range Kidnappers Vineyard
 Chardonnay →

Dog Point Vineyard Chardonnay

Felton Road Bannockburn Chardonnay

Kumeu River Estate Chardonnay

SPECIAL OCCASION

Clearview Reserve Chardonnay

Kumeu River Maté's Vineyard Chardonnay

Mt. Beautiful Chardonnay

Villa Maria Keltern Vineyard Chardonnay

LEFT Chardonnay harvest at Craggy Range in New Zealand

SOUTH AFRICA

Facing strict quarantine regulations in the 1970s, a group of South African winemakers devised a scheme to smuggle Chardonnay cuttings into the country. But they wound up planting what turned out to be Auxerrois Blanc, Chardonnay's less famous sibling. Chardonnay eventually established a presence here in the 1980s. Since then, South African Chardonnay, dwarfed in comparison to Chenin Blanc, has made a name for itself in the wider world.

The best appellations include Robertson, which benefits from cool Indian Ocean breezes; Elgin, which offers high altitudes in the Hottentot-Holland Mountains; and Stellenbosch, which perfectly combines the attributes of the prior two regions. Made in versions from light and crisp to well oaked, South African Chardonnay features flavors of pineapple and grapefruit.

RECOMMENDED WINES: SOUTH AFRICA

BARGAIN

De Wetshof Limestone Hill Chardonnay
Graham Beck The Game Reserve Chardonnay
Spier Signature Collection Chardonnay
Warwick The First Lady Chardonnay

VALUE

Glenelly Estate Reserve Chardonnay
Kara-Tara Chardonnay
Meerlust Chardonnay
Tokara Chardonnay

SPECIAL OCCASION

Capensis Chardonnay
Hamilton Russell Vineyards Chardonnay
Jardin Nine Yards Chardonnay
Rustenberg Five Soldiers Chardonnay

WINEMAKER WISDOM

"I love Chardonnay's lack of excessively aromatic varietal fruit, its seemingly effortless layers, and generous texture, regardless of origin. Our Chardonnay tends to combine lemon, lime, and pears when physiologically ripe, sometimes with a hint of green and yellow apple and perhaps white peach. We are known for an aesthetic far closer to white Burgundy than to a generalised 'New World' style. The world is full of great Chardonnay in a range of styles, as it should be. You just need to pick the aesthetic that resonates most with you."

—*Anthony Hamilton Russell, proprietor, Hamilton Russell Vineyards*

"Chardonnay talks about soil, making it a conduit for understanding terroir. It can go from place to place and shine a light on what that vineyard can do. Today, the clonal selections we work with are very similar, if not the same, from country to country. We all share material and knowledge all the time, so the differences really come down to site expression and growing conditions. The farming practices, crop load, and vine age all contribute to the singular expressions which define a site/region. In the Western Cape, the soils are extremely old and weathered. With careful farming practices, these sites express that complexity. Chardonnay is also about evolution. With Capensis, the approach centers on quality and longevity with the understanding of how Chardonnay gains complexity with age."

—*Graham Weerts, winemaker, Capensis*

USA

Every state in the union makes wine, and some Chardonnay grows in each of them. As the nation's winemaking heart, California naturally receives the most recognition, with New York and Oregon not far behind. Washington, Virginia, and Texas have excellent reputations with this variety as well. Beyond those, it succeeds in states that don't immediately come to mind as wine regions: Alabama, Arizona, Arkansas, Colorado, Connecticut, Georgia, Idaho, Illinois, Indiana, Iowa, Maryland, Massachusetts, Michigan, Minnesota, Missouri, New Hampshire, New Jersey, New Mexico, North Carolina, Ohio, Oklahoma, South Carolina, Tennessee, and Vermont. Most wines from these states don't have wide distribution, so visit tasting rooms at local wineries or check out websites devoted to the local wine industry to learn more.

California

The number one choice among American wine drinkers and the number one grape planted in California, Chardonnay grows stem to stern in the Golden State. It has thrived here since the 1880s, when Charles Wetmore imported cuttings from Meursault and planted them in his vineyard in Livermore. Often called the father of the California wine industry, Wetmore at the time was serving as secretary of the California Viticultural Commission. In 1896, Paul Masson also brought plantings from Burgundy to Livermore, followed by German winemaker C. H. Wente in 1912. Today the Wente Clone accounts for 80 percent of the variety in the entire country.

Fast-forward through a world war, Prohibition, the Great Depression, and another world war, and you'll understand why the first half of the 20th century wasn't a great time for wine in America—or anywhere, for that matter. Then, in 1976, the wine tasting known as the Judgment of Paris pitted top French wines against their counterparts from California, shining new light on Chardonnay. Chateau Montelena Chardonnay 1973, the white wine that placed first, beat out wines from Burgundy's best regions, including Meursault and Puligny-Montrachet. Around this time, Americans developed the habit of drinking wines designated by variety rather than region, scoring another hit for Chardonnay's popularity.

Today more than 90,000 acres of Chardonnay grow in California, with the largest acreage in Monterey, Sonoma, San Joaquin, Napa, and Yolo counties. You can find it in every possible style, from cheap and cheerful—sold in boxes or cans—to luscious and superb with just the right amount of oak. Past California Chards were overoaked almost to undrinkability, but most vintners are producing versions of the wine noted for balance and finesse.

In addition to Napa and Sonoma, other regions known for high-quality Chardonnay include Mendocino, Monterey, and Santa Barbara, each region featuring cooling ocean breezes and cold nights that help preserve acidity. Chardonnay is the most planted variety in Mendocino, just north of Sonoma County. Monterey accounts for about a fifth of the state's vineyards, while Mendocino and Santa Barbara each have around 5 percent of the total. Down the coast in Southern California, Santa Barbara and its sub-AVA Santa Maria Valley both have strong reputations for high-quality Chardonnay.

LEFT Chardonnay on the vine at Foley Estate Vineyards in Santa Barbara, California

WINEMAKER WISDOM

"We demonstrate our oceanic soils and marine-impacted landscape with as much luxury, precision, and purpose as possible. A salty underpinning corrals intense elements of lemon and lime."

—*Greg Brewer, winemaker, Brewer-Clifton*

"I love the structure and flavor of Chardonnay. I love that it can express a range of styles very well, from ripe, tropical, and creamy with malolactic fermentation to fresh and vibrant with citrus notes. For example, Clone 809 at Spanish Springs in the San Luis Obispo Coast will give you bright citrus and stone fruit if picked earlier. The same 809 in Coombsville, Napa Valley, picked a little later on the curve, will give you tropical fruit flavors and ripe florals."

—*Marbue Marke, winemaker, Oceano*

"Chardonnay is a blank slate with such a wide range. You can go from no oak, no malo, all the way to a barrel-fermented Chardonnay with malo that's richer in texture and age-worthy. Chardonnay with oak and malo comes through as brioche and biscuity, with lemon curd, and sometimes buttery notes and a broad texture. We do two caviar pairings that are out of this world. One is with our Unoaked Chardonnay paired with wild Tennessee sturgeon, always a fan favorite at the winery."

—*Alex McGregor, director of winemaking, Saracina Vineyards*

RECOMMENDED WINES: CALIFORNIA

BARGAIN

Charles Woodson's Intercept Chardonnay

Harken Barrel Fermented Chardonnay

J. Lohr Riverstone Chardonnay

Kendall-Jackson Vintner's Reserve Chardonnay

Saracina Unoaked Chardonnay

Save Me San Francisco Calling All Angels Chardonnay

VALUE

Alma Rosa Sta. Rita Hills Chardonnay

Brewer-Clifton Sta. Rita Hills Chardonnay

Cambria Katherine's Vineyard Chardonnay

Chalone Vineyard Estate Chardonnay

Diatom Bar-M Chardonnay

Foley Estates Sta. Rita Hills Chardonnay

Metz Road Riverview Vineyard Estate Grown Chardonnay

Oceano Spanish Springs Vineyard Chardonnay

SPECIAL OCCASION

Au Bon Climat Nuits-Blanches au Bouge Chardonnay

Copain Wines DuPratt Chardonnay

The Hilt Estate Chardonnay

Maggy Hawk Skycrest Vineyard Chardonnay

Paul Lato Le Souvenir Sierra Madre Vineyard

Talbott Vineyards Sleepy Hollow Chardonnay

Napa

First, let's never forget that Napa Valley put California *and* Chardonnay on the American wine map in 1976 at the Judgment of Paris. In the northern reaches of the region, Chardonnay grown on the valley floor will yield prominent tropical fruit flavors, while higher-altitude mountain vineyards coax out citrus notes and minerality. At the southern end, the colder climate of the Carneros AVA, which straddles Napa and Sonoma, benefits from cooling breezes off San Pablo Bay as well as early morning fog, both of which prevent the grapes from overripening and losing their freshness and acidity.

RECOMMENDED WINES: NAPA

BARGAIN

Beringer Napa Valley Chardonnay

Ca' Momi Napa Valley Chardonnay

Raymond Napa Valley Reserve Chardonnay

Sterling Vineyards Napa Valley Chardonnay

Trefethen Double T Napa Valley Chardonnay

VALUE

Michael Mondavi Family Estate Isabel Mondavi Chardonnay

Post & Beam Napa Valley Chardonnay

Sequoia Grove Winery Napa Valley Chardonnay

Smith-Madrone Estate Grown Chardonnay

Stags' Leap Napa Valley Chardonnay

SPECIAL OCCASION

Cakebread Cellars Napa Valley Chardonnay

Far Niente Estate Bottled Chardonnay

Freemark Abbey Napa Valley Chardonnay

JCB N°76 Chardonnay, Napa Valley

William Hill Napa Valley Chardonnay

SPLURGE

Grgich Hills Paris Tasting Commemorative Estate Grown Chardonnay

La Jota WS Keyes Vineyard Chardonnay

Kongsgaard The Judge Chardonnay

Pahlmeyer Napa Valley Chardonnay

RECOMMENDED WINES: CARNEROS

BARGAIN

Benziger Chardonnay Sangiacomo Vineyard Chardonnay

Clos Agnes Carneros Sonoma County Chardonnay

Imagery Ricci Vineyard Chardonnay

RouteStock Carneros Chardonnay

VALUE

Artesa Estate Vineyard Chardonnay

Bouchaine Estate Chardonnay

Buena Vista Chateau Buena Vista Carneros Chardonnay

Frank Family Vineyards Carneros Chardonnay

Merryvale Carneros Chardonnay

Oberon Los Carneros Chardonnay →

Rombauer Vineyards Carneros Chardonnay

SPECIAL OCCASION

Cakebread Cellars Chardonnay Reserve

Hyde de Villaine Hyde Vineyard Chardonnay

Patz & Hall Hyde Vineyard Chardonnay

Ram's Gate Estate Chardonnay

Schug Carneros Estate Chardonnay

WINEMAKER WISDOM

"There's a wonderful varietal purity and clarity of character to Chardonnay, and no matter what style you make, from fresh styles to fuller-bodied, that purity and clarity express themselves all the way from grape to bottle. One defining characteristic I love is the white, crushed-seashell minerality. When I'm tasting the grapes in the vineyard, they have that green-apple tartness and brightness. When the grapes are ready to pick, that flavor turns into a richer apple-pie flavor. It's something you can take a bite out of, a perfect ripeness that you can connect directly to orchard fruit."

—*Tony Coltrin, head winemaker, Oberon Wines*

"Napa Valley Chardonnay differs in its ability to achieve ripeness early and sometimes even overripeness. Sugar can accumulate quickly, and acids can drop out because it can get so warm here. Wines from our region are sometimes big, creamy, and viscous; the best ones have acidity to bring balance. In other regions, such as Burgundy and Sonoma Coast, the weather is much cooler. Grapes often are picked with less sugar and much more acid, resulting in crisp, structured, bright wines. What I love about making Chardonnay from Napa Valley is that it offers the opportunity to craft wines with intense flavor and texture but also with nuanced aromatics and refreshing acidity. Barrel fermentation adds layers of toasted hazelnuts and subtle hints of vanilla. Additional aromas sometimes include flint and wet stone."

—*Nicole Marchesi, winemaker, Far Niente Winery*

"Chardonnay from Napa Valley has a great purity of fruit, more citrusy in wines made from Carneros, more apple and pear qualities in those a little farther away from the water. Most also will include some elements of vanilla, brioche, or toast. For pairings, if I'm feeling casual, roast chicken and potatoes. If I'm feeling fancy, I love it with seared scallops over a bed of leeks and/or fennel."

—*Kristy Melton, winemaker, Freemark Abbey*

"Napa is a relatively small region for growing Chardonnay, but when you dive into all the unique sub-AVAs, you'll find a plethora of opportunities to make distinct, site-driven wines. When you add the winemaker's touch with such techniques as barrel fermentation, lees stirring, and malolactic fermentation, you can create a very layered, complex, and age-worthy Chardonnay. Choosing to avoid those techniques would lead to a completely different style, showcasing its chameleon nature."

—*Mark Williams, winemaker, William Hill Estate Winery*

Sonoma

Farther west than neighboring Napa, Sonoma boasts a number of cool-climate regions ideal for cultivating Chardonnay. About half of the Carneros AVA sits within Sonoma County. In the 1980s and '90s, it reigned as the region's coolest appellation, but as winemaking moved west and to higher altitudes, that assertion no longer goes unchallenged. With more than 15,000 acres, Sonoma is the second-highest producer of the grape in the state. But a good portion goes into high-quality sparkling wine made by wineries founded by families with roots in Champagne. Coastal fog and cool nights help achieve Chardonnay's freshest flavor profile, especially in the Russian River Valley, Alexander Valley, Sonoma Coast, and Petaluma Gap AVAs.

WINEMAKER WISDOM

"I'm most inspired by the wines in Côte d'Or because of the variety of styles there and the region's unique micro-climates. Compared to our Sonoma County Chardonnay, the wines from this region of France can have higher acidity with more delicate flavors. In Sonoma Valley, the warm days with cool nights showcase more floral and spice flavors, and as you move west into Russian River Valley, I see more 'coastal cool' flavors of green apple and citrus. Up in the northern part of the county, in Alexander Valley, I find more tropical pineapple and melon flavors expressed from that warm-weather environment."

— *Katie Madigan, winemaker, St. Francis*

"In Sonoma County, thin top soils of fractured sandstone intermixed with volcanic ash make for a fascinating interplay of flavor, texture, and length."

— *Brian Maloney, winemaker, JCB*

RECOMMENDED WINES: SONOMA

BARGAIN
Au Contraire Russian River Valley Chardonnay
Coppola Director's Cut Chardonnay
Frei Brothers Chardonnay Reserve
St. Francis Winery & Vineyards Sonoma County Chardonnay

VALUE
Arista Russian River Valley Chardonnay
DeLoach OFS Our Finest Selection Chardonnay
Emblem Rodgers Creek Petaluma Gap AVA
    Chardonnay
Hartford Court Four Hearts Vineyard Russian River
    Valley Chardonnay
J Vineyards & Winery Russian River Valley
    Chardonnay

SPECIAL OCCASION
Buena Vista Winery Viticultural Society
    Natalia's Selection Chardonnay
Hartford Court Four Hearts Vineyard Russian
    River Valley Chardonnay
JCB N°33 Chardonnay →
Stonestreet Estate Vineyards Estate
    Chardonnay

SPLURGE
Flowers Camp Ridge Meeting Estate Ridge Vineyards
    Chardonnay
Kosta Browne El Diablo Chardonnay
Stonestreet Estate Vineyards Upper Barn Vineyard
    Chardonnay
Williams Selyem Olivet Lane Vineyard Chardonnay

New York

Like Burgundy, coastal California, and Oregon, New York is a cold-climate wine region, and the Empire State found much of its vinous success with *Vitis labrusca* and hybrid grapes. Charles Fournier and Konstantin Frank, experimenting here with European varieties to make into sparkling wine, first successfully grew Chardonnay in the Finger Lakes region in the 1950s. The variety tolerates New York's cold, wet winters, while cool growing season delays ripening, permitting the grapes to mature to greater complexity without overripening. It grows in the Finger Lakes, Hudson Valley, and Long Island. Expect flavors of green pear and Granny Smith apple with notes of citrus and spice.

RECOMMENDED WINES: NEW YORK

BARGAIN
Fox Run Doyle Family Chardonnay
Lakewood Chardonnay
Lamoreaux Landing Reserve Estate Bottled Chardonnay
Macari Vineyards Estate Chardonnay
Millbrook Unoaked Chardonnay

VALUE
Anthony Road Barrel Ferment Chardonnay
Dr. Konstantin Frank Hilda Chardonnay
Jamesport Saddleback Chardonnay
One Woman Estate Chardonnay
Wölffer Estate Perle Chardonnay

Oregon

The rest of the wine world first discovered Oregon's potential for great Burgundy-style wines when prominent French winemaking families bought land and built wineries here. The first commercial vineyards took root in the Willamette Valley in the early 1970s, but the first round of Oregon Chardonnays suffered from poor clonal selection and heavy oaking. Today's leaner versions, often made from French clones planted on carefully selected sites, vinify in stainless steel and concrete, which allows the fruit and minerality to shine. In the last 20 years, Oregon Chardonnay has hit its stride. Look for wines from Willamette Valley and its sub-AVAs, especially Dundee Hills, Eola-Amity Hills, and Yamhill-Carlton. Flavors include pineapple and pear and a pronounced note of flint.

RECOMMENDED WINES: OREGON

BARGAIN
A to Z Wineworks Oregon Chardonnay
Acrobat Chardonnay
Chehalem Inox Chardonnay
Wine by Joe Chardonnay

VALUE
Argyle Willamette Valley Chardonnay
Domaine Drouhin Oregon Arthur Chardonnay
Maison Noir Knock On Wood Chardonnay
Rose Rock Chardonnay
Siduri Willamette Valley Chardonnay

SPECIAL OCCASION
00 Wines VGW Very Good White Chardonnay
Domaine Serene Evenstad Reserve Chardonnay
Gran Moraine Yamhill-Carlton Chardonnay
Penner-Ash Wine Cellars Willamette Valley
   Chardonnay →
WillaKenzie Estate Chardonnay

RIGHT Gran Moraine Winery in Oregon

WINEMAKER WISDOM

"Chardonnay can express, in the most refined, complex, and elegant way, the multiple qualities of a soil. When grown well, in the right place and made with skilled hands, it always will deliver the beautiful secrets of its birthplace. We all can find the style—from steely and crisp to multilayered, ample, long palate, complex, rich, oaky—that suits our palates."

—*Véronique Boss-Drouhin, winemaker,*
Maison Joseph Drouhin and Domaine Drouhin Oregon

"Chardonnay is my desert-island grape. It's the only variety to which I could devote the rest of my life. No other grape is so versatile. If it were an animal, it would be a *Homo sapiens*. I love the power from the acidity, the complexity from long native ferments, and the precision from judicious oak use. Great Chardonnay from the Willamette Valley achieves balanced alcohol and acidity, has ample but not over-the-top fruit, and, dare I say, minerality. As an industry, we are just beginning to tease out how the different soil types in the Willamette Valley influence the character of Chardonnay. Yamhill-Carlton and specifically the Gran Moraine Vineyard have soils that are a result of ancient seafloor uplift. From my tastings, these soils give a slightly gravelly feel and structure that I find immensely pleasing. Willamette Chardonnays are svelte. They often exhibit more grace than power and have more tertiary flavors that most other New World wines."

—*Shane Moore, winemaker, Gran Moraine*

"It's very much a winemaker's wine. You can be very cerebral about approaching it, but the enjoyment of it is a pretty visceral experience. You don't have to analyze every detail. The range of styles, flavors, growing areas, and winemaker input create such a diverse array of Chardonnays, and it's so much fun to explore. I love Chardonnays that have palate weight at lower alcohols with fresh flavors and crisp acid, so the Willamette Valley was the first—well, really the only—place that we looked for making our first Chardonnay for Siduri."

—*Matt Revelette, winemaker, Siduri*

AROUND THE WORLD

One of the most well-traveled varieties, Chardonnay grows in practically every winemaking country you can name. In addition to France and the other notable countries already discussed, you can find it elsewhere in Europe, including: Austria, Bulgaria, Croatia, Germany, Greece, Hungary, Macedonia, Moldova, Portugal, Romania, Slovakia, Slovenia, Spain, and Switzerland; in Morocco in Africa; in the Middle East and Central Asia: Georgia, India, Israel, Lebanon, and Turkey; in North America: Canada and Washington State; and in South America: Brazil and Uruguay.

RECOMMENDED WINES: AROUND THE WORLD

BARGAIN

Adega de Monção Chardonnay, Portugal

Enate Chardonnay 234, Spain

Murfatlar Chardonnay, Romania

Raimat Chardonnay, Spain

Rough Day Chardonnay, Bulgaria

VALUE

Christina Orange Chardonnay, Austria

Dalton Estate Unoaked Chardonnay, Israel

The Electric Chardonnay Acid Test, Germany

Golan Heights Winery Chardonnay, Israel

Marjan Simčič Chardonnay, Slovenia

Recanati Reserve Chardonnay, Israel

SPECIAL OCCASION

Familia Torres Milmanda, Spain

Saints Hills Le Chiffre, Croatia

Weingut Emmerich Knoll Loibner Chardonnay, Austria

WINEMAKER WISDOM

"At the beginning, 30 years ago, our barrel-fermented Chardonnay showed a more intense, buttery or butterscotch character, associated with a high concentration of diacetyl. Today, we know that extended contact with lees, when stirred, can reduce the diacetyl content and lends stability and longevity. We have changed the butterscotch style for a fresher, fruitier, and more exotic profile. The oft-forgotten truth is that white wines match better with cheese than reds."

—*Jesús Artajona Serrano, winemaker, Enate*

"Some time ago, consumers knew only a handful of wines from a country or wine region. Today, their knowledge has increased tremendously, and now people know that not only different climates are important for specific grape varieties but also the specific valley/vineyard, the specific type of soil, and the different winemaking techniques. We should embrace that!"

—*Miguel Torres Maczassek, general manager, Familia Torres*

CHASSELAS

(shah-suh-LAH)

IN THE GLASS

SMALL BORDEAUX GLASS, PALE STRAW IN COLOR

TASTING PROFILE

ACIDITY

BODY

SWEETNESS

LOW   MEDIUM   HIGH

TASTING NOTES

GREEN APPLE   LEMON   WHITE FLOWERS

Wines made from Chasselas tend to taste dry, acidic, and aromatic. They have aromas and flavors of green apple, lemon, lime, white peach, white flowers, jasmine, fresh green herbs, and a touch of river rock or slate. Crisp and zesty in the mouth, they have a clean finish.

YOU SHOULD KNOW

Chasselas grows widely in Switzerland, ranking as the country's most planted white variety. In the Valais region, it goes by the name Fendant.

FOOD PAIRINGS

CHEESE   SALAD   SHRIMP

The Swiss love to pair Chasselas with cheeses, such as Gruyère and Emmentaler, and it goes perfectly with fondue. Its high acidity means that it also pairs well with green salads, grilled vegetables, shrimp, seafood, and veal dishes.

RECOMMENDED WINES: SWITZERLAND

BARGAIN

Domaine du Daley Le Chasselas Grand Reserve Grand Cru

Les Fils de Charles Favre Fendant de la Dame de Sion

Jean-René Germanier Vétroz Fendant Les Terrasses

VALUE

Avalanche Fendant

Château d'Auvernier Neuchâtel Blanc →

Henri Badoux Aigle Les Murailles

Luc Massy Chemin de Fer Dézaley Grand Cru

Olivier Roten Caves du Paradis Fendant

Raymond Chappuis Dézaley Grand Cru Les
    Embleyres

Robert Gilliard Les Murettes Fendant Sion

Testuz Dézaley L'Arbalète Chasselas

SPECIAL OCCASION

Les Frères Dubois et Fils Dézaley-Marsens Grand
    Cru de la Tour

Louis Bovard Médinette Dézaley Grand Cru

Pierre Gonon Chasselas, France

SINCE THE 1600S, Chasselas has grown north of Lake Geneva, mainly in the Vaud, Geneva, Neuchâtel, and Valais cantons. Fendant has had appellation protection since 1966. Vaud also adds appellation names to the label, such as Lavaux, Vully, or Bonvillars, so look for those. Many people assumed that the grape came from the eponymous village in Burgundy, but recent research shows that it most likely grew in Switzerland first and subsequently traveled to the French village.

Vineyard altitudes range from 270 meters to 1,100 meters (885 feet to 3,600 feet), making it challenging to grow wine here, and you usually can spot snow on vineyards in early spring. Winemakers plant their vineyards only on the south-facing slopes so the grapes can ripen fully. Chasselas ripens earlier than other grapes, which suits this unique climate and terroir. Vineyards lie on steep slopes, making machine harvesting difficult to almost nonexistent. Many growers tend vines by hand, with the occasional cow, ox, or horse to lighten the load.

The Swiss like to drink their own wine and rank fourth internationally in annual wine consumption. According to 2022 statistics, they drink 33 liters per person per year, but little of their wine makes it to the American or British

Château d'Auvernier in Switzerland

markets. They consume about a third of it themselves, export roughly a quarter to Italy, sell 15 percent to France, and the remaining 10 percent goes to what they call the "New World." But Swiss winemakers are seeking new markets, particularly China.

Chasselas also grows in France's Loire Valley and in Baden, Germany. Some French winemakers purportedly have been looking for land in England on which to plant it. The variety grows in small quantities in Portugal and Croatia, as well as in Hungary and Turkey as table grapes.

ABOVE Aging cellar at Château d'Auvernier
LEFT Chasselas harvest at Château d'Auvernier

CHENIN BLANC

(SHEHN-in BLAHNK)

IN THE GLASS

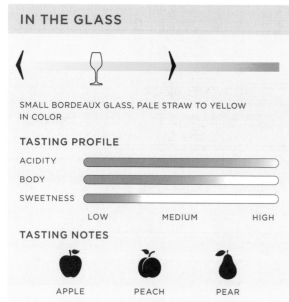

SMALL BORDEAUX GLASS, PALE STRAW TO YELLOW IN COLOR

TASTING PROFILE

	LOW	MEDIUM	HIGH
ACIDITY			
BODY			
SWEETNESS			

TASTING NOTES

APPLE   PEACH   PEAR

Dry Chenin Blanc has aromas and flavors of apple, pear, and river rocks. Off-dry versions go floral with jasmine and orange blossom as well as more lush fruits, such as peach and passion fruit. Sweet Chenin Blanc evokes orange marmalade, honey, and fresh ginger. Expert tasters sometimes use lanolin to describe its full body, rich mouthfeel, and otherwise indescribable earthiness.

YOU SHOULD KNOW

Chenin Blanc comes in a variety of styles, from bone dry to dessert sweet, the latter especially in France and South Africa. Vintners in Vouvray and the Loire Valley often vinify into sparkling wine. If the label doesn't list the residual sugar content, look for the French words *doux* (sweet) or *sec* (dry). Also check the alcohol level—the lower the ABV, the higher the sugar—and the color: the darker, the sweeter. When in doubt, ask!

FOOD PAIRINGS

CHICKEN   PORK   CHEESE

Dry or off-dry Chenin Blanc tastes spectacular with poultry, especially fried chicken or turkey. Open a bottle for your next Thanksgiving, Christmas, or other cold-weather holiday feast because it pairs well with a medley of savory and sweet dishes, including cranberry sauce and sweet potatoes. It's also terrific with all different styles of pork: grilled, sweet-and-sour, and so on. Its high acidity also stands up nicely to soft, tangy goat cheese.

RECOMMENDED WINES: FRANCE

BARGAIN

Château Moncontour Vouvray Demi-Sec (semisweet)

Domaine de la Gaverie Vouvray Sec

Domaine du Petit Coteau Sec

VALUE

Château de la Roulerie Coteaux du Layon (sweet)

Domaine de Vodanis François Gilet Vouvray Sec

Domaine du Petit Clocher Les Audacieuses

Domaine Xavier & Agnès Amirault Les Quarterons Anjou Blanc

Saget La Perrière Marie de Beauregard

SPECIAL OCCASION

Château de Fesles La Chapelle Vieilles Vignes

Domaine des Baumard Quarts de Chaume (sweet)

Domaine Bourillon d'Orleans La Coulée d'Argent Sec Montgouverne

Domaine du Closel Clos du Papillon

Domaine de la Taille aux Loups Clos de Mosny

L IKE YOUR BEST FRIEND at a house party, Chenin Blanc is the first to arrive and the last to leave. Its vines bud early in spring, but it fully ripens well into fall. Also like a good best friend, this wine proves wildly versatile. The sugar content and acidity render it suitable for every possible style: dry, off-dry, sweet, botrytized (noble rot), and even sparkling.

Named for Mt. Chenin in Touraine, a wine region in France's Loire Valley, Chenin Blanc has grown in France for more than 1,300 years. In the early 1500s, French thinker and author François Rabelais wrote of the variety in his masterwork, *Gargantua and Pantagruel*, calling the grape by its local name, Pineau de Loire: "Pineau wine. Oh the nice white wine! And for my soul, it is nothing else than taffeta." Now, that's a tasting note!

In France, Chenin Blanc has many other synonyms, including: Anjou, Blanc d'Anjou, Gros Chenin, Gros Pineau, Pineau d'Anjou, Pineau de Loire, Pineau de Savennières, Plant d'Anjou, and Rouchelin. Several of these names have to do with the main areas where it grows. Like other traditional Old World wines, most French Chenin Blanc bears the name of the appellation on the label, rather than the variety name. When choosing a bottle, it helps to know the French terms for dry (*sec*), off-dry (*demi-sec*), semisweet (*moelleux*), sweet (*doux*), and sparkling (*crémant*, which technically means "creamy" as a description of the mouthfeel). In shops and on wine lists, you'll find bottles from the following appellations.

Reyneke Chenin Blanc vineyard in South Africa

VOUVRAY

The region most familiar to consumers, Vouvray produces Chenin Blanc in dry, off-dry, and sweet styles as well as sparkling wines. Producers make dry or sparkling versions for cool vintages and off-dry versions in warmer years to harness higher sugar levels and tropical fruit flavors. These wines have high acidity and flavors of pineapple and mango, and they mature gracefully for many years.

SAVENIÈRRES

These dry, full-bodied, age-worthy Chenin Blancs have flavors of green apple and pear and strong minerality. Vintners here make other styles, but almost all exported Savenièrres tastes dry.

MONTLOUIS-SUR-LOIRE

This is Vouvray's neighbor to the south, on the opposite bank of the Loire River. Winemakers make dry, off-dry, and sweet styles. If you can find them, these wines usually offer better value than those from across the river.

COTEAUX DU LAYON

This sweet wine appellation runs along the banks of the Layon River, a tributary of the Loire in Anjou. Chenin Blanc often goes by the moniker Pineau de Loire here, and winemakers either harvest the grapes late or botrytize them. The wines range from off-dry to very sweet, and the designation Sélection de Grains Nobles (selection of noble berries) applies to noble-rot versions. Expect flavors of canned peach, dried apricot, and apple pie with notes of honeycomb and spice. Six communes may add their names after the larger appellation, and two others, Quarts de Chaume and Bonnezeaux, may go by their more specific names rather than this broader appellation.

Quarts de Chaume

The only Grand Cru appellation in the Loire Valley, Quarts de Charme has a reputation for sweet wines, made from noble rot or not, often compared to Sauternes. Bottles can age for up to 50 years. Pair these wines with blue cheese, foie gras, or creamy desserts, such as flan or crème brûlée.

Bonnezeaux

The wines of Bonnezeaux consist entirely of Chenin Blanc made sweet, either with *Botrytis cinerea*—a beneficial fungus poetically called noble rot—or not. This appellation offers a level of complexity similar to Quarts de Chaume. Notes of vanilla and orange blossom join flavors of mango, peach preserves, and orange marmalade. Pair with apple or peach pie, vanilla or butter pecan ice cream, or pork rillettes.

CRÉMANT DE LOIRE

This AOC includes sparkling wine made with the traditional method in Anjou, Touraine, and Cheverny in the central Loire Valley. The rules allow for 10 different grapes, but winemakers here favor Chenin Blanc. Dry versions bear the designation *brut* and off-dry bottles are called *demi-sec*. Expect aromas of orchard fruit, white flowers, and hazelnut with flavors of Granny Smith apple, green pear, and lemon with notes of toasted almond and spice. Demi-sec Crémant de Loire has flavors of peach and pineapple with honey and vanilla.

....

WINEMAKER WISDOM

"Chenin Blanc always delivers its extensive array of aromatics with great panache. On the nose, the wines are rich with subtle aromas of almond and acacia, complemented by fresh honey notes. On the palate, the wines are soft and well-balanced with lovely length due to the freshness provided by specific terroirs of siliceous clay soils."

—*Laurent Saget and Bruno Mineur, winemakers, Saget La Perrière*

....

RIGHT Chenin Blanc grapes on the vine at Chalone Vineyard in California

OTHER NOTABLE COUNTRIES

Chenin Blanc has grown in South Africa since the 1600s. Today it's the country's most widely planted wine grape, which goes by the alias Steen. In California in the 1960s and '70s, producers used it as a blending grape for inexpensive white wines, but Golden State winemakers are producing quality single-variety bottlings now. Chenin Blanc also grows in Australia and New Zealand, usually for white blends, though you can find single-varietal versions. Small plantings exist in the traditional South American wine countries of Argentina, Brazil, Chile, and Uruguay, as well as farther afield in Canada, Mexico, China, Spain, India, and Israel.

SOUTH AFRICA

The most widely planted grape in South Africa, Chenin Blanc accounts for around 18 percent of all vineyards in the country. South Africa grows twice as much acreage of it as France. Purportedly the Dutch East India Company brought cuttings here in the 1650s. For many years, producers used it, because of its high yields, to make bulk wine and brandy. It grows throughout the nation's winelands, but the best Chenin Blancs hail from Swartland, Paarl, Stellenbosch, and Wellington. The variety's versatility offers an almost blank slate for terroir and the winemaker's hand, which is why, as in France, it comes in a broad range of styles, including bone dry, syrupy sweet, and sparkling. Dry South African Chenin Blanc often has flavors of apple and green pear with full-throttle acidity and strong minerality, while sweeter bottlings offer pineapple and canned peaches backed by bold acidity that keeps them from tasting cloying.

WINEMAKER WISDOM

"Chenin Blanc performs exceptionally well here—at high altitude and on decomposed granite soils—with minimal intervention required in the vineyard or cellar. Chenin Blancs from the Loire and in particular Vouvray generally have a higher acidity and resultant freshness than their South African counterparts."

—*Johan Reyneke, owner, Reyneke Wines*

USA

A lot of Chenin Blanc used to grow throughout California, used mainly for inexpensive white blends, but growers tore much of it up and replanted different vines as American tastes turned to Cabernet Sauvignon, Chardonnay, and Sauvignon Blanc. Today, the highest concentrations of Chenin Blanc in California occur in Mendocino, Napa Valley, and the Clarksburg AVA. It grows in the Texas High Plains AVA and in Washington's Yakima and Columbia valleys. Small but significant plantings thrive throughout America, including in Arizona, Colorado, Idaho, Maryland, Minnesota, Missouri, New Mexico, New York, North Carolina, and Virginia.

WINEMAKER WISDOM

"Most European or South African Chenins can taste sweeter, with much different fruit profiles. Due to our unique limestone and decomposed granite site, the profile remains quite special. I love the opulent textures combined with high-desert aromas. The thick viscosity is unique, as is the combination of acidity, minerality, and fruit expression."

—*Greg Freeman, winemaker, Chalone Vineyard*

BELOW Aerial view of Chalone Vineyard and Pinnacles National Park

FIANO

(fee-AH-no)

IN THE GLASS

SMALL BORDEAUX GLASS, MEDIUM STRAW TO LIGHT YELLOW IN COLOR

TASTING PROFILE

ACIDITY
BODY
SWEETNESS

LOW   MEDIUM   HIGH

TASTING NOTES

PEAR   MELON   NUTS

Aromas of fresh fruit join mineral notes and strong floral scents. Flavors of pear, honeydew melon, citrus, and apple accompany smoke, oyster shell, dried herbs, and almond or hazelnut. Most Fiano tastes surprisingly complex, with rich mouthfeel and bold acidity.

YOU SHOULD KNOW

It's easy to classify all southern Italian white wines as easy-drinking pours to consume within a year or two of harvest, but Fiano—and especially Fiano di Avellino—can age. Fiano made in stainless steel matures beautifully for 5 to 7 years, and the best versions last up to 10.

FOOD PAIRINGS

CHICKEN   FISH   PASTA

Richly textured Fiano holds up to flavorful chicken dishes such as chicken tagine or lemon chicken. It also tastes terrific alongside grilled or sautéed salmon, flounder Française or Florentine, or salade Niçoise. Fiano matches naturally with pasta with clam sauce, linguine with shrimp scampi, or even spicy sesame noodles.

RECOMMENDED WINES: ITALY

BARGAIN

La Capranera Paestum Fiano
Donnachiara Fiano di Avellino
Mandrarossa Fiano Ciaca Bianca
Petilia Fiano di Avellino →
Villa Matilde Fiano di Avellino

VALUE

Ape Petilia Fiano di Avellino
Cantine di Marzo Fiano di Avellino
Donnachiara Empatia Fiano di Avellino
Luigi Maffini Kratos Fiano
Mastroberardino Radici Fiano di Avellino
Planeta Cometa Fiano, Sicilia Menfi DOC
Villa Raiano Alimata Fiano di Avellino

SPECIAL OCCASION

Feudi di San Gregorio Studi Arianello Fiano
    di Avellino
Planeta Cometa Fiano
San Salvatore Pian di Stio

FIANO HAS ONE OF THOSE unprovable backstories that wine people love and party poopers love to decry. In ancient Roman times, producers made a wine called *apianum* using a grape species called *apiana*, from the Latin word for "bees," which swarmed around the sweet bunches of grapes. Fiano *could* descend from a garbled pronunciation of *apiana*. Without DNA testing, it's impossible to know if it's the same grape, but we like that contemporary bees love this plant as much as their ancient ancestors.

A lot of Fiano grew in southern Italy before the phylloxera blight hit in the 1800s. Many winemakers eagerly replanted stricken vineyards with heartier varieties, such as Sangiovese and Trebbiano. In the 1970s, Antonio Mastroberardino—who has worked to identify and preserve Fiano and other ancient Italian grape varieties—brought it back in force. Fiano has low yields, meaning not a lot of grapes on the vine, and the grapes themselves don't give much juice, so overall output runs low. The fruit grows in small, loose bunches with tough skins well adapted to widely ranging temperatures, day and night, during the long growing season.

It serves as a blending grape in around 15 Italian DOCs, including Sannio, Costa d'Amalfi, Monreale, and Penisola Sorrentina. It grows widely in Sicily, where it has achieved great success, and it grows throughout Marche in central Italy and Campania in the south, where it forms the basis for Fiano di Avellino DOCG.

Fiano harvest at Planeta in Sicily

The most acclaimed Fiano grows in hillside vineyards of the Apennine Mountains not far from Avellino, in the Irpinia region, in Avellino province. Vineyards here range in altitude and soil types, which include volcanic, clay, and limestone. Bottles of Fiano di Avellino offer strong minerality and excellent aging potential, and some producers, such as Villa Raino and Feudi di San Gregorio, are releasing single-vineyard versions. Quite a few producers use lees contact to create nuanced wines with more complex flavors and textures. Fiano di Avellino DOCG must contain at least 85 percent Fiano, with up to 15 percent of Greco, Coda di Volpe Bianca, or Trebbiano Toscano allowed.

Over the last 20 years, plantings in Sicily have increased. Winemakers here often used it in blends, but Sicilian Fiano is gaining attention as a single-varietal wine, producing riper, fuller versions than those from the mainland. Vineyards near Menfi, in the Southwest, produce a style known for strong minerality and notes of dried herbs, citrus, and tropical fruit.

Outside Italy, Fiano also grows in the Hunter and Clare valleys and McLaren Vale of Australia, where it has adapted well to the Mediterranean-style climate. It has also found a home in Argentina, mainly in the La Rioja region in the west of the country. You can find small amounts in California, too.

WINEMAKER WISDOM

"Fiano di Avellino is one of the most complex and elegant white wines of Italy. It is among the few white wines that have real aging potential, about 20 years. A semi-aromatic wine in its young and fresh version, it's able to express all the characteristics of the territory in which it takes root. It changes a lot over the years and evolves toward tertiary hints of oil and notes of honey combined with balsamic hints."

—*Riccardo Cotarella, consultant enologist, Donnachiara*

"Working with these grapes with small but beautiful clusters and reaching an attractive golden color made me completely fall in love. In their birthplace, Campania, the wines are firm, sapid, and austere. In Sicily, they gain a more tropical, rounder aroma profile. The capital of the variety, from where we often taste examples from colleagues and friends, is Irpinia, which has a mountain ambience that gives such an inspiring balance to the wines. Classically, Fiano is one of those grapes that works all round for an entire seafood dinner—on the beach if you're lucky."

—*Patricia Toth, winemaker, Planeta*

RIGHT Fiano vineyard at Donnachiara winery in Italy

FRIULANO

(free-oo-LAH-no)

IN THE GLASS

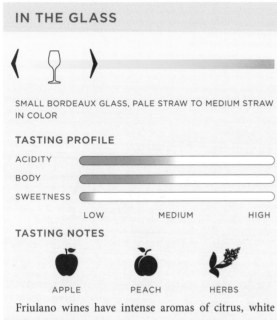

SMALL BORDEAUX GLASS, PALE STRAW TO MEDIUM STRAW IN COLOR

TASTING PROFILE

ACIDITY

BODY

SWEETNESS

LOW   MEDIUM   HIGH

TASTING NOTES

APPLE   PEACH   HERBS

Friulano wines have intense aromas of citrus, white peach, and yellow apple along with touches of green herbs and bitter almonds. Flavors include white flowers with strong minerality before a zesty finish.

YOU SHOULD KNOW

People have called Friulano many things and confused it with many other grapes. It traveled from Italy, through France, to Chile, and winemakers planted it in South America, thinking it was Sauvignon Blanc. Not until the 1990s, using DNA testing, did Chilean winemakers realize the mistake, at which point they pulled out the Friulano vines and planted Sauvignon Blanc.

FOOD PAIRINGS

OLIVES   HAM   ASPARAGUS

Friulano is ideal with antipasto. It pairs well with stuffed hot peppers, olives, pickled vegetables, sliced meats, and salty cubes of cured provolone. It also stands up nicely to asparagus and artichokes.

RECOMMENDED WINES: ITALY

BARGAIN
Bastianich Vigne Orsone Friulano
Borgo Conventi Friulano
Cantina Puiatti Friulano →
Torre Rosazza Friulano
La Tunella Friulano

VALUE
I Clivi di Ferdinando Zanusso Clivi Galea
Gradis'ciutta Friulano
Livio Felluga Friulano
La Vigne di Zamò Friulano
La Vigne di Zamò, Vigne Cinquant'anni Friulano

SPECIAL OCCASION
Bastianich Plus

SPLURGE
Miani Buri Friulano
Miani Filip Friulano

RIGHT Friulano vineyard at Livio Felluga in Friuli, Italy

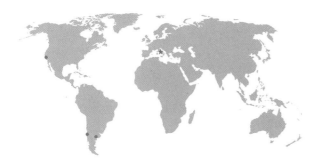

T HIS MYSTERIOUS WHITE GRAPE—the signature of Friuli, north of Venice, in the Friuli–Venezia Giulia region—also goes by the names Sauvignonasse, especially in Argentina and Chile, and Sauvignon Vert in California. We prefer to use its most common name so you can find it in the wine shop. Italians used to call it Tocai Friulano, but Hungary ordered Italy to desist because that name caused confusion with Hungary's Tokaj region and its Tokaji wines. In 2007, the Hungarians prevailed in the European Court of Justice, so now it's just Friulano. (They also forced growers in Alsace to rename their Tokay Pinot Gris or Tokay d'Alsace to Pinot Gris.)

History claims that Julius Caesar and his soldiers came to this region in 53 BCE and founded the Forum Julii, which later became known as the Cividale del Friuli. The Romans planted grapevines on the slopes of the eastern hills here, and their descendants tended those vines for centuries.

One of the area's most important DOCs is Consorzio Tutela Vini Friuli Colli Orientali. The others are Ramandolo, Colli Orientali del Friuli Picolit, and Rosazzo. Terraced on rolling hillsides, most of the vineyards stand at an altitude of 400 meters (1,300 feet). The foothills of the Alps protect the vines from cold northern winds, so the grapes have a long growing season that allows them to concentrate sugars and develop good acidity.

Friulano wines tend to taste zesty, with good acidity, and drink nicely on their own or pair with lighter fare. If growers harvest after full ripeness, the resulting increases in body and richness. Some winemakers allow their wines to sit on the lees for months or permit malolactic fermentation. Those wines have a rich, creamy mouthfeel that rivals some of the best Chardonnays. Other winemakers age their Friulano in oak barrels, which of course adds additional aromas of vanilla, toast, and baking spices.

WINEMAKER WISDOM

"When my father, Livio, began our family's journey among the hills surrounding the village of Rosazzo, he started by restoring some of the oldest vineyards of Friulano, which are still part of our estate. These wines embody our wish to share the aging potential, beauty, identity, and millenary viticultural tradition of our hills in Friuli. The terroir of Rosazzo is quite eclectic, and Friulano wines coming from different sites in the same area can be surprisingly diverse in their profiles: some fuller, exuberant, and tropical; others elegant, with herbal notes of a Mediterranean garden, with a touch of that savory finish that takes us back to the days when the Adriatic Sea covered the hills."

—*Andrea Felluga, owner and director, Livio Felluga*

FURMINT

(FOOR-mint)

IN THE GLASS

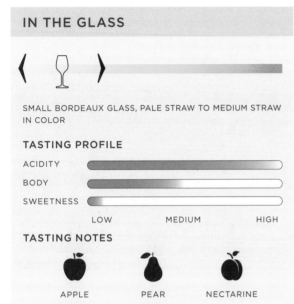

SMALL BORDEAUX GLASS, PALE STRAW TO MEDIUM STRAW IN COLOR

TASTING PROFILE

ACIDITY

BODY

SWEETNESS

LOW   MEDIUM   HIGH

TASTING NOTES

APPLE   PEAR   NECTARINE

Dry Furmints have aromas of Bartlett pear, yellow peach, nectarine, honeysuckle, and apple, along with a note of flint or smoke from the volcanic soils in which it grows. Expect flavors of stone fruits, great minerality, and a crisp, clean finish.

YOU SHOULD KNOW

Producers use botrytized Furmint grapes to make Tokaji wines (page 244), but vintners also are making it as a single varietal in a dry style, which appeals younger, adventurous drinkers.

FOOD PAIRINGS

CHICKEN   SHRIMP   CHEESE

Dry Furmint pairs with many dishes, including seafood, shrimp, fried calamari, chicken, and pork. Its bright acidity stands up to cream sauces, such as in chicken paprikash, and to fried foods. Try it with pad thai or Thai green curry. It also tastes delicious with soft cheeses, such as Gouda, Brie, and Havarti.

RECOMMENDED WINES: HUNGARY

BARGAIN

Bodrog Borműhely Dry Furmint

Disznókő Dry Furmint

Gróf Degenfeld Tokaji Off-Dry Furmint

Patricius Dry Furmint

Royal Tokaji Dry Furmint →

VALUE

Holdvölgy Winery Vision Furmint

The Oddity Tokaji Dry Furmint

Oremus Tokaji Dry Furmint Mandolás

Royal Tokaji Vineyard Selection Dry Furmint

Samuel Tinon Birtok Dry Furmint

Tokaj-Hétszőlő Dry Furmint

SPECIAL OCCASION

Barta Winery Old King Furmint

Erzsébet Cellar Zafur Furmint

SPLURGE

Oremus Tokaji Dry Furmint Petracs

RIGHT Vineyards at Tokaj-Oremus in Tokaj, Hungary

F URMINT IS A DISTINCTLY Hungarian grape . . . just ask any Hungarian! (Jeff is half.) Researchers believe that, after the Mongolian invasion, it came to Hungary in the Middle Ages. The transport reportedly occurred during the reign of King Béla IV. Said to be an active participant in replanting damaged vineyards, he supposedly eased immigration laws to entice winemakers to settle in his kingdom. Other researchers speculate that Italian missionaries brought the grape with them from the city of Formia in Lazio, and one Hungarian winemaker said the name comes from *froment*, the French word for "wheat," because of its light color. We can't say which story is true, but we do know that winemakers and consumers alike hold Furmint in high regard.

The Tokaji wine region, north of Budapest, consists of gentle rolling hills covered in grapevines and grand Austro-Hungarian palaces and hunting lodges. It sits at the confluence of the Tisza and Bodrog rivers, which supply this historic region with water and provide the humidity for the formation of botrytis (noble rot). King Louis XIV of France famously declared Tokaji "the king of wines, the wine of kings."

Some 15 years ago, when we first visited Tokaj, producers were making only sweet wines, but in the last decade, they have begun to produce dry Furmint. Except for special occasions, people aren't drinking sweet wines anymore, especially for regular drinking. Young Hungarians respect the culture of their forebears' sweet wines but want less sugar in their diet.

Hungarian winemakers responded by producing dry white wines from ripe but nonbotrytized Furmint grapes. Dry Furmint wines have wonderful aromatics including white flowers, honeysuckle, green apple, pear, and even white peach, but they taste completely dry, most with fewer than 3 grams of residual sugar per liter. This new style has taken the market here by storm, and producers are struggling to keep up with demand. Many Budapest restaurants have more than 20 dry Furmint wines by the glass and even more offerings by the bottle.

These dry Furmint wines are gaining popularity in British and American markets as well, generally consumed by younger drinkers eager to try something new. Many Hungarian companies are capitalizing on this development, using trendy names to entice adventurous drinkers. Growers in Croatia, Slovakia, and Slovenia have planted the grape, as have some California vineyards. You'll find dry Furmint wines on the wine lists of some of the world's best restaurants in New York City, Paris, Tel Aviv, and Dubai, as well as by the glass in popular wine bars in Singapore and Hong Kong.

LEFT Barrel cellar at Tokaj-Oremus

GEWÜRZTRAMINER

(geh-VOORTS-tra-MEE-nuhr)

IN THE GLASS

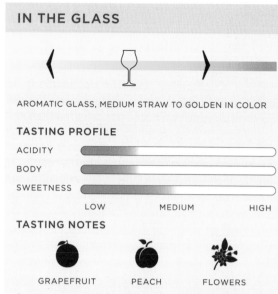

AROMATIC GLASS, MEDIUM STRAW TO GOLDEN IN COLOR

TASTING PROFILE

	LOW	MEDIUM	HIGH
ACIDITY			
BODY			
SWEETNESS			

TASTING NOTES

GRAPEFRUIT   PEACH   FLOWERS

Sweetness ranges from low to high, but all styles of Gewürztraminer have a pronounced floral aroma: rose, lily, orange blossom, jasmine, even lilac. You will find citrus and orchard-fruit aromas as well, notably grapefruit, lemon, peach, and lychee, joined by notes of ginger and baking spices. On the palate, fruit will outweigh the floral and spice notes.

FOOD PAIRINGS

CHICKEN   PORK   CURRY

Bright fruit flavors with notes of ginger and flowers pair perfectly with dishes that combine savory, spicy, and even sweet elements. Try it with Moroccan-style tagine or General Tso's. It also works well with ham or pork dishes, such as glazed baby back ribs, pork fried rice, or Hawaiian pizza (no hating!). It's also tastes great with red and green curries, whether Indian, Thai, or Malaysian.

RECOMMENDED WINES: FRANCE

BARGAIN

Joseph Cattin Gewurztraminer
Pierre Sparr Gewurztraminer Grande Reserve
Ruhlmann Gewurztraminer Vieilles Vignes

VALUE

Rolly Gassmann Gewurztraminer
Trimbach Classic Gewurztraminer
Zind Humbrecht Gewurztraminer Turckheim

SPECIAL OCCASION

Domaine Weinbach Cuvée Laurence Gewurztraminer →
Domaine Weinbach Gewurztraminer Furstentum
Domaine Zind Humbrecht Gewurztraminer Clos
    Windsbuhl
Domaine Zind Humbrecht Gewurztraminer Roche
    Calcaire
Pierre Sparr Gewurztraminer Grand Cru Mambourg

SPLURGE

Domaine Marcel Deiss Gewurztraminer Selection de Grains
Domaines Schlumberger Gewurztraminer Cuvée Anne

YOU SHOULD KNOW

Gewürztraminer's ancestral home lies in Germany, probably Pfalz, but it has found its forever home in Alsace, France, where regulations allow it in Alsace Grand Cru Wines. Many families who make wine in Alsace have Germanic surnames, as do producers in Italy's Alto Adige region. These areas across the Rhine and in the Alpine foothills have more in common viticulturally, culinarily, and even architecturally with their neighbors in Austria and Switzerland than with other parts of France or Italy.

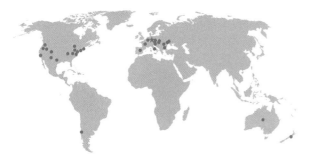

I T WAS THE BEST OF TIMES, it was *gewürzt* of times. Like a character in a novel, the nondescript Traminer grape made its way from Italy to Germany, transforming into something glorious, and then found fame in Italy and France before alighting in America.

Just as Pinot Gris is a naturally occurring variant of Pinot Noir, so Gewürztraminer is a mutation of Traminer, also called Savagnin Blanc in France's Jura region.

But here the deviation occurred the opposite way. The paler Traminer grape evolved into a pink-skinned berry that gives Gewürztraminer its deep color. With this metamorphosis, the new variety also took on distinct tropical aromas and flavors of fruit and flowers, the profile it has today. *Gewürz*, German for "spice" or "seasoning," serves as a descriptive prefix and, at least in English-speaking countries, often a shorthand for a bottle or glass of this aromatic variety.

In Alsace, France, Gewurztraminer—generally spelled without the umlaut—ranks as the second most widely planted variety, accounting for around 20 percent of the region's vineyards. Producers vinify it into dry versions as well as sweet Vendange Tardive (late-harvest) wines and Sélection de Grains Nobles (selection of noble berries) made with noble-rot grapes.

Gewurztraminer grapes at Zind-Humbrecht in Alsace

When grown in specific subregions here, it can go into Grand Cru bottles, and many producers also make single-vineyard versions. Bottles bear the designation of Alsace or Alsace Grand Cru, and the region has 51 Grand Cru sites. A Grand Cru bottle can sport just that description or include the site name as well. Better-known Gewurztraminer Alsace Grand Crus include Hengst, Mambourg, Steingrubler, Furstentum, Kitterlé, Goldert, Frankstein, and Turckheim. Many producers leave the designation and site name off their labels, though, believing that vineyard names have more recognition than Grand Cru sites.

Gewurztraminer (French, no umlaut) tends to have high alcohol levels for a white wine. If you're trying to determine whether a bottle from Alsace tastes sweet or dry but the label doesn't indicate residual sugar (RS), check the alcohol level. If it's 13 percent ABV or higher, the wine will taste dry. Bottles labeled "Alsace" may taste semisweet or off-dry. Grand Cru Alsace Gewurztraminer will drink full-bodied and dry, with a deep straw or yellow color and bold minerality. It's not a high-acid grape, but the region produces examples with acidity strong enough to counter cloying sweetness in wines with higher sugar levels. When properly stored, Grand Cru Gewurztraminer or well-made single-vineyard bottlings age beautifully and can rest for 10 to 20 years in a cellar before opening.

Gewürztraminer grows across central Europe. In its native Germany, winemakers cultivate more Traminer than Gewürztraminer, which also holds true in Austria. Those two markets have many excellent examples, but few make it to the wider world via export, which also holds true of versions from Luxembourg. Gewürztraminer also grows in Hungary, where it goes by the name Tramini, and Bulgaria as Mala Dinka. The Slovenians call it Traminac, while the Romanians call it Rusa. You can find plantings in Ukraine, Moldova, Slovakia, and Czechia. Farther west, Alto Adige, in northern Italy, grows a lot of it, while a few Spanish regions grow small amounts. In America, it concentrates heavily on the coastal wine regions. In the Southern Hemisphere, Gewürztraminer grows in Australia, New Zealand, and Chile.

WINEMAKER WISDOM

"Many people say it's a love-or-hate wine. I disagree! It has a similar balance to most lighter red wines. The phenolics of a good Gewurztraminer are similar to an unoaked red Burgundy. So people who find most white grapes too acidic or hard to digest should taste dry Gewurztraminer. It always has a certain floral element, but ripeness and great terroir will hide its perfumy side and reveal more noble and elegant spicy/peppery aromas. With age, the spicy character will get stronger, and these perfumy floral flavors will disappear. With time, the sweetness also will tone down, and the tannins will take over the wine, allowing for more food pairings."

—Olivier Humbrecht, owner and general manager, Zind-Humbrecht

"Alsace has 13 major types of soils, which gives us the opportunity to produce amazing terroir-driven wines. It is, as we say, liquid gold. You can never grow tired of the diversity of Alsace wines. Each terroir brings something different; each grape variety makes it unique. A dry Gewurz, with its spiciness, exoticism, and floral characteristics, would taste perfect with duck, but we also love it with a spicy steak tartare or lobster and mango/ginger twist."

—Pierre Trimbach, winemaker and technical director, Trimbach

Nussbaumer Tramin in Italy

LEFT Horse-drawn plow at Zind-Humbrecht in Alsace

OTHER NOTABLE COUNTRIES

ITALY

Tramin grapes reportedly originated in Alto Adige, no doubt near the town of Tramin. Experts believe the Gewürztraminer variant first occurred in Germany, but it has returned gloriously to its roots, becoming one of the celebrated white aromatic grapes of the region. Gewürztraminer ripens quickly, so high-altitude vineyards in this cool region help preserve the grape's perfume and maintain all or most of its low acidity. Slightly more than 1,500 acres grow in Alto Adige, accounting for about 11 percent of the region's total vineyard area. If you don't want sweet, Alto Adige Gewürztraminer is a safe bet because almost all of the versions made here taste bone dry, despite the tropical fruit and floral notes on the nose. The Italians also call it Traminer Aromatico.

- -

WINEMAKER WISDOM

"Gewürztraminer is definitely my favourite grape, one of the oldest varieties, and the parent of many of today's most renowned varieties, such as Pinot. The variety has slept a Sleeping Beauty's sleep for a very long time. Especially in our area, its potential had not been recognized. In the 1970s and '80s, it received little consideration, a complicated wine, not as aromatic, with little appeal. Quantity prevailed over quality. In the 1980s and '90s, as we started reducing the yield per hectare, we realised that we could produce a very particular wine. For many years now, we have committed ourselves entirely to this variety. Now it has a clearly identifiable aromatic profile, which has contributed greatly to its allure. Contrary to Alsace or Germany, Gewürztraminer from Alto Adige/South Tyrol is dry."

—*Willi Stürz, winemaker, Cantina Tramin*

- -

RECOMMENDED WINES: ITALY

BARGAIN

Albino Armani 1607 Gewürztraminer
Cantina Tramin Kellerei Gewürztraminer
Castel Sallegg Gewürztraminer
Castelfeder Vom Lehm Gewürztraminer
Colterenzio Schreckbichl Gewürztraminer
Kellerei Kaltern Südtiroler Gewürztraminer

VALUE

Alois Lageder Gewürztraminer
Cantina Terlano Kellerei Terlan Classico Gewürztraminer
Elena Walch Kastelaz Gewürztraminer
Terlano Gewürztraminer
Tramin Nussbaumer Gewürztraminer
Weingut Köfererhof Valle Isarco Gewürztraminer

SPECIAL OCCASION

J. Hoffstätter Kolbenhof Gewürztraminer
Kurtatsch Gewürztraminer Riserva
Maso Thaler Gewürztraminer
St. Michael-Eppan San Michele Appiano Sanct Valentin
  Gewürztraminer

SPLURGE

Baron di Pauli Exilissi Gewürztraminer
Cantina Termeno–Kellerei Tramin Epokale Gewürztraminer

RIGHT Manual harvest at Nussbaumer Tramin

USA

Quite a bit of Gewürztraminer grows in California, especially Mendocino, Sonoma, and Monterey counties. Farther north, you'll find planting in the Columbia Valley AVA straddling Washington and Oregon and the Snake River Valley AVA shared by Oregon and Idaho. In New York, it grows both on Long Island and in the Finger Lakes. Both the Pacific Northwest and New York offer the cool climate in which the variety thrives. In between, it grows in a long list of states, including Texas, New Mexico, Colorado, Michigan, Ohio, Kentucky, Pennsylvania, Maryland, Virginia, and New Hampshire.

RECOMMENDED WINES: NEW YORK

BARGAIN

Lakewood Vineyards Gewürztraminer

Palmer Gewürztraminer

Red Newt Cellars Gewürztraminer

Stony Lonesome Gewürztraminer

Weis Vineyards Gewürztraminer

VALUE

Channing Daughters Sparkling Gewürztraminer

Damiani Rebel Gewürztraminer

Dr. Konstantin Frank Gewürztraminer

Hermann J. Wiemer Vineyard Gewürztraminer

Lenz Old Vines Gewürztraminer

Ryan William Vineyard Gewürztraminer

WINEMAKER WISDOM

"In the Finger Lakes region, we are still on our own path of discovery when it comes to vineyard location and the level of ripeness that we can achieve consistently. It's one of the more difficult varieties, if not the most difficult, to strike the optimal harmony of power and finesse because it isn't a simple question of sugar and acid. In some instances, it can be floral, opulent, and lacking in complexity, not a style that I'm fond of. Finding balance while maintaining complexity and not drowning the delicate flavors are crucial and ultimately very rewarding in the finished wine."

—*Fred Merwarth, co-owner and head winemaker,*
Hermann J. Wiemer Vineyard

ABOVE Wine analysis at Hermann J. Wiemer Vineyard in New York

RECOMMENDED WINES: USA

BARGAIN

Alexander Valley Vineyards Wetzel Gewürztraminer, California

Balletto Gewürztraminer, California

Canoe Ridge Vineyard Oak Ridge Gewürztraminer, Washington

Chateau Ste. Michelle Gewürztraminer, Washington

Foris Dry Gewürztraminer, Oregon

Hobo Wines Banyan Gewürztraminer, California

Hyland Estates Gewürztraminer, Oregon

Ovum To Love Somebody Gerber Vineyard Gewürztraminer, Oregon

Treveri Cellars Sparkling Gewürztraminer, Washington

VALUE

Gundlach Bundschu Estate Vineyard Gewürztraminer, California

Handley Cellars Gewürztraminer, California

Navarro Vineyards Estate Dry Gewürztraminer, California

Reddy Vineyards Gewürztraminer, Texas

Thomas Fogarty Gewürztraminer, California

WINEMAKER WISDOM

"Gewurztraminer is one of the most complex grapes in the world and, for me, equals the complexities found in some of the most complex red wines of the world. If done right, this variety should exude a beautiful spiciness and richness that can't be found in any other. Add to this beautiful notes of lychee and tropical fruits, and you have one of the most unique, delicious wines in the world. With less restrictive laws in how wine should be made in the New World, we have room to explore, and making our wine a sparkling adds that much additional joy to the variety and its complexities."

—*Christian Grieb, winemaker, Treveri Cellars*

ABOVE Bottles resting at Treveri Cellars in Washington State

GODELLO

(go-DAY-yo)

IN THE GLASS

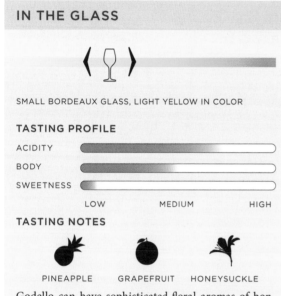

SMALL BORDEAUX GLASS, LIGHT YELLOW IN COLOR

TASTING PROFILE

	LOW	MEDIUM	HIGH
ACIDITY			
BODY			
SWEETNESS			

TASTING NOTES

PINEAPPLE   GRAPEFRUIT   HONEYSUCKLE

Godello can have sophisticated floral aromas of honeysuckle or lavender layered atop notes of citrus and tropical fruit. On the palate, it offers a medley of fruits: apple and pear, pineapple and green papaya, lime and grapefruit. Notes of thyme or oregano often make an appearance, and lees or barrel aging add density and creaminess to the mouthfeel.

YOU SHOULD KNOW

Earlier versions of Godello mainly fermented in steel for drinking young, but winemakers frequently age it on the lees or in barrels, producing a more sophisticated style meant to age. Because of its rise in popularity, Godello has become more expensive recently.

FOOD PAIRINGS

SHRIMP   SUSHI   CHICKEN

Spaniards almost always drink it with seafood, especially shellfish. Unoaked versions go perfectly with oysters, boiled shrimp, or sushi. Creamy, lees-aged versions taste terrific alongside grilled chicken or pork chops. For a special treat, try a rich, barrel-aged Godello with fried chicken.

RECOMMENDED WINES: SPAIN

BARGAIN

Bodegas Godeval Godello →
Bodegas Valdesil Montenovo Godello
Dominio de la Tares La Sonrisa Godello
Godelia Godello
Palacio de Canedo Agricultura Ecológica Godello
Palacio de Canedo Godello

VALUE

Alberto Orte Escalada do Sil Blanco
Pago de los Abuelos Viñas Centenarias Godello
Rafael Palacios Godello Louro do Bolo
Silva Daponte Godello
Tilenus Godello Monteseiros

SPECIAL OCCASION

Alveredo-Hobbs Godello
Bodegas Avancia Nobleza Old Vines Godello
Bodegas Emilio Moro La Revelia
Rafael Palacios As Sortes Godello

RIGHT Godello harvest at Bodegas Godelia in Bierzo, Spain

G ODELLO MOST LIKELY AROSE near Galicia's Río Sil in northwest Spain. In his 1532 treatise *Description of the Terrain around the City of Lamego*, Rui Fernandes, an overseer in the Douro Valley for King João III of Portugal, wrote about Godello under two of its many synonyms, Agudelho and Trincadente. A later origin story posits that Godello first grew in a town called Godella, near Valencia, in the 1800s and that a trader brought cuttings to Galicia shortly after. But experts see it as a local grape rather than a late transplant from across the kingdom.

The phylloxera scourge of the late 1800s decimated most of Galicia's Godello plantings. Growers largely planted Palomino, the main grape used for Sherry, in its stead. In the 1970s, viticulturists Horacio Fernández Presa and Luis Hidalgo started the Godello REVIVAL Project, an acronym that stands for Restructuring the Vineyards of Valdeorras, a subregion of Galicia. They researched and implemented best rootstock and vineyard practices, sought the finest locations among the chalky hillsides of Valdeorras, and repropagated a grape reduced, at its nadir, to just 11,000 square *feet* of total plantings. It took time, but Fernández Presa's Godeval winery produced the first known single variety Godello in the mid-1980s, attracting national attention to the Valdeorras DO and the grape. The area's reputation as a premier growing region solidified when Rafael Palacios and his family moved there in 2004 and began producing Godello as well. In recent years, Godello has become so popular that it's among the most expensive in Spain for winemakers to purchase from grape farmers. Several small producers who don't have their own vineyards can't afford to buy it and have had to drop it from their offerings.

In addition to Valdeorras, Godello grows throughout Galicia in the Ribeiro, Ribeira Sacra, and Monterrei DOs as well as Bierzo in neighboring Castilla y León. It thrives on steep, rocky hillsides with mineral-laden soil, which adds notes of oyster shell, gravel, and river rocks to bold fruit flavors. Godello most often draws comparisons to Chardonnay in that it responds well to a variety of winemaking techniques, including stainless steel, aging on lees, and barrel aging. But it has more of an aromatic and mineral component than Chardonnay. Pleasant notes of honeysuckle, jasmine, and orange blossom meet fruit flavors and notes of dried herbs and minerals.

Like local rival Albariño, which grows on both sides of the border, Godello also grows in significant amounts in Portugal, where, in addition to the two synonyms noted earlier, it mostly goes by the name Gouveio. To confuse matters even more, it also is called Verdelho in Portugal's Dão region, but it bears no immediate relation to the Verdelho grape used in Madeira. A few California producers make Godello wines as well.

WINEMAKER WISDOM

"What I like most about Godello wines is their versatility. Godellos from Valdeorras taste more citric and fresh, compared to those from Bierzo, which are more mature and deep. I love pairing them with the umami of Japanese food."

—*Olga Verde Viéitez, winemaker, Bodegas Godelia*

GRAŠEVINA

(GRAHSH-eh-VEE-nah)

IN THE GLASS

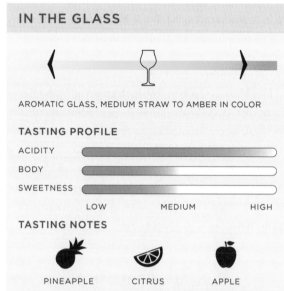

AROMATIC GLASS, MEDIUM STRAW TO AMBER IN COLOR

TASTING PROFILE

	LOW	MEDIUM	HIGH
ACIDITY			
BODY			
SWEETNESS			

TASTING NOTES

PINEAPPLE   CITRUS   APPLE

Sweetness ranges from low to high. Dry Graševina wines have aromas and flavors of mango, papaya, Winesap apple, and citrus blossoms. Aromatic and enticing, they taste refreshing. In sweet versions, the same aromas and flavors concentrate and heighten with citrus blossoms, honeysuckle, freesia, caramelized pineapple, honeycomb, and beeswax.

YOU SHOULD KNOW

Graševina goes by many names around the world, most commonly as Welschriesling in Germany and German-speaking regions, Olaszrizling in Hungary, Riesling Italico in northern Italy and China, and by 20 or so other terms. Most experts agree that it's indigenous to Croatia, where it's the most widely planted white variety.

FOOD PAIRINGS

SHRIMP

PORK

ICE CREAM

Dry Graševina's high acidity pairs nicely with seafood and shrimp dishes, such as shrimp scampi or jambalaya. It makes a nice match with steamed mussels and clams as well as light meats, such as veal or pork in cream sauces. Enjoy it with your next takeout order of General Tso's chicken because the acidity excellently accompanies the hot peppers and spice. In its sweeter form, it goes excellently with creamy desserts, such as rice pudding, crème brûlée, flan, or ice cream.

RECOMMENDED WINES: AROUND THE WORLD

BARGAIN
Enjingi Graševina, Croatia
Gere Attila Pinceszete Olaszrizling, Hungary
Krauthaker Graševina, Croatia
Kutjevo Graševina, Croatia
Peter Wetzer Olaszrizling, Hungary

VALUE
Kolfok Nolens Volens Welschriesling, Austria
Weingut Hermann Fink Welschriesling TBA, Austria (sweet)
Weingut Werlitsch Welschriesling vom Opok, Austria

SPECIAL OCCASION
Antunović Graševina Tradition, Croatia
Durnberg Welschriesling Elementum, Austria
Weingut K+ K Kirnbauer Eiswein, Austria (sweet)

SPLURGE
Kutjevo Graševina Ice Wine, Croatia (sweet)
Weingut Höpler Noble Reserve, Austria (sweet)

G RAŠEVINA CROATICA, the Croatian society of Graševina winemakers, maintains that during his reign from 276 to 282 CE, Emperor Marcus Aurelius of Rome brought the Graševina grape to what is now the Kutjevo region of Croatia. Almost 1,000 years later, Cistercian monks built one of the area's oldest wine cellars here, and sections of it remain in use today.

Croatian winemakers tell us the variety's name Graševina derives from *grašak*, the Croatian word for "peas"—which the grapes resemble during the growing season—and *vinova loza*, "grapevine." Today, most winemakers make a fresh, stainless-steel version bottled and consumed within a year of harvest, a style that younger consumers prefer. But many vintners also continue make their forebears' styles: barrel fermented, aged in oak, ice wine, or botrytized grapes.

Winemakers here constantly note that their vineyards grow at the 45th parallel, the same latitude as Bordeaux and Piedmont. Three large rivers supply water to the region: the Sava, the Drava, and the Danube. Graševina grows in eastern Croatia and Slavonia, with some excellent wines coming from the Danube River basin, where the vines thrive in alluvial soils.

You can find some of Slavonia's best vineyards in Vetovo, Krnjevac, Vinkomir, Mandičevac, Mitrovac, and Turković. Near the Danube River, look for Graševina

Graševina vineyard in Croatia

from Baranja, Srijem, Ilok, and Vukovar as well as bottles from vineyards in Vukovo, Vučedol, Principovac, and Goldberg. Some of the region's absolute best wines come from Kutjevo and other surrounding hilly areas, such as Zagorje, Prigorje, Moslavina, and Medimurje.

Austria has more than 7,000 acres of Graševina, planted mostly in Burgenland and Styria, and much of that harvest goes into sparkling wines. The Hungarians grow it in the Lake Balaton and Tokaji regions to make both dry and sweet wines. Chinese producers call this grape variety Welschriesling, and it ranks there as one of the most widely planted white varieties—definitely one to watch in the future.

RIGHT Graševina/Welschriesling vineyard marker

GRECO

(GREH-ko)

IN THE GLASS

SMALL BORDEAUX GLASS, PALE STRAW TO MEDIUM STRAW IN COLOR

TASTING PROFILE

ACIDITY

BODY

SWEETNESS

LOW   MEDIUM   HIGH

TASTING NOTES

LEMON   PEACH   FLINT

Greco has aromas of citrus and white flowers and, when fermented in stainless steel, flavors of apple, lemon, cantaloupe, peach, and fresh herbs. It generally grows in volcanic soils, which impart aromas and flavors of flint, smoke, and good minerality. The crisp, clean finish sometimes can feature a touch of bitter almond. Oaked versions taste more complex, with notes of vanilla, pear, apple, and brown baking spices.

YOU SHOULD KNOW

The predominant grape grown in the Greco di Tufo DOCG in Campania, southern Italy, Greco must comprise at least 85 percent of those wines to obtain the DOCG's seal of approval.

FOOD PAIRINGS

SUSHI   FISH   SALAD

It pairs excellently with seafood, sushi, and sashimi and goes well with grilled or broiled fish and seafood pastas. It stands up to the vinegar in most salads and tastes delicious with sliced tomatoes. Try having it with soft cheeses, such as Brie and mozzarella.

RECOMMENDED WINES: ITALY

BARGAIN

Cantine di Marzo Greco di Tufo

Donnachiara Greco di Tufo

Feudi di San Gregorio Cutizzi

Macchialupa Greco di Tufo

Petilia Greco di Tufo

Quattro Venti 420

Vadiaperti

Vesuvium Greco di Tufo

VALUE

Benito Ferrara Vigna Cicogna Greco di Tufo

Calafà Ariavecchia Greco di Tufo

Donnachiara Aletheia →

I Favati Terrantica Etichetta Bianca

Feudi di San Gregorio Greco di Tufo

Mastroberardino Greco di Tufo

Mastroberardino Nova Serra

Pietracupa Greco di Tufo

Villa Matilde Greco di Tufo

RIGHT Mastroberardino vineyard in Campania during winter

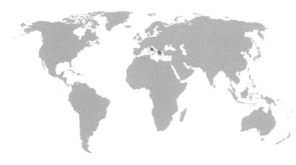

IN THE 700S BCE, the ancient Greeks colonized Mediterranean lands, including southern Italy, bringing with them their ways of life, food culture, and vines. They planted Greco in what became known in antiquity as Magna Graecia (Greater Greece), today the regions of Apulia, Basilicata, Calabria, and Campania. These regions enjoyed Greco wine for many years, but World War II destroyed many of the vineyards in these regions, and many more vines suffered neglect afterward as villagers migrated to cities for work. Thankfully winemakers today, including the Mastroberardino family, have dedicated themselves to saving Greco and preserving its historical significance.

Some ampelographers (the technical term for "wine researchers") consider Greco a single variety with multiple clones, while others classify it as a group of distinctly different varieties with a common origin. DNA testing has linked Greco to other varieties, including Asprinio Bianco. Researchers still argue about the differences among Greco di Tufo, Greco di Bianco—where many wines come in a dessert style made from raisinated grapes—and other Italian regions, but we'll concentrate on the crisp, fruity, mineral-rich wines from Tufo, a DOCG that centers on an eponymous town named for its volcanic soils, or *tuff*.

Winemaking techniques in Greco di Tufo vary widely. Some vintners make their wine only in stainless-steel vats, while others age it in oak barrels. Wines made in stainless

steel retain a crisp, light, fruity, acidic profile, and some oak-aged examples feel rounder in the mouth and have woody aromas and such flavors as vanilla, toast, hazelnuts, almonds, and even cinnamon. Oaked wines also can lean more toward stone fruits, such as white and yellow peach, apple, and pear. More complex oak-aged wines pair well with cream sauces, white meats, and cheeses. Light and easy drinking, the wines work equally well as an aperitif or paired with light summer fare.

In their native region, they grace practically every table in seaside restaurants, which serve them alongside fresh seafood from the Mediterranean, prepared simply, and served just hours after it was caught. If you have the luck or means, the absolute best way to enjoy Greco di Tufo wines is on the beach or a boat in southern Italy during the summer.

WINEMAKER WISDOM

"Ours is a 'heroic' viticulture. It's a continuous climbing on impervious paths. It's a set of 'tiles' in which men, ancient vines, and unique territories merge. The noblest and most ancient of these grapes is Greco di Tufo. This vine in ancient times was called Aminea Gemina (Soul Mate), which my sister Teresa and I are: twin souls with one goal, respect for our Irpinia territory."

—Roberto Bruno, enologist, Petilia

"I love its density, structure, and minerality. It's refreshing and intensely fruity. It pairs well with risottos and seafood dishes."

—Massimo di Renzo, winemaker,
Mastroberardino

LEFT Harvested grapes at Petilia in Italy

GRILLO

(GREE-lo)

IN THE GLASS

(🍷)

SMALL BORDEAUX GLASS, PALE STRAW IN COLOR

TASTING PROFILE

ACIDITY

BODY

SWEETNESS

LOW   MEDIUM   HIGH

TASTING NOTES

LEMON   APPLE   PEAR

Dry Grillos taste crisp, zesty, and refreshing. They have aromas of lemon zest, Granny Smith apple, citrus blossoms, and acacia flowers. Flavors include lemon-lime, Bartlett pear, grapefruit, and fresh green herbs.

YOU SHOULD KNOW

In the early 1800s, Grillo proved very popular in Sicily, where producers mostly made it into sweet, Marsala-style wines. The variety fell out of favor, but winemakers today are planting more Grillo to make crisp white wines for younger drinkers who prefer dry wines with less sugar and alcohol.

FOOD PAIRINGS

SALAD   CHICKEN   CHEESE

Dry Grillo pairs well with dishes containing lemon, such as salads, lemon chicken, shrimp in a lemon sauce, or fried calamari sprinkled with lemon juice. It also goes great with such cheeses as Gouda or Havarti.

RECOMMENDED WINES: ITALY

BARGAIN

Cantina Cellar Luma Grillo

Corvo Grillo

Duca di Salaparuta Grillo

Feudo Arancio Grillo Sicilia

Feudo Maccari Olli Grillo

Feudo Montoni Vigna della Timpa Grillo

Firriato Altavilla della Corte Grillo

Irmana Grillo

Mandrarossa Costadune Grillo

Planeta La Segreta Grillo Sicilia

Valle dell'Acate Zagra Grillo

VALUE

Alessandro Viola Note di Grillo

Caruso & Minini Naturalmente Bio Grillo

Donnafugata SurSur Grillo

Duca di Salaparuta Kados Grillo

Feudo Maccari Family and Friends Grillo

Feudo Montoni Grillo della Timpa

Marco De Bartoli Grappoli di Grillo Bianco

Tasca d'Almerita Fondazione Whitaker Mozia Grillo

Some historians believe that Roman soldiers under the command of Julius Caesar brought Grillo vines from mainland Italy to Sicily. Others think it developed as a spontaneous, native crossing of other grape varieties on the island. Either way, Grillo wines, whether made dry or sweet, taste delicious. For centuries, winemakers used it in the production of sweet Marsala wine, but today's producers, rather than repeating the heavy, sweet, boozy Marsalas of old, are making dry, crisp, clean white wines with less alcohol, following in the footsteps of other Italian whites such as Pinot Grigio, Gavi, and Soave.

Resistant to high temperatures and full sun, Grillo does well on windswept Sicily. Better winemakers tend trellised vines with care while paying special attention to canopy management, which limits the sun the grapes receive. The variety generally produces grapes with high sugar content, so vintners also carefully monitor the final alcohol levels.

Dry Grillo wines sell extremely well in Sicily and other coastal areas of Italy, driven by better winemaking techniques and lower prices. Young, fashionable Italians drink these zesty whites while on the beach or floating in the Mediterranean Sea, pairing them with lighter cuisine, such as fish, shellfish, and salads, popular in beachfront restaurants. Many good dry Grillo wines have made it to the American and British markets as well.

Grillo grapes on the vine at Planeta in Sicily

WINEMAKER WISDOM

"I love their aromas, freshness, longevity, and versatility. I find a delicate sapidity that recalls the closeness to the sea."

—Antonio Moretti, owner, Feudo Maccari

"Wines made with Grillo can have very distinct personalities, depending on the winemaking technique. It can produce a variety of styles, from easy-drinking, crisp, fruit-driven expressions to more complex, terroir-driven, mineral wines. As a Sicilian living by the coast, I like to pair it with seafood and vegetarian pasta dishes, but it also matches perfectly with white meat. New World areas with Mediterranean climates, such as Australia (Riverina), have planted Grillo due to its suitability for this growing area and interesting resilience to climate change."

—Antonio Rallo, CEO and winemaker, Donnafugata

Donnafugata Tenuta di Contessa Entellina winery in Sicily

GRÜNER VELTLINER

(GROO-nuhr VEHLT-lee-nuhr)

IN THE GLASS

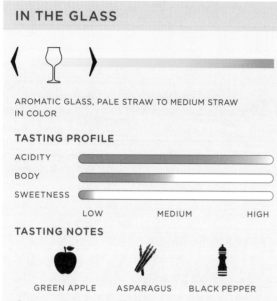

AROMATIC GLASS, PALE STRAW TO MEDIUM STRAW IN COLOR

TASTING PROFILE

ACIDITY

BODY

SWEETNESS

LOW   MEDIUM   HIGH

TASTING NOTES

GREEN APPLE   ASPARAGUS   BLACK PEPPER

Grüner wines typically have a vegetal, herbaceous aroma, like steamed asparagus. You'll find a bit of white or black pepper both in the bouquet and on the palate. They have high acidity and minerality, which make them taste crisp with a zesty, bright burst of citrus in the finish.

YOU SHOULD KNOW

Most producers bottle Grüners with screw caps, and many bottles come in a generous 1-liter size. They often contain a small amount of carbon dioxide, which gives them a little fizz when opened. But don't misconstrue this slight spritz as a fault or refermentation in the bottle. Most vintners make it to be drunk young, but some winemakers also create food-friendly, barrel-aged styles made to age.

FOOD PAIRINGS

CHICKEN   ASPARAGUS   CHEESE

The high acidity makes it a great partner for fried foods, such as fried chicken, Wiener schnitzel, and fried seafood. The peppery notes allow it to pair well with asparagus and goat cheeses.

RECOMMENDED WINES: AUSTRIA

BARGAIN

Anton Bauer Gmork Grüner Veltliner
Getränk Grüner Veltliner
Loimer Lois Grüner Veltliner
Pfaffl Grüner Veltliner Zeisen →
Pratsch Grüner Veltliner
Weingut Fred Loimer Grüner Veltliner
Wolfgang Vineyards Gru-Vee

VALUE

Laurenz V. Charming Grüner Veltliner
Pratsch Grüner Veltliner Rotenpullen
Weingut Emmerich Knoll Loibner Grüner Veltliner
Weingut Franz Hirtzberger Rotes Tor Grüner Veltliner
Weingut Rudi Pichler Grüner Veltliner

SPECIAL OCCASION

Schloss Gobelsburg Ried Lamm Grüner Veltliner
Veyder Malberg Alter.Native Grüner Veltliner
Weingut Bründlmayer Lamm Reserve Grüner Veltliner

SPLURGE

Weingut Franz Hirtzberger Honivogl Grüner Veltliner

Outside Europe, Grüner grows in Australia, New Zealand, and Canada. In America, you can find it in California, Washington, and Oregon, with smaller plantations in Pennsylvania and Maryland.

WINEMAKER WISDOM

"If you look after Grüner in the vineyard, it'll be your friend in the wine cellar and, depending on the chosen picking date, will give you a wine that sings right after bottling and will continue to give you joy after many years, sometimes decades, of cellar aging. It's much like a chameleon, as it takes in all the climate and mineral qualities of where it is grown and expresses these back to you in the glass. It grows alongside Sauvignon Blanc very well. We were very impressed by the wines we tasted in New Zealand and California, and we're happy that the Grüner message is going across the world."

—Dieter Hübler, owner, with Peter Schweiger, head winemaker; and Peter Schweiger Jr., associate winemaker, Laurenz V.

"I love the diversity, from easy-drinking and uncomplicated to complex, deep, and mineral. If, as we do, you work traditionally, with low intervention—meaning spontaneous fermentation, higher temperatures, more sediments, and fine oxidation in wooden casks—then you get very classy GVs. If you compare apples with apples, Austrian versions have a more traditional style, meaning pepper, herbs, and minerality. In the New World, you find more of a fruit-driven style."

—Fred Loimer, winemaker, Loimer Lois

OF ALL THE AROMATIC GRAPES that have gained popularity in the last few years, Grüner Veltliner has the coolest nickname among wine lovers: Gru-Vee. It's Austria's most important grape, but it also grows in Czechia, Slovakia, Bulgaria, and Hungary. You can find small plantings in Alto Adige, Italy, and Stuttgart, Germany.

Ampelographers think that one of Grüner's parents is Traminer, which most likely imparts its aromatic traits. They think the other parent is Saint George, a very old, rare vine. The spontaneous crossing probably occurred in the Niederösterreich area of Austria, but the name "Veltliner" points toward the Italian town of Valtellina, near the Swiss border.

In the 1950s, Grüner grew widely in Austria, and it remains the most widely planted white grape there today, representing more than 30 percent of Austria's total vineyards. It grows predominately in the Burgenland, Niederösterreich, and Steiermark regions. Kamptal and Kremstal, two small DACs in the center of Austria, have a reputation for producing quality Grüner Vetliners, as do the Weinviertel, Traisental, and Wachau areas.

Since 1980, Austrian wine consumption has decreased steadily, following a larger European trend, yet per capita wine consumption for the average Austrian still pours out to the tune of more than 20 liters per year. A good portion of that is Grüner Veltliner. Domestic consumption has decreased, but happily for the rest of the world, Austrian exports have increased steadily. Grüner Veltliner proves extremely popular with Austrians both young and young at heart. Vienna's wine bars often pair it with small plates and snacks. Some producers make sparkling Grüner, but very little of it makes its way to the export market.

KERNER

(KUHR-nuhr)

IN THE GLASS

SMALL BORDEAUX GLASS, MEDIUM STRAW IN COLOR

TASTING PROFILE

	LOW	MEDIUM	HIGH
ACIDITY			
BODY			
SWEETNESS			

TASTING NOTES

MANGO · APPLE · CITRUS

Styles vary from dry to sweet. As a child of Riesling, Kerner exhibits many of the same characteristics, though not identical aromas. You'll smell tropical fruits, apple, citrus blossoms, and acacia flowers and detect flavors of mixed fruit salad, red currants, Granny Smith apple, and mango with a racy, citric finish.

YOU SHOULD KNOW

The variety takes its name from German physician Justinus Kerner (1786–1862), famous, among other accomplishments, for writing drinking songs. He had a caustic sense of humor, and some count him as one of the first doctors to suggest drinking a glass of wine a day.

FOOD PAIRINGS

CHICKEN · PASTA · CHEESE

Kerner has milder acidity than Riesling, so it pairs better with less tart or spicy foods. It matches nicely with herb-roasted chicken, pasta dishes with cream sauces, roasted vegetables, and soft cheeses.

RECOMMENDED WINES: AROUND THE WORLD

BARGAIN

Abbazia di Novacella-Kloster Neustift Sudtirol Eisacktaler Kerner, Italy

Chitose Winery Kimura Vineyard Kerner, Japan

Hokkaido Wine Kerner, Japan

Weingut Fritz Windisch Niersteiner Kirchplatte Kerner Auslese, Germany

Weingut Niklas Südtiroler Luxs Kerner, Italy

Weingut Schlosshof Dr. Heimers Schatzkammer Kerner Auslese, Germany

VALUE

Borreo Single Vineyard Kerner, USA: California

Camel Farm Winery Private Reseve Kerner, Japan

Eisacktaler Kellerei Cantina Valle Isarco Kerner, Italy →

Kurtatsch Kerner, Italy

Siebe Dupf Kellerei Magdener Kerner, Switzerland

Silverado Vineyards R&D, USA: California

Takizawa Vinery Kerner, Japan

SPECIAL OCCASION

Eisacktaler Kellerei Cantina Kerner Nectaris Passito, Italy

Schenk Westhofener Bergkloster Kerner Spätlese, Germany

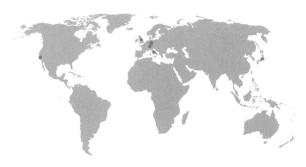

I N 1929, agronomist August Herold, working for the Baden-Württemberg state government in Lauffen, Germany, crossed Riesling with Trollinger (Schiava Grossa), which hails from the Trentino area of Italy. In 1969, the new variety, which growers had planted widely, received official recognition and approval for use in many German winegrowing regions. It now ranks in the top five white varieties grown in Germany.

Kerner tends to do well in cooler climates, higher altitudes, and partial shade. It generally ripens in early October, making for a longer growing season that produces fresh and fruity wines with lower acidity but still well balanced. The vines produce large crops and high yields, so many German winemakers grow Kerner instead of Riesling. The trick is to find vintners who control their yields, which results in a concentrated wine instead of a thin, watery version. Good Kerner tastes elegant, with aromas of citrus blossoms and a full, fruity palate. Some of the best come from Germany, especially the Pfalz, Mosel, and Rheinhessen regions, and Italy's Alto Adige.

Growers have planted Kerner in Switzerland, Britain, California, and even Japan. Most wines available in the American market tend to come from Trentino–Alto Adige, Italy.

WINEMAKER WISDOM

"I love Kerner because it's not Cabernet or Chardonnay! It's just different. The aroma and acidity are unlike anything else we make. It's refreshing but with a completely different minerality than Sauvignon Blanc. It balances any Asian spices. We serve it with caviar, crème fraîche, and potato chips, a delicious pairing. I tasted one from Alto Adige, which inspired us to plant Kerner in the first place. Our Napa version is more floral forward. It has minerality but not in the forefront as much as the Italian version, which is stonier than our California style."

—*Jon Emmerich, winemaker, Silverado Vineyards*

"Kerner is easy to understand because of its aromatics and body. I appreciate Kerner often by itself as an aperitif. The best food pairing for me is shellfish or grilled fish. Kerners from Switzerland have a more herbal and spicy character and are less fruit-driven but with a similar body. Definitely nice!"

—*Andreas Kofler, president, Cantina Kurtatsch*

"Due to our altitudes, temperature fluctuations, and lower yields, our Kerners develop more aromas and a crispier acidity. In Germany, Kerner is grown more in an easy-drinking way, with higher yields and therefore not as complex as the Kerners from Alto Adige."

—*Hannes Munter, winemaker, Cantina Valle Isarco*

MACABEO

(mah-kah-BAY-oh)

IN THE GLASS

⟨ 🍷 ⟩

SMALL BORDEAUX GLASS, PALE STRAW TO MEDIUM STRAW IN COLOR

TASTING PROFILE

ACIDITY

BODY

SWEETNESS

LOW   MEDIUM   HIGH

TASTING NOTES

PEAR   CITRUS BLOSSOMS   HERBS

When picked early and fermented in stainless steel, Macabeo wines taste fresh and crisp, with aromas and flavors of citrus flowers, fresh green herbs, freesia blossoms, and lemon pith. When harvested later and aged in oak, they have fuller body with aromas and flavors peaches, apricots, pears, vanilla, and toasted hazelnuts.

YOU SHOULD KNOW

Macabeo grows all over Spain, but in Rioja it goes by the name Viura. Many bottles available in the American and British markets come from Rioja, so look for "Viura" on the labels.

FOOD PAIRINGS

CURRY   SALAD   SUSHI

Young, crisp, clean Macabeo pairs nicely with spicy food, including Thai green curries, Singapore chili crab, or Szechuan seafood. It also makes a great match with green vegetables, lightly dressed salads, or raw seafood, such as clams, oysters, sushi, and sashimi. When oak-aged, it complements more substantial dishes: grilled pork chops, oven-roasted chicken, and oven-baked fish, such as branzino or salmon.

RECOMMENDED WINES: SPAIN

BARGAIN

Bodegas Muriel Tierras de Lastra

Bodegas Valdemar Finca Alto Cantabria

El Coto Blanco

Viña Bujanda Viura →

VALUE

Bodegas Alegre Valgañón Blanco

Bodegas Palacios Remondo Placet Valtomelloso

CVNE Monopole Clasico Blanco

Marqués de Murrieta Capellanía Reserva

Merce Carme Macabeo

Vara Viura

SPECIAL OCCASION

Bodegas Pujanza Anteportalatina Blanco

R. López de Heredia Viña Tondonia Viña Gravonia

SPLURGE

Bodegas Frontonio El Jardín de las Iguales Macabeo

Remirez de Ganuza Gran Reserva Blanco

RIGHT Macabeo/Viura vine at Viña Bujanda in Rioja, Spain

I F YOU SEE "VIURA" on the label, the wine comes from Macabeo grapes grown, vinified, and bottled in the Rioja region of Spain. Just the word "Macabeo" on the label indicates that the grapes grew in a different region of Spain, perhaps Catalonia. In France, Maccabeu grows mostly in the Languedoc-Roussillon region. French producers make it into dry wines labeled "Minervois" or "Corbières" or into sweet wines labeled "Rivesaltes" or "Maury." Spain has more than 100,000 acres of it, while France grows just about 7,000 acres, so you more likely will see single-varietal bottlings of Macabeo / Viura on shop shelves.

Macabeo ranks as the most widely planted white variety in northern Spain. It grows predominately in Rioja, Badajoz, Tarragona, Castilla-La Mancha, Aragon, Valencia, and Zaragoza. It serves as the main variety in many Spanish DOs and DOCs, including Terra Alta, Tarragona, Somontano, Rioja Penedès, Navarra, Costers del Segre, Conca de Barberà, and Calatayud. In Catalonia, producers usually blend Macabeo with Parellada and Xarel·lo to make Cava.

The young, fresh, and fruity style normally ferments in stainless steel and ages in stainless steel or neutral tanks so the aromas and flavors remain lively with good acidity. Aromas and flavors include citrus peel, citrus blossoms, white flowers, fresh herbs, and grapefruit zest. This style drinks nicely as an aperitif on any of Spain's beautiful beaches, and it pairs perfectly with seafood tapas, such as clams, oysters, mussels, and anchovies in vinegar.

Quite a few vintners are making fuller-bodied, aged Macabeos. Typically these wines also ferment in stainless steel, but then they transfer to oak barrels for aging. This process produces wines with more heft on the palate and more complex aromas and flavors, including Bartlett pear, Fuji apple, peaches, and apricots along with vanilla and toasted hazelnut from the wood. This oaked style can age in the bottle for a few years before drinking and pairs with more complex foods, such as seafood in cream sauce or grilled or roasted meats, such as chicken and pork.

Depending on where it grows, Macabeo has many other names. Some of these include Alcanon, Macabeu, Maccabeo, Maccabeou, Makkobeo, and Viuna, to name only a few.

ABOVE Viura vineyard at Viña Bujanda in Rioja
RIGHT Harvested Viura grapes at Viña Bujanda

WINEMAKER WISDOM

"Its freshness gives personality both to the youngest and aged wines, making them very elegant wines at the table, capable of enhancing any dish. From Catalonia, they taste more neutral and watery, and in Castilla they taste acidic. In all cases, the aging potential remains good, and maturation in the bottle leads to mineral and noble aromas. If I had to look for a similar grape in the world, I would think of Chenin Blanc from South Africa."

—*Lauren Rosillo, agronomist, Viña Bujanda*

MALVASIA

(MAHL-vah-ZEE-ah)

IN THE GLASS

SMALL BORDEAUX GLASS, MEDIUM STRAW TO AMBER IN COLOR

TASTING PROFILE

ACIDITY

BODY

SWEETNESS

LOW   MEDIUM   HIGH

TASTING NOTES

APPLE   PEACH   NUTS

Sweetness ranges from low to high. Made dry, it has aromas of citrus blossoms, white peach, and green apple and flavors of stone fruits and lemon curd. Made sweet, such as a *passito*-style (made from raisinated grapes and named for an ancient Carthaginian wine) Italian wine or Madeira, it has flavors of peach, apricot, and honey with nutty, oxidized characteristics.

FOOD PAIRINGS

FISH   CHEESE   APPLE PIE

Dry Malvasia pairs great with grilled fish and oven-roasted chicken. It also complements soft cheeses and white pizzas. When made into a passito- or Madeira-style wine, it stands up to hard cheeses, such as Parmigiano-Reggiano and aged Gouda, and fruity desserts, including apple pie and raspberry tart.

RECOMMENDED WINES

See recommendations later in chapter.

YOU SHOULD KNOW

In the 1400s, the English began referring to sweet wines made from this variety and imported from Monemvasia in Greece (medieval Latin name: Malmasia) as Malmsey. The name stuck. Many literary scholars still refer to Malvasia as Malmsey, but most wine writers use the word only when referring to sweet wines made from Malvasia in Madeira, Portugal. For Madeira recommendations, see page 206.

M ALVASIA ENCOMPASSES a group of grapes usually named for where they grow. For example, Malvasia Bianca refers to Malvasia grown more generally in Italy, Malvasia Toscana specifically in Tuscany; and Malvazija Istarska to Istria in Croatia. The wines produced in these areas differ as a result of slight genetic variations, climate, terroir, and winemaking styles. The variety has many subvarieties, but around the world, Malvasia grapes exhibit similar likes and dislikes and grow in similar regions and climates.

Experts believe that Malvasia originated in Crete, which lies southeast of Monemvasia, an important Greek port in antiquity. Malmasia, the medieval Latin name for the city, gave rise to Malmsey in English and, in Italian, to the name of the grape variety. In addition to Greece, Italy, and Croatia, Malvasia also grows in Slovenia, Spain, Portugal, and California.

In Greece, it still grows on a few of the Cycladic islands. In Italy, Malvasia Bianca generally makes crisp, dry wines with some of the best bottlings hailing from the Friuli–Venezia Guila region. Italian winemakers often blend Malvasia with Trebbiano to enhance the texture and flavor of their wines. Producers make very interesting sparkling versions in Emilia-Romagna and sweet passito-style

Saints Hills Malvasia vineyard in Istria, Croatia

wines in southern Italy. Historians believe that Venetian traders brought vines from Greece to the Istrian Peninsula (mostly) in Croatia. It's the most popular white wine in Istria, often paired with seafood recently harvested from the Adriatic Sea. In Spain, excellent dry versions of Malvasia begin with vines growing in the volcanic soils of the Canary Islands, and California's San Joaquin Valley also produces an excellent varietal expression of Malvasia Bianca.

More than a dozen grape varieties go by the name Malvasia in Portugal, but some researchers question whether they all are true relatives. Malvasia Candida grows on Madeira, a Portuguese island, and producers use it make the traditional aged, sweet wine known as Malmsey. Malvasia Fina, sometimes known as Boal (no relation to Bual), grows in the Douro Valley and goes into white Port wine.

WINEMAKER WISDOM

"It's produced mostly as a fresh style of wine, but it also behaves nicely as a sparkling wine. It can undergo long maceration, after which we get a harmonious orange wine. It also can be made as a sweet passito. Istrian Malvasia gives notes of spiciness, acacia flower, grapefruit peel, citrus, and chives. As it opens, we taste fruitiness, apricots, apples. In the end, you can feel the minerality and the smell of the sea the most."

—*Marko Fakin, oenologist, Fakinwines*

"It's interesting to taste all the varieties and biotypes of Malvasia. The common feature that I find fascinating is always the aromaticity that makes this vine unique in the world. In Emilia-Romagna, we mainly cultivate a variety called Malvasia di Candia, which has an extraordinary aroma and incredible acidity. My favorite food pairing with our Malvasia is an amberjack with pink pepper and a lemon citronette."

—*Alessandro Medici, owner, Medici Ermete*

"Malvazija is a beautiful, aromatic variety, a true representative of Istria and Croatia. It has many faces, can be made fresh, ready to drink, but also, as we make it, aged and with layered aromas, blended with a bit of Chardonnay from the same vineyard. I love Malvazijas's seductiveness and her ability to show terroir and the art of winemaking."

—*Ernest Tolj, owner, Saints Hills Winery*

RECOMMENDED SWEET WINES: AROUND THE WORLD

BARGAIN
Cantina Valtidone Venus Malvasia Dolce, Italy

Cougar Vineyards Dulce Bubbly Malvasia Bianca, USA: California

Vega de Yuco Yaiza Malvasía Semidulce, Spain

VALUE
Fenech Malvasia, Italy

SPECIAL OCCASION
Bodegas Los Bermejos Malvasía Naturalmente Dulce, Spain

Caravaglio Malvasia, Italy

Hauner Malvasia, Italy

Tenuta Capofaro Malvasia, Italy

SPLURGE
El Grifo Canari, Spain

RECOMMENDED DRY WINES: AROUND THE WORLD

BARGAIN
Bodega Vulcano de Lanzarote Malvasía Volcánica Seco, Spain

Bodegas Los Bermejos Malvasía Volcánica Seco, Spain

Caravaglio Salina Malvasia Bianco, Italy

El Grifo Malvasía Seco, Spain

Fakin Malvazija, Croatia

Mario Schiopetto Collio Malvasia, Italy

Poggio le Volpi Malvasia Puntinata Roma, Italy

Vega de Yuco Yaiza Malvasía Seco, Spain

VALUE
Bodega Abel Mendoza Monge Malvasía, Spain

Bodegas Rubicón Amalia Malvasía Seco, Spain

Bodegas Stratvs Malvasía Seco, Spain

Edi Kante Malvasia Carso, Italy

Medici Ermete Daphne Sparkling Malvasia Secco, Italy

Saints Hills Mala Nevina, Croatia →

Sterling Vineyards California Malvasia Bianca, USA: California

Tenuta Capofaro Didyme Malvasia, Italy

SPECIAL OCCASION
Damijan Podversic Malvasia, Italy (orange wine)

Hauner Malvasia delle Lipari, Italy

Victoria Torres Pecis Malvasía Aromática Piezas No. 3, Spain

ABOVE Fermentation tanks at Fakin in Croatia

MÜLLER-THURGAU

(MEW-luhr TOOR-gow)

IN THE GLASS

AROMATIC GLASS, PALE STRAW TO MEDIUM STRAW
IN COLOR

TASTING PROFILE

ACIDITY

BODY

SWEETNESS

LOW   MEDIUM   HIGH

TASTING NOTES

FLOWERS   WHITE PEACH   APPLE

They have delightful floral aromas and flavors of white peach, Golden Delicious apple, and gooseberry.

YOU SHOULD KNOW

In the 1950s, postwar Europe loved sweet and off-dry Müller-Thurgau wines. Producers often blended the variety with other grapes and labeled the bottles as "Liebfraumilch" (Dear Mrs. Milk) for exportation to British and American markets. Blue Nun Leibfraumilch and Black Tower Liebfraumilch enjoyed decades of popularity in the USA. Still available today, they don't attract the attention of dedicated wine lovers.

FOOD PAIRINGS

EGGS   SHRIMP   FISH

Müller-Thurgau pairs nicely with quiche and omelets. It's great for light lunches, including seafood salad or a spicy shrimp cocktail. It also goes nicely with cedar-plank salmon and grilled swordfish.

RECOMMENDED WINES: AROUND THE WORLD

BARGAIN

Alois Lageder Müller-Thurgau Eisacktaler, Italy

Anne Amie Vineyards Cuvée A Müller-Thurgau, USA: Oregon

Elena Walch Müller-Thurgau, Italy

Erste + Neue Kellerei Müller-Thurgau, Italy

Kurtatsch Kellerei Müller-Thurgau, ItalyNadine Saxer Nobler
   Weisser, Switzerland

Stefan Vetter Müller-Thurgau, Germany

Weingut Garlider Müller-Thurgau Südtirol, Italy

VALUE

Enderle & Moll Pur Müller-Thurgau, Germany

Kettmeir Müller-Thurgau Trentino, Italy

Markgraf Von Baden Müller-Thurgau, Germany

Montinore Estate Müller-Thurgau, USA: Oregon

Pacherhof Müller Thurgau, Italy

Staffelter Hof Jan Matthias Klein Müller-Thurgau, Germany

SPECIAL OCCASION

Tiefenbrunner Feldmarschall von Fenner, Italy

RIGHT Müller-Thurgau grapes at Cantina Kurtatsch in Italy

IN 1882, HERMANN MÜLLER, a Swiss botanist, crossed Riesling and a little-known grape called Madeleine Royale, resulting in Müller-Thurgau, which ripens early, requires less sunshine, and yields 30 percent more grapes than Riesling. He added "Thurgau" to it from the Swiss canton in which he lived.

After Riesling, it ranks as Germany's second-most-planted grape, and it accounts for approximately 12 percent of the country's vines. It grows mostly in Baden, Franken, Pfalz, Mosel, and Rheinhessen. Eschewing the Liebfraumilch wines made by their ancestors, many winemakers today craft good, dry expressions of the variety. Meant to be drunk young, usually within two or three years of harvest, Müller-Thurgau wines generally taste uncomplicated and drink easy.

The variety also proves popular in Luxembourg's Moselle region, though Luxembourgish labels often call it Rivaner. In small amounts, it grows in Switzerland, where it commonly goes by the name Riesling-Sylvaner. In the cool climate and high altitude of Italy's Alto-Adige and Dolomiti regions, the grape performs very well. Eger and Lake Balaton in Hungary, where it's called Rizling-szilváni, have sizable plantations. It grows in Moravia, Czechia, and in smaller numbers in Slovenia, Moldova, Russia, and Austria. In America, Oregon and Washington also have limited plantings.

. . . .

WINEMAKER WISDOM

"I really like the Müller-Thurgau from Germany, especially from Franconia, often very mineral-driven and less fruity. In those examples, Riesling as a parent is more recognizable than in the ones from Alto Adige. I can't think of a better wine for an aperitif. Müller-Thurgau tastes fresh with high acidity, so I love it most with raw seafood, such as sushi or ceviche, especially in summer—so delicious!"

—*Andreas Kofler, president, Cantina Kurtatsch*

. . . .

MUSCAT

(MOO-skaht)

IN THE GLASS

AROMATIC GLASS, PALE STRAW TO MEDIUM STRAW IN COLOR

TASTING PROFILE

ACIDITY

BODY

SWEETNESS

LOW   MEDIUM   HIGH

TASTING NOTES

WHITE FLOWERS   PEACH   CITRUS

Muscat wines have beautiful floral aromas of freesia, jasmine, honeysuckle, and orange blossom. They come in dry, off-dry, slightly sweet, or very sweet styles with flavors of white peach, Meyer lemon, apricot, and acacia honey.

FOOD PAIRINGS

SALAD   CURRY   ICE CREAM

They taste delightful on their own as an aperitif or paired with sweet and savory foods. Dry Muscat pairs with fresh fruit and salads. Slightly sweeter versions make excellent matches with spicy food, including Thai curries, other spicy Asian dishes, and hot chili. When sparkling, it goes beautifully with creamy desserts, ice cream, and sponge cake.

RECOMMENDED WINES

See recommendations later in chapter.

YOU SHOULD KNOW

The grape name has many variations, and most people probably know it by its Italian name, Moscato, which California winemakers have adopted. Its other names include Moscatel in Spain, Muskateller in Germany, and Misket in Bulgaria, to name a few. Most widely available wines come from Muscat Blanc à Petits Grains, Moscato Bianco, and Muscat of Alexandria. The fruit has a naturally high sugar content that also makes it great as a table grape.

Muscat grapes at Bodega Jorge Ordóñez in Malaga, Spain

AMPELOGRAPHERS POINT to more than 200 varieties belonging to the Muscat family, and some experts even hold that many noble grape varieties descend from Muscat. Historians consider the Muscat grape one of the oldest, if not *the* oldest cultivated variety. Most scientists agree that Muscat has been around for a long time, and some suggest that the ancient Persians and Egyptians vinified it.

The name has speculative origins as well. It could come from the city of Muscat in Oman, and many of our Spanish friends like to think it takes its name from *mosca*, Spanish for "fly," because the wine's sweetness attracts fruit flies. Whatever the case, most Muscat family members have in common a sweet floral aroma reminiscent of jasmine, freesia, or honeysuckle.

Muscat produces many distinct wines and styles around the world. Dry wines have gained in popularity, and even in southern Spain, where Moscatel traditionally becomes a semisweet or sweet wine, vintners are making dry versions with fewer than 6 grams of residual sugar per liter.

French producers make a sweet wine called Muscat de Beaumes de Venise from Muscat Blanc à Petit Grains, known locally as Muscat de Frontignan. The vines grow on hillsides of the Dentelles de Montmirail, a small mountain range in Provence, and the ripe grapes have high sugar levels. The winemakers fortify it with a 95 percent ABV spirit that stops fermentation and preserves the sweetness of the final wine. Muscat de Beaumes de Venise ranges in color from medium gold to light amber and has luscious flavors of dried apricot, canned peaches, honeycomb, orange marmalade, jasmine blossoms, and honeysuckle. See page 227 for more information.

Other French Muscats include Muscat d'Alsace, Muscat du Cap Corse (Corsica), and Muscat de Frontignan in the Languedoc region. Languedoc Muscat wine must contain at least 15 percent alcohol, so many producers add alcohol during fermentation. Muscat de Lunel, Muscat de Rivesaltes, and Muscat de Mireval all take their names from towns where they're made. Muscat de St-Jean-de-Minervois, one of France's rarest wines, is certainly worth the effort and cost.

Other subvarieties from the family—Muscat de Hamburg, Muscat Ottonel, Sárgamuskotály—grow in Moldova, Romania, Hungary, Bulgaria, Ukraine, and Czechia. Greek producers grow it on some of the islands and in the Peloponnese region. Brazil makes good sparkling Muscat wines near Bento Gonçalves, the nation's wine center, that young drinkers enjoy at chic discotheques across the country.

Muscat of Alexandria originated in Africa, where the ancient Egyptians vinified it, and it now grows around the world. South Africa alone boasts four subvarieties: Muscat d'Alexandrie (also called Hanepoot), Muscat de Frontignan (Muscadel in South Africa), Muscat de Hambourg

(Black Muscat), and Muscat Ottonel. The last of these four, one of the lightest in color of all Muscats, grows mostly in Constantia, Breede River Valley, Klein Karoo, and Lower Orange. Muscat de Frontignan planted in Constantia goes into the eponymous wines of the region, Klein Constantia Vin de Constance, one of the country's finest sweet wines.

Australians have been making Muscat wines for a century. Many of the best, made in the fortified style, come from Rutherglen and Glenrowan in Victoria. Winemakers in New Zealand also make quality Muscats in semi-sweet, fortified, and botrytized versions. In Austria, Muscat Blanc à Petits Grains goes by the names Muscateller or Gelber Muskateller, and the wines come mostly from Sudsteiermark, Burgenland, and Wachau. Also in Austria, producers in the Neusiedlersee region grow Muscat Ottonel to make late-harvest wine. In America, lots of California winemakers make inexpensive, sweet Moscato wines, many with brightly colored, eye-catching labels. Winemakers in Cyprus, Indonesia, Japan, and Tunisia also vinify grapes from the Muscat family.

WINEMAKER WISDOM

"Phoenicians first planted Moscatel de Alejandría in Málaga more than 2,700 years ago. At the end of the 18th century, the British heavily introduced fortification to Andalusian winemaking. Before that, all Málaga wines were unfortified. We were the first producer in Málaga to resurrect the tradition of unfortified sweet winemaking since phylloxera. There's no trellising or terracing, resulting in a 'heroic' style of viticulture that's completely ancient. The age of the vines, high altitudes, and slate soils result in an extremely high-acid sweet wine with tremendous balance. Even with sugar concentrations exceeding 100 g/L and reaching 450 g/L, the wines don't taste cloying. The acidity also contributes to tremendous ageability. When compared to sweet Muscat wines made internationally, the Muscat of Málaga shows more complexity, more refinement, and better freshness."

—Jorge Ordóñez, founder and owner,
Jorge Ordóñez Málaga

RIGHT Manual harvest at Bodega Jorge Ordóñez in Malaga

RECOMMENDED DRY WINES: AROUND THE WORLD

BARGAIN
Botani Moscatel Old Vines, Spain
Yarden Mount Hermon Moscato, Israel

VALUE
Planeta Moscato Allemanda Noto, Italy
Riofavara Sicilia Noto Mizzica, Italy

SPECIAL OCCASION
Albert Boxler Muscat, France

RECOMMENDED SWEET WINES: AROUND THE WORLD

BARGAIN
Bulletin Place Moscato, Australia
Caposaldo Moscato, Italy
Eberle Muscat, USA: California
Mirassou Moscato, USA: California
Vino Noceto Moscato Frivolo, USA: California

VALUE
Gallivant Moscato, USA: California

SPECIAL OCCASION
Jorge Ordóñez Malaga No. 2 Victoria, Spain →
Klein Constantia Vin de Constance, South Africa
Molino Real, Spain

OTHER NOTABLE COUNTRIES

ITALY

Italian regulations allow Moscato Bianco, one of the country's most common white grapes, in many DOCs, most famously Piedmont's sweet Asti wines. Few people living outside Italy have tried the dry wines made in the Aosta Valley from Muscat de Chambave. Tuscany vintners use Moscadello di Montalcino to make a lightly sweet version, while their Calabrian counterparts make sweet, passito-style wines. Muscat also goes into dessert wines on the island of Pantelleria, where the grape goes by the name Zibibbo. You can find further examples in a variety of styles from Emilia-Romagna, Friuli-Venezia Giulia, Lombardy, Puglia, Sardinia, Sicily, Trentino, and the Veneto.

Asti producers make both still and sparkling versions, but many of the sparklers are *frizzante* or only slightly fizzy because many Asti wines undergo just one fermentation, not two as with most other sparkling wines. Compared to others, Asti are less bubbly and have lower alcohol levels.

Growers pick the grapes at their highest sugar level, fermenting the juice quickly and stopping fermentation with cold refrigeration, resulting in sweet wines with ABVs between 4.5 to 6.5 percent.

The Asti DOCG covers more than 50 towns in the provinces of Alessandria, Asti, and Cuneo. A portion of the land has steep slopes, and historically these vineyards can be harvested only by hand. A bottle labeled "Asti DOCG" must contain 100 percent Moscato Bianco, and the alcohol level will range a bit higher than other Asti wines, generally 7 to 11 percent. When looking for an Asti DOCG bottle, note that most Italians consider wines from Canelli as having some of the best quality. Bottles labeled "Asti Spumante DOCG" have more bubbles and more pressure. For bottles labeled "Brut, Extra Brut," or "Pas Dosé," secondary fermentation can occur via the traditional method in the bottle or the Martinotti-Charmat method in large steel tanks. The Asti Protection Consortium—founded in 1932, making it one of the oldest wine consortiums in Italy—recently allowed for dryer wines labeled "Asti Seco."

WINEMAKER WISDOM

"Moscato d'Asti is embedded with the DNA of our territory. It's a unique white wine, delicately fizzy, approachable, and yet complex, with a surprising balance between sweetness and freshness. It's also versatile: perfect for desserts, such as hazelnut cake, cookies, a cup of strawberries, but capable of matching with oysters, Parma ham, and seasoned cheese as well. It's enjoyable every moment of the day with equal pleasure, from brunch till aperitivo."

—*Luigi Coppo, CEO, Coppo*

"The most important aspect of Moscato has to be that finite balance between acid and sugar, as well as the general generosity of flavour. For something savoury, I like to pair Moscato with a Thai green curry or any spicy Indian or Southeast Asian cuisine, as it helps temper that heat. For something sweet, you can't go wrong with a pineapple upside-down cake! The fresh, vibrant acid of the Moscato helps cut all that sweetness."

—*Jeremy Nascimben, senior winemaker,*
Calabria Family Wines

RECOMMENDED WINES: ITALY

BARGAIN

Beni di Batasiolo Bosc Dla Rei
Borgo Maragliano La Caliera
Coppo Moncalvina →
Dogliotti 1870
Fontanafredda Le Fronde
La Spinetta Bricco Quaglia
Vietti Cascinetta

VALUE

Albino Rocca
Ceretto I Vignaioli di S. Stefano
Elvio Cogno
Marco Negri Marsilio
Marenco Scrapona
Massolino
Mauro Sebaste
Michele Chiarlo Nivole
Rinaldi Vini

SPECIAL OCCASION

Ca' d'Gal Vite Vecchia

LEFT Aerial view of Jorge Ordóñez vineyards in Malaga, Spain

PINOT BLANC

(PEE-no BLAHNK)

IN THE GLASS

SMALL BORDEAUX GLASS, PALE STRAW TO MEDIUM STRAW IN COLOR

TASTING PROFILE

ACIDITY

BODY

SWEETNESS

LOW   MEDIUM   HIGH

TASTING NOTES

PEACH   PEAR   RIVER ROCKS

Pinot Blanc has soft fruit aromas of white peach, Bartlett pear, lemon zest, and river rocks. Generally lighter and less aromatic than its fraternal triplet Pinot Gris, it features flavors of Granny Smith apple, nectarine, and citrus zest with strong minerality.

YOU SHOULD KNOW

Besides Alsace, some of the best Pinot Blanc comes from Alto Adige, where it goes by two other names: Pinot Bianco and Weissburgunder, depending on the producer's language preference. In Italy, it comes in unoaked and oaked styles, but the most popular versions, refreshing and racy, have bold citrus flavors and distinctive minerality.

FOOD PAIRINGS

CHEESE   CHICKEN   EGGS

Pinot Blanc tastes terrific with soft, gooey, melted cheeses. Go for raclette, fondue, Brie en croûte, or white pizza. It's a natural alongside chicken dishes, especially grilled with lemon and herbs or chicken Française. Also try it with quiche, cheese omelets, or eggs Benedict.

RECOMMENDED WINES: FRANCE

BARGAIN

Cave de Ribeauville Pinot Blanc

Domaine Charles Baur Pinot Blanc

Dopff & Irion Alsace Pinot Blanc

Hugel & Fils Pinot Blanc Cuvée Les Amours

Joseph Cattin Pinot Blanc

Pierre Sparr Pinot Blanc

Rolly Gassmann Pinot Blanc

Willm Pinot Blanc Reserve

VALUE

Albert Boxler Pinot Blanc

Albert Mann Pinot Blanc

Domaine Amélie & Charles Sparr Pinot Blanc Pensée

Trimbach Classic Pinot Blanc

Zind-Humbrecht Pinot Blanc

SPECIAL OCCASION

Marc Kreydenweiss La Fontaine aux Enfants Pinot Blanc

RIGHT Harvested Pinot Blanc grapes at Lieb Cellars on Long Island, New York

A THREEQUEL, POOR PINOT BLANC isn't as well known or loved as its Pinot Noir and Pinot Gris/ Grigio relatives. Pinot Noir gave rise to Pinot Gris, and genetically speaking, Pinot Blanc evolved from the latter of those two varieties. In the late 1800s, viticulturists first observed Pinot Blanc in Burgundy, frequently confusing the vine with Chardonnay and often calling it Chardonnet Pinot Blanc or Pinot Blanc Chardonnet. In Burgundy, Pinot Noir and Chardonnay grow in close proximity to each other, and a single Pinot Noir plant can contain grapes in a spectrum of color variations, including purple, gray, white, and even mixed stripes. So, it's easy to understand how confusion arose. All the varieties take their first name from the French word for "pine" because the small, tight grape clusters look like pinecones. *Noir, Gris,* and *Blanc* translate to "black," "gray," and "white," respectively. Like Chardonnay, Pinot Blanc functions as somewhat of a blank slate, receiving most its final characteristics not from the vineyard but rather from the winemaking process.

Some Pinot Blanc still grows in Burgundy, where regulations allow it for blending in small amounts with Chardonnay in white Burgundy, and in Champagne, where it serves as one of the four allowed additional grapes. But Pinot Blanc has found a good home in Alsace, with many wine lovers considering its expression here more elegant and voluptuous than Pinot Gris from the same region. Bottlings here may contain small blending amounts of

Auxerrois Blanc and often draw comparisons to racy Chablis, although they can have more floral notes and touches of smoke on the nose and increased floral, almond, and spice notes on the palate. The grape also goes by the name Klevner here, and it grows across the Moselle River in Luxembourg, where its blending partner Auxerrois proves more popular. Pinot Blanc also serves as one of the mainstays of Crémant d'Alsace (page 197).

In Austria and Germany, the variety is called Weissburgunder, meaning "white Burgundy," and some Italian producers also use that moniker. Some Austrian winemakers blend it with Chardonnay and age it in oak, while others mature it in barrels as a single varietal. It grows in Burgenland, Styria, and Neusiedlersee, where vintners also make an off-dry, botrytized style. In Germany, you can find it in light, bright versions as well as a *Spätlese trocken*, or late-harvest style, which can drink dry or off-dry. The vine's largest concentrations grow in Mosel, Pfalz, and Baden. But both Austrian Grüner Veltliner and German Riesling dwarf the Pinot Blanc from those countries in the export market.

In Italy, the variety goes by Pinot Bianco, while Croatia and Slovenia call it Beli Pinot. (*Beli* means "white" in both languages.) It also grows in Hungary, Serbia, Slovakia, Czechia, and America. In Canada, Pinot Blanc thrives in the Okanagan Valley, and producers on the Niagara Peninsula in Ontario make it into ice wine.

WINEMAKER WISDOM

"Pinot Blanc is what we call a 'glouglouglou' wine, an easy aperitif but also perfect with salad, terrines, mussels, oysters, or anything easy you would share on a table with friends and family!"

—*Pierre Trimbach, winemaker and technical director, Trimbach*

ABOVE Pinot Blanc harvest at Lieb Cellars on Long Island's North Fork
RIGHT Vineyards at Elena Walch in Alto Adige, Italy

OTHER NOTABLE COUNTRIES

ITALY

Pinot Blanc has a dual identity in bilingual Alto Adige, where it goes by Pinot Bianco and Weissburgunder, depending on which language the producer prefers. Coolness at higher vineyard altitudes here, around 1,500 feet, helps maintain acidity. It grows in Friuli–Venezia Giulia, especially in the Friuli Colli Orientali and Collio subzones near the Adriatic. Italian vintners make it in a fresh, crisp style entirely in stainless steel as well as Riserva versions in a mix of steel and oak. It also goes into the Italian sparkling wine Franciacorta (page 216).

. . . .

WINEMAKER WISDOM

"In Alto Adige, we have a long tradition of planting Pinot Bianco, and we feel that it has found its ideal home here. It's planted mainly at higher elevations to preserve its natural acidity, thanks to the temperature fluctuations between day and night. With the calcareous and porphyric soils, you find not only delicate fruit-driven aromas but also an incredible minerality and salinity with a crisp acidity. It's really the mineral aspect that's unique to Alto Adige Pinot Bianco. Delicate oak adds another layer and palate weight."

—*Karoline Walch, co-owner, Elena Walch*

. . . .

RECOMMENDED WINES: ITALY

BARGAIN

Alois Lageder Terra Alpina Pinot Bianco

St. Michael Eppan Appiano Pinot Bianco

Tiefenbrunner Anna Weissburgunder

VALUE

Alois Lageder Haberle Pinot Bianco

Cantina Produttori San Michele Appiano Pinot Bianco

Elena Walch Pinot Bianco Kristallberg →

Erste + Neue Pinot Bianco

Livio Felluga Illivio Bianco

St. Pauls Kalkberg Pinot Bianco

SPECIAL OCCASION

Castel Sallegg Pratum Pinot Bianco

Girlan Flora Riserva Pinot Bianco

Kellerei Kaltern Caldaro Quintessenz Pinot Bianco

Terlan Vorberg Riserva Pinot Bianco

WINEMAKER WISDOM

"Alsace is most prominently associated with Pinot Blanc, but I appreciate lighter, crisp, unoaked versions from Alto Adige more. Long Island is a cool-climate region surrounded by moderating water on three sides, so we benefit from high acid levels and an extended growing season that gives us solid flavor development. Pinot Blanc here excellently expresses freshness and depth of fruit flavor. Pinot Blanc often is described as bland, and we're happy to challenge that perception. As a winemaker, underdog grapes are fun to work with, and when grown in the correct climate, they can shine. I've been working with this grape for 30 years and still find it interesting and challenging."

—*Russell Hearn, winemaker, Lieb Cellars*

"Pinot Blanc offers a fresh, crisp, versatile style that pairs well with a range of foods, including roast chicken and white-fish dishes. In the riper vintages, it offers tropical characteristics such as pineapple."

—*Kareem Massoud, winemaker, Palmer Vineyards*

"Few people are familiar with Pinot Blanc and typically fall quickly in love with it once they have tried ours. Our vineyard has a rather cool growing season. The grapes ripen slowly, and as a result we often pick at lower sugar levels but have exceptional fruit intensity."

—*Joe Nielsen, general manager and winemaker, Ram's Gate Winery*

USA

Quite a bit of Pinot Blanc grows in California, notably Carneros, used for producing sparkling wine. It also grows in Monterey and in some areas of the Central Coast, though some older Monterey plantings turned out to be Melon de Bourgogne. Growers cultivate it in Oregon's Willamette Valley and in the Finger Lakes and Long Island regions of New York. These temperate-to-cool regions preserve the freshness, acidity, and aromatic qualities of the grapes, giving them profiles of apple and peach with notes of almond and white flowers.

RECOMMENDED WINES: USA

BARGAIN
The Four Graces Pinot Blanc, Oregon
Glenora Pinot Blanc, New York
St. Innocent Freedom Hill Vineyard Pinot Blanc, Oregon

VALUE
Chalone Vineyard Estate Grown Pinot Blanc, California
Harper Voit Surlie Pinot Blanc, Washington
Kelley Fox Wines Freedom Hill Vineyard Pinot Blanc, Oregon
Lieb Cellars Estate Pinot Blanc, New York
Palmer Pinot Blanc, New York →
Ram's Gate Estate Pinot Blanc, California
Ryan William Vineyard Pinot Blanc, New York
Weis Vineyards Pinot Blanc, New York

SPECIAL OCCASION
Foundry Schrader Ranch Pinot Blanc, California
Robert Sinskey Vineyard Pinot Blanc, California
Seabold Cellars Rodnick Farm Old Vines Pinot Blanc, California
Three Sticks Durell Vineyard Pinot Blanc, California

PINOT GRIGIO

(PEE-no GREE-jo)

IN THE GLASS

SMALL BORDEAUX GLASS, PALE STRAW TO LIGHT YELLOW IN COLOR

TASTING PROFILE

	LOW	MEDIUM	HIGH
ACIDITY			
BODY			
SWEETNESS			

TASTING NOTES

LEMON   APPLE   PEACH

Pinot Grigio has aromas of citrus and green apple with light floral notes joined on the palate by zippy flavors of lemon, lime, and Granny Smith apple. When made in a more serious style, it has notes of clove and baking spices on the nose and more body than Italian versions. Expect flavors of pear and peach with notes of almond and ginger.

FOOD PAIRINGS

SUSHI   PASTA   CHICKEN

Italian or Californian bottles taste terrific alongside sushi, sashimi, or other seafood from the raw bar. They pair well with "white" pasta dishes, such as linguine with clam sauce, spaghetti aglio e olio, or shrimp scampi over capellini. Mineral-driven expressions from France or elsewhere—labeled "Pinot Gris"—complement salty cheeses, such as feta or Parmigiano-Reggiano, or dishes with a touch of bright spice, including tandoori chicken or chicken tagine. If you have the opportunity, sip one with the famed Alsatian *flammekueche*, a flatbread topped with melted cheese, onion, and bacon.

RECOMMENDED WINES

See regional recommendations throughout the chapter.

YOU SHOULD KNOW

Outside Italy and France, you can tell a lot about a winemaker's style by whether a bottle bears the name Pinot Grigio or Pinot Gris. New World Pinot Gris has soft aromatics and feels somewhat weighty on the palate, with a sense of elegance and complexity. New World Pinot Grigio, on the other hand, boasts citrus and green apple flavors and high acidity in a crisp, refreshing style.

Pinot Grigio harvest at Infiné 1939 in northern Italy

THE RISE OF SUPERHERO FRANCHISES has taught us that dual identities can be good, as can mutations. Let's start with identities—or, in this case, something more like multiple personalities. Pinot Grigio and Pinot Gris are the same grape that goes by two different names. Pinot Grigio is the Italian name, and Pinot Gris the French. In both languages, Pinot means "pinecone," referring to the shape of the tight clusters of grapes. In this part of the book, we usually name a chapter according to the grape's place of origin, but in this case we're using the Italian name because Pinot Grigio is more familiar to more drinkers.

The variety goes by other names as well, including Grauburgunder or Grauer Burgunder in Austria and Germany, Sivi Pinot in Slovenia, and Szürkebarát in Hungary. The Hungarian word means "gray monk," a nod to the tale that in 1375 Holy Roman Emperor Charles IV ordered Pinot Gris vines brought from to Hungary from France. There, Cistercian monks planted the vines on the shores of Lake Balaton, earning the grape its Hungarian moniker. Even within France, Pinot Gris has several aliases, such as Fromenteau in Champagne, Malvoisie in the Loire, and Tokay in Alsace until 2007.

Both *grigio* and *gris* mean "gray" in their respective languages. We refer to just about every other grape in this book as white—in reality, green—but both of these Pinots look grayish-purple. Individual bunches may have multiple colors within them, with grapes ranging from gold and green to gray to lavender. Nevertheless they produce a white wine when pressed.

As you may recall from the prior chapter, Pinot comes in three chromatic and chronological classifications: Noir, meaning "black"; Grigio for "gray"; and Blanc,

which translates to "white." The latter two mutations of Pinot Noir happened spontaneously, meaning that they arose in the field rather than a lab. Scientists believe that the transition that produced Pinot Gris took place at least 800 years ago.

Written evidence of grapes in France that may have been Pinot Gris date as far back as the early 1200s, but we can't confirm the variety with any certainty. Experts believe that it originated in Burgundy, the birthplace of Pinot Noir, where locals called the gray variety Fromenteau. From Burgundy, it spread to Switzerland, Germany, and northern Italy. In the early 1700s, winemakers in Germany and France were producing Pinot Gris. German wine merchant Johann Ruland came across wild Pinot Gris vines in the Palatinate. The wine he made became known as Rülander, another name for Pinot Gris that remains in use today. Viticulturists in France wrote about the mutation at about the same time, calling it Auvernat Gris. By the end of the 1700s, "Pinot Gris" had come into common usage within France.

Perhaps the variety's most important migration took it to Italy. Pinot Grigio suddenly appears in a variety of regions, including Alto Adige, Trentino, and Friuli–Venezia Giulia. Like many other European varieties, Italian immigrants brought Pinot Grigio vines to America during the

California gold rush that began in 1848, the year of revolutions. But the true revolution in Pinot Grigio began in the 1970s, when it became the number one imported variety in America. Many wine snobs turn their noses up at it, but it's one of the most popular varieties almost everywhere that people drink wine. Crisp and refreshing, Pinot Grigio led the charge against overoaked, buttery Chardonnays. If Pinot Gris represents Clark Kent, understated and mild-mannered, then Pinot Grigio embodies Superman, with the power to make bottles fly off store shelves.

By any name, this prolific grape grows in seemingly every wine-producing country in the world. In Europe, you also can find it in Czechia, Luxembourg, Moldova, Romania, Turkey, and Ukraine. It thrives throughout the New World as well, including America, Canada, Argentina, Chile, South Africa, and Australia.

OTHER NOTABLE COUNTRIES

CENTRAL EUROPE

Germany has the third-largest amount of Pinot Gris in the world, earning the bronze behind Italy and France. The variety goes by three names here. Grauburgunder and Grauer Burgunder both mean "gray Burgundy," nodding to its region of origin, while Rülander pays homage to the merchant who supposedly discovered it in Germany. In this part of Europe, most of it comes from Rheinhessen, Pfalz, and Baden. German Grauburgunder tends to have higher acidity and minerality than examples from other countries. Rheinhessen and Pfalz versions usually drink fresh and dry. Winemakers in Baden use skin contact, bâtonnage, and oak aging to produce fuller-bodied, more fragrant wines that tend to taste off-dry.

In the 1200s or 1300s, Cistercian monks purportedly brought it from France to Austria, where locals called it Grauer Mönch, "gray monk," as well as Grauburgunder. Growers here cultivate it mainly in Steirmark and Burgenland. Picked young, it makes dry still or sparkling wines. Riper grapes with higher sugar content or botrytis become off-dry or sweet late-harvest wines.

Pinot Gris grows widely along the Mosel River in Luxembourg. Most winemakers here make a fresh, crisp version with little to no oak aging, but some prefer to age their wines in oak for a rounder, more complex style that pairs with the region's rich cuisine.

RECOMMENDED WINES: CENTRAL EUROPE

BARGAIN

Domaine Viticole Laurent & Rita Kox Pinot Gris, Luxembourg

Leo Hillinger Pinot Gris, Austria

Villa Wolf Pinot Gris, Germany

Weingut Steindorfer Fuchsloch Pinot Gris, Austria

VALUE

Domaine Clos de Rochers Pinot Gris, Luxembourg

Domaine Mathis Bastian Wellenstein Foulschette Pinot Gris, Luxembourg

Philip Lardot Pinot Gris Landwein, Germany

Weingut Friedrich Becker Family Pinot Gris, Germany

Weinlaubenhof Alois Kracher Illmitz Pinot Gris, Austria

Wenzel Wild and Free Pinot Gris, Austria

FRANCE

Pinot Gris may have originated in Burgundy, but its French home lies in Alsace, which shares a border with Germany along the Rhine River, where yield largely determines quality. Limiting the tons per hectare, which in effect limits bunches per vine, allows for concentration of flavor and maximal ripeness. Producers here make it in a precise, dry style with flavors of pear and lemon zest aided by bold minerality that goes extraordinarily well with food. Off-dry versions have flavors of peach and apricot. In Alsace, you also can find sweet, Vendange Tardive (late-harvest) Pinot Gris that has notes of honey, caramel, and ginger.

Alsace has 51 Grand Cru vineyards, which by definition producer higher-quality wine. They face south, southeast, and east to maximize sun exposure and allow grapes to ripen to their fullest. High altitudes provide cooler nighttime temperatures to preserve acidity, while rocky soils add mineral notes. The finest sites among the Alsatian Grand Crus include Geisberg, Rangen, Vorbourg, Muenchberg, Schlossberg, and Schoenenbourg.

Elsewhere in France, Pinot Gris grows in small amounts, used mainly as a blending grape.

RECOMMENDED WINES: FRANCE

BARGAIN
Joseph Cattin Pinot Gris
Pfaffenheim Pfaff Pinot Gris Tradition
Pierre Sparr Pinot Gris Reserve
Willm Pinot Gris Reserve
Wolfberger Pinot Gris Signature

VALUE
Domaines Schlumberger Les Princes Abbés Pinot Gris
Gustave Lorentz Pinot Gris Reserve
Leon Beyer Pinot Gris
Meyer-Fonné Pinot Gris Reserve

SPECIAL OCCASION
Domaine Weinbach Cuvée Sainte Catherine Pinot Gris
Domaine Zind-Humbrecht Pinot Gris Roche Calcaire
Domaine Zind-Humbrecht Pinot Gris Roche Volcanique
FE Trimbach Pinot Gris Réserve Personnelle

SPLURGE
Domaine Ostertag Pinot Gris Muenchberg
Hugel & Fils Pinot Gris Sélection de Grains Nobles

WINEMAKER WISDOM

"In the rest of the world (North America, Germany, Australia, New Zealand), Pinot Gris is made like Chardonnay: often in small barrels with some wood influence. The Alsace style is quite unique. It probably has the most fruit-driven style and makes Pinot Gris capable of very long aging. It isn't made in new oak, so the wine retains elegance and energy. The wine shows strong vineyard character and can be quite intense without being heavy. It can go with an entire menu that doesn't have red meat!"

—*Olivier Humbrecht, owner and general manager,*
Zind-Humbrecht

ITALY

Thriving in cold weather, Pinot Grigio grows mainly in northern wine regions, offering different expressions, depending on terroir and climate. Some of the largest brands offer refreshing, easy-drinking, cheap, and cheerful wines. You can find some of these crowd-pleasers that we consider great "party pours" in the following bargain listings. But they drink worlds apart from single-varietal DOC wines made using sustainable practices. Alto Adige/Südtiroler and Trentino, two of the best regions for Pinot Grigio, both lie within the larger Trentino–Alto Adige region. Regulations for each location stipulate that at least 85 percent of the wine in the bottle must come from Pinot Grigio, with other varieties allowed for blending.

Trentino, a DOC with the same percentage split, covers the whole province, with many vineyards in the foothills of the Dolomites. It constitutes the southern half of the region, and grows more Pinot Grigio than any other grape, accounting for a third of production. Just over half of the wine made here exports to America.

With a mild climate and more than 300 days of sun per year, Alto Adige, north of Trentino, is Italy's northernmost wine region and one of its most popular holiday destinations. Alpine villages reminiscent of Germany or neighboring Switzerland sit atop many of its hillsides. Among more than 20 varieties in cultivation, Pinot Grigio grows most widely, accounting for more than 10 percent of total production. Expect flavors of lemon and pear with soft floral notes. Many producers have Germanic names, and bottles from the Alto Adige/Südtiroler DOC may be labeled "Pinot Grigio" as well as "Rülander." They also may contain up to 15 percent of other local white grapes. Pinot Grigio here comes in two distinct styles, either lean with strong minerality and pronounced floral aromas or full-bodied with bold flavors of apple, pear, and citrus.

Friuli–Venezia Giulia sits north of Venice, and its best growing areas for Pinot Grigio include Collio and Colli Orientali, hilly areas with limestone soils and good sun exposure. Flavors of pear and apple join spice and floral notes. Oltrepò Pavese DOC in Lombardy specializes in still and sparkling wines made with at least 85 percent Pinot Grigio. Grapes grown on alluvial soils near the Po River produce wines noted for flavors of peach and apple.

WINEMAKER WISDOM

"I love the elegance, crispness, fragrance, and longevity of our wines. I love their being modern but always linked to traditions and their historical roots. In all wines, we constantly look for elegance and maximum finesse. Burgundy is the region whose wines are closest to our style, and we are inspired by some of them to make Jermann wine taste even more emotional."

—Luca Belluzzo, oenologist, Jermann

"As a family, we have a long tradition cultivating Pinot Grigio. My father, Livio, bet on it many years before its popularity beyond the Friulian borders. We consider it a noble grape with great complexity and good aging potential. Terroir and low yield are crucial. The best ones taste well balanced, quite complex, with a rich aromatic profile and a distinct mineral component."

—Andrea Felluga, owner and director, Livio Felluga

"I have enjoyed excellent expressions of Pinot Grigios from other regions of Italy and around the world, as well as outstanding Pinot Gris wines from Alsace and Oregon, among others. Pinot Grigio from Trentino has incredible aromatics and minerality due to its mountainous origin."

—Fabrizio Marinconz, winemaker, Infiné 1939

RECOMMENDED WINES: ITALY

BARGAIN

Bollini Pinot Grigio

Borghi Ad Est Pinot Grigio

Bottega Vinaia Pinot Grigio

Caposaldo Pinot Grigio

Ecco Domani Pinot Grigio →

Pighin Pinot Grigio

Villa Sandi Pinot Grigio

Zenato Pinot Grigio

VALUE

Alois Lageder Porer Pinot Grigio

Attems Pinot Grigio

Gradis'ciutta Pinot Grigio

Infiné 1939 Pinot Grigio

Jermann Pinot Grigio

Livio Felluga Pinot Grigio

Marco Felluga Pinot Grigio

Peter Zemmer Giatl Pinot Grigio Riserva

Pighin Pinot Grigio

Rottensteiner Pinot Grigio

LEFT Pinot Grigio vineyard at Infiné 1939

NEW ZEALAND

Despite Sauvignon Blanc's preeminence in the Land of the Long White Cloud, many winemakers here grow and produce Pinot Gris—about 6 percent of total production—most of which remains in the domestic market. As the name indicates, New Zealand Pinot Gris owes more to Alsace than to Italy. About a third of it grows in Marlborough, and another 40 percent divides evenly between Hawke's Bay and Gisborne. Warmer North Island bottlings from Auckland, Hawke's Bay, and Gisborne favor fuller, riper profiles of apple pie, canned peaches, and soft spice, while cooler South Island versions from Marlborough, Central Otago, and Nelson tend to come in a more austere but well-structured style.

RECOMMENDED WINES: NEW ZEALAND

BARGAIN

Giesen Pinot Gris

Huia Pinot Gris

Lawson's Dry Hills Pinot Gris

Leefield Station Pinot Gris

Yealands Pinot Gris

VALUE

Astrolabe Province Voyage Pinot Gris

Drumsara Pinot Gris

Kumeu River Estate Pinot Gris

Man O' War Exiled Pinot Gris

Peregrine Pinot Gris

Tinpot Hut Pinot Gris

SPECIAL OCCASION

Dry River Pinot Gris, Martinborough

USA

Going by both its Italian and French names, this variety grows widely throughout America. Perhaps surprisingly, it's Oregon's most widely grown white grape. Unlike many other varieties, we can trace its Oregon origin to a single event. David Lett of Eyrie Vineyards planted it in 1965 and marketed it as the perfect wine pairing with northwest salmon. In the 1990s, Oregon Pinot Gris took off, and today it comes in a wide variety of styles from fresh and crisp to plump and full-bodied with lees aging or light touches of oak.

In California, it grows in almost every winegrowing county. The majority lies in the Central Valley, where producers make it in an easy-drinking style usually labeled "Pinot Grigio." Higher-end, small-lot versions from cool-climate areas near the Pacific often say "Pinot Gris" on the label.

The variety thrives throughout New York State in the Finger Lakes, Long Island, and Hudson Valley, particularly alongside Riesling, its counterpart from Alsace and Germany. Small amounts grow in northern Ohio as well.

ABOVE Aerial view of J Vineyards and Winery Bow Tie vineyard in Sonoma, California

RECOMMENDED WINES: USA

BARGAIN
Airfield Estates Pinot Gris, Washington
Boeger Winery Pinot Gris, California
Channing Daughters Pinot Grigio, New York
La Crema Pinot Gris, California
Edna Valley Vineyard Pinot Gris, California
Elk Cove Vineyards Estate Pinot Gris, Oregon
Estancia Pinot Gris, California
Hossmer Estate Pinot Gris, New York
King Estate Pinot Gris, Oregon
Lakewood Vineyards Gigliotti Vineyards Pinot Gris, New York
Mazza Chautauqua Cellars Pinot Grigio, New York
William Grassie Wine Estates Pinot Gris, Washington

VALUE
Anthony Road Wine Company Barrel Ferment Pinot Gris, New York
J Vineyards and Winery Pinot Gris, California
Keeler Estate Vineyard Barrel Aged Pinot Gris, Oregon
Lenz Estate Selection Pinot Gris, New York
Living Roots Pinot Gris, New York
Sokol Blosser Pinot Gris, Oregon
WillaKenzie Estate Pinot Gris, Oregon
Wölffer Estate Pinot Gris, New York

WINEMAKER WISDOM

"Our growing region is surrounded by bodies of water on three sides that moderate temperature, which delays spring bud-break but provides an extended growing season. Cool climate regions, such as the North Fork of Long Island, also retain high acidity levels with longer flavor development. A light but complex Pinot Grigio is a combination of the correct growing region, good vineyard management, and a light touch from the winemaker. If the fruit is ripe, don't get in the way of it expressing itself in the glass."

—*Russell Hearn, winemaker, Suhru Wines*

"Crisp but full, Pinot Gris from Russian River Valley beautifully balances its viscosity and weight with vibrant, food-friendly acidity. Alsatian-style Pinot Gris I would generally describe as having a fleshy, voluptuous mouthfeel with exotic bouquets of green apple, honeysuckle, slate, white nectarine, and bright acidity. Pinot Gris from Oregon tends to have similar qualities, but oftentimes with more crispness, citrus, and delicate minerality. This style differs from the Pinot Grigio of northern Italy, which tends to be leaner with more subtle flavors and aromas of pear, citrus, and hay."

—*Nicole Hitchcock, winemaker, J Vineyards and Winery*

"Pinot Gris can be many things, from richer, riper, sweeter Alsatian versions to lighter, high-acid, citrus, mineral-driven dry northern Italian versions. Washington State Pinot Gris is sunshine in a glass. The Washington State flavor profile runs from citrus, stone fruit, pink apple, and pear with wet stone and underlying herbal grassy notes."

—*Chad Johnson, co-owner and winegrower, Boomtown by Dusted Valley*

"The grape responds to an array of winemaking inputs, specifically skin contact, time, and temperature. Italian Pinot Grigio I find generally lighter bodied and more gravely with harder phenolics, while Alsatian Pinot Gris can be a bit more opulent. Also, clean botrytis influence can be a fantastic element. Its naturally delicate aromatics allow so many winemaking decisions to show through. Our work leans toward slate, honeydew, and grapefruit with a touch of honey on years the grapes have some botrytis."

—*Chris Stamp, head winemaker, Lakewood Vineyards*

RIGHT Machine harvest at Lakewood Vineyards in New York

POŠIP

(PO-ship)

IN THE GLASS

AROMATIC GLASS, PALE STRAW TO MEDIUM STRAW IN COLOR

TASTING PROFILE

ACIDITY

BODY

SWEETNESS

LOW   MEDIUM   HIGH

TASTING NOTES

APPLE   CITRUS   ALMONDS

Pošip has aromas and flavors of Winesap and Fuji apples, citrus blossom, orange peel, grapefruit zest, and marzipan in the finish.

YOU SHOULD KNOW

Croatian winemaker Mike Grgich famously made the Chateau Montelena Chardonnay that won first prize at the Judgment of Paris in 1976, and in Croatia his Pošip garnered the prestigious Vrhunska Vina, the top premium wine accolade. His daughter Violet and nephew Ivo now run his winery in Trstenik, where they concentrate on making wines from indigenous varieties.

FOOD PAIRINGS

OCTOPUS   SALAD   CHEESE

It makes the perfect pairing with just about every type of seafood, including briny oysters, clams, and steamed mussels. Try it with octopus grilled on a wood fire. It also nicely accompanies seafood paella and salads. Drink an oak-aged version with your next charcuterie board of soft cheeses and smoked meats. Our absolute favorite pairing is with watching the sun set over the Adriatic from one of Croatia's beautiful islands.

RECOMMENDED WINES: CROATIA

BARGAIN

Merga Victa Pošip

Pecotić Baran Pod Korita Pošip

Pošip Cara Marco Polo Pošip

Rizman Pošip

Senjković Sentiment Pošip

Testament Pošip

Zlatan Otok Makarska Pošip

VALUE

Ahearne Pošip

Grgić Vina Pošip

Korta Katarina Pošip

Saints Hills Posh →

Stina Majstor Barrique Pošip

Terre Madre Premium Pošip

Toreta Special Pošip

Vinarija Krajančič Pošip Sur Lie

RIGHT Barrel cellar at Saints Hills in Croatia

UNLIKE KORČULA'S MOST FAMOUS SON, Marco Polo, Pošip didn't travel too far from its island home. Planted on steep slopes that run from mountaintops to the sea, the vines grow on the Pelješac Peninsula and the Dalmatian Coast. It's nearly impossible for producers to use machinery or even farm animals to manage the vines clinging to precipitous hillsides, so the process takes place by human hand alone. Growers here tell us that the grape gets its name from the handheld, curved soil tiller called a *sip* that its bunches resemble.

Some of the most acclaimed Pošip wines come from Smokvisko–Carsko Polje on Korčula, where the grapes ripen early due to constant sunlight, retaining good acidity because of cool nightly northern breezes. The harvest often finishes by the last week of August or the first week of September, and that early ripening helps to prevent Pošip grapes from developing molds or mildews that occur later in the fall. Most winemakers harvest early in the morning or late at night to prevent the grapes from overheating in the strong sunlight. Most also prefer a slow, controlled fermentation in water-cooled stainless-steel tanks that also preserve flavors and acidity.

Roughly 9 or 10 months after harvest, Pošip wine is ready to drink, and most of it is consumed within the year. Producers here don't need to export their wines because they sell virtually all of it within the domestic market, with many Croatians drinking it at beach bars and seafront restaurants. Most winemakers prefer the fresh, younger style, but a few age their Pošip in barrels and rest it on its lees to create creamier, woody versions. Luckily for the rest of us, vintners are starting to share their delicious bottles with wine-loving consumers across the globe.

WINEMAKER WISDOM

"Pošip, our most-loved white variety, represents the character of Dalmatia. It is at first a very difficult variety, but if you learn how to please it, it gives you more than any other white grape from Dalmatia. No rules apply with it, and I love it!"

—*Ernest Tolj, owner, Saints Hills Winery*

RIESLING

(REEZ-ling)

IN THE GLASS

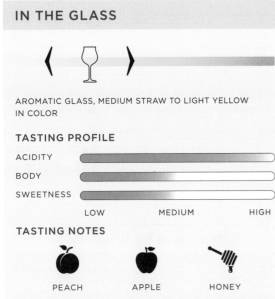

AROMATIC GLASS, MEDIUM STRAW TO LIGHT YELLOW IN COLOR

TASTING PROFILE

	LOW	MEDIUM	HIGH
ACIDITY			
BODY			
SWEETNESS			

TASTING NOTES

PEACH   APPLE   HONEY

Sweetness ranges from low to high. Dry Riesling has aromas of grapefruit, stone fruits, and rose petal with flavors of apple, peach, and lemon-lime. Sweet Riesling shares those notes and adds honeycomb or dried apricot on the nose, with flavors of canned peaches, apricot preserves, orange marmalade, and honey.

YOU SHOULD KNOW

Because it can be hard to figure out if a bottle is dry, sweet, or somewhere in between, some people avoid Riesling altogether, which is a shame. German Riesling comes in five different styles, always clearly labeled. You just have to know what the terms mean. Some producers now include a sweetness scale on the back label. Older Rieslings can have a scent of petrol, a hallmark of a high-quality bottle—not a flaw.

RIGHT Harvest at Schloss Johannisberg in Germany

FOOD PAIRINGS

PORK   SUSHI   CURRY

The classic dry pairing is Wiener schnitzel with potato and cucumber salad. Dry Riesling also tastes great with sushi or seafood crudo. Medium dry or medium sweet Riesling pairs excellently with curry and Thai dishes combining sweet, sour, and spicy elements. Sweet Riesling also pairs well with Thai dishes, and we love it with flan or crème brûlée. Sugar proportions of specific wines follow in our recommendations.

RECOMMENDED WINES: GERMANY

BARGAIN

August Kesseler Riesling (30 g/L)

Clean Slate Riesling (23 g/L)

Dr. Pauly Bergweiler Noble House Riesling (35 g/L)

George Albrecht Schneider Niersteiner Paterberg Riesling Kabinett (35 g/L)

Raimund Prüm Solitär Riesling Dry (6 g/L)

The Seeker Riesling (25 g/L)

VALUE

Dr. H. Thanisch Bernkasteler Badstube Riesling Kabinett (36 g/L)

Dr. Loosen Wehlener Sonnenuhr Riesling Kabinett

Schloss Johannisberg Riesling Grünlack Spätlese

SPECIAL OCCASION

S.A. Prüm Wehlener Sonnenuhr Riesling (9 g/L)

Schloss Johannisberg Silberlack Erstes Gewächs

SPLURGE

Fritz Haag Brauneberger Juffer Sonnenuhr Riesling Auslese

Weingut Wittmann Morstein Riesling Grosses Gewächs

RIESLING ISN'T THE MOST popular grape in the world, but it sure gets around. It grows in just about every winemaking country across the globe. As an offspring of the prolific yet hardly known Gouais Blanc, it also has a lot of field relatives. The variety's half siblings include Aligoté, Blaufränkisch, Chardonnay, Colombard, and Furmint.

We'll start of course with Germany, where it most likely originated. The first written mention of the variety dates to 1435, documenting the sale of Riesling vines to a German count, spelled as "Riesslingen." The modern spelling came along in 1552, when German physician and botanist Hieronymus Bock wrote about it, albeit in Latin, in his *Kreutterbuch* (plant book). In 1787, the archbishop of Trier commanded that growers rip out all "bad" grapevines in the Rhineland and replant with Riesling, thus creating a large area growing almost nothing but this one variety. By the 1850s, German Riesling's popularity had grown to the point that it sold for higher prices than wine from Champagne or Bordeaux. Today it ranks as Germany's most widely planted grape.

Riesling loves cold weather for several reasons. It has thick vines, making it less susceptible to cold temperatures. Its buds develop late in the season, so sudden spring frosts or storms don't harm its flowers or buds as much. It ripens late in the season as well, doing best on south-facing slopes that receive long hours of daylight. It grows in every one of Germany's 13 main wine regions. The best include Mosel, Rheingau, Pfalz, Nahe, and Rheinhessen. Wineries that meet strict standards can join the Verband Deutscher Prädikats (VDP), an organization of the country's best producers, but members must comply with standards stricter than governmental regulations.

The Mosel River, a tributary of the Rhine, has its own tributaries, including the Saar and Ruwer. Only about 75 miles northwest of the French border, these miles of waterways feature many hairpin twists and turns. Extremely steep hillsides host vineyards that rise from the riverbanks, the soils topped with blue slate, which adds strong minerality to the finished wines. The slate also reflects sunlight, offering additional heat to the vines. Among the finest in the world, Mosel Rieslings have light body, pale color, and refreshing acidity.

Pfalz, Germany second-largest wine region by vineyard

acreage, begins at the border with France near the town of Schweigen. It runs north for about 50 miles, ending just south of Rheinhessen. Plantings of Riesling in Pfalz grow on the broad plain between the Hardt Mountains and the Rhine River. Soil types include sandstone, slate, basalt, and limestone, which also lend minerality to wines with less acidity than versions from Mosel.

Almost 80 percent of Rheingau's more than 7,500 acres grow Riesling, a tradition stretching back to the Middle Ages. The 18th-century tradition of picking Riesling at different ripeness levels here eventually led to the formation of the VDP. Rheingau Riesling features spicy aromas and prominent acidity.

Between Rheingau to the north, Pfalz to the south, and Nahe to the west, Rheinhessen is Germany's largest region, known for many crops besides grapes. Easy-drinking Rheinhessen wines have medium body and approachable acidity.

East of Mosel and west of Rheinhessen, Nahe has been a center for wine since the 700s. Most of its vineyards stretch along the Nahe River, and the region's volcanic soils give the Riesling here strong minerality. Until recently, most white wines from here were blends labeled "Rhine Wine," but quality Nahe Riesling ranks among the finest in the country.

German Riesling classifications reflect ripeness and sugar levels at time of harvest and don't establish guidelines for residual sugar. They are as follows:

KABINETT: The lightest and driest style, produced with grapes picked early in the harvest, Kabinett usually tastes dry or off-dry but can run sweeter. The lower the alcohol, the sweeter the wine. Bottles with ABVs 10 percent or higher should taste dry.

SPÄTLESE: Meaning "late harvest," Spätlese wine comes from grapes allowed to ripen longer, allowing for a richer, sweeter liquid. It can range from dry to sweet.

AUSLESE: The word translates to "selection," meaning these wines come from grapes selected for advanced ripeness and sugar levels late in the season, sometimes with botrytis. Expect robust flavors, vivid acidity, and higher alcohol. A fruity style with high residual sugar, Auslese goes best with savory food rather than dessert.

BEERENAUSLESE: Meaning "berry selection," Beerenauslese (or BA) wine uses completely botrytized grapes and has a concentrated sweetness balanced by the fruit's high acidity. It always drinks sweet.

TROCKENBEERENAUSLESE: This "dry berry selection" wine, made in very small quantities, comes from hand-selected individual grapes completely raisinated from botrytis.

EISWEIN: Producers make this always sweet dessert "ice wine" from grapes with the same ripeness level as Beerenauslese but that have remained on the vine until frozen solid (often in January) before picking. Look for bottles from Austria, Canada, and New York as well.

From its home in central Europe, Riesling has travelled the world and grows wherever Germanic immigrants planted their vines. It thrives across the border in France, Luxembourg, Austria, and Switzerland, and French viticulturists included it in their grouping of otherwise French grapes called the "noble varieties," which, according to them, have the inherent potential to make the best wine. The other two white grapes they selected are Chardonnay and Sauvignon Blanc. Behind those two varieties, Riesling ranks as the world's third-most-popular single-varietal white wine. For other growing nations, the usual suspects include Australia, New Zealand, and America, but for a deeper dive go to bottles from Slovenia, Ukraine, Israel, Italy, India, Chile, and China.

Riesling likes to get around and also go under cover. It goes by Rheinriesling in Austria, Risling in Bulgaria, Raisin du Rhin in Alsace, Renski Rizling in Slovenia, and both Weisser Riesling and White Riesling in America, where it grows in significant amounts in New York, California, Washington, Michigan, and Oregon.

RIGHT Winemaking at Stadt Krems in Austria

WINEMAKER WISDOM

"It's easy to drink and invites you to linger. There's probably no other grape variety in the world where the second bottle tastes even better than the first! The farther south you plant it, the more opulent it becomes. Nevertheless, you have to be able to drink it against thirst, which you can't do with Rieslings from southern climates."

—*Max Himstedt and Simon Batarseh, oenologists, August Kesseler*

"No other white grape variety is more versatile in style, allowing for the production of light to full-bodied styles, very dry to very sweet wines, not to forget about ageability. A matured great Riesling is second to none. Austrian Rieslings as well as many examples from Alsace, Washington, and Australia also reflect the variety very well, more often in a fuller style than their German counterparts."

—*Dominik Meyer, head winemaker, Moselland eG, Clean Slate*

"I love the character of vines grown on slate. I also love the brightness and low alcohol of great Kabinett wines. Even after 50 years, they stay powerful in the glass. Spätleses are enormous in fruit and depth, and they are nicely concentrated, perfect for an aperitif. Riesling from Mosel shows a perfect combination of elegant mineral notes, refreshing acidity and fruit flavors—sharp as a knife or with a distinguished concentration of perfect ripened grapes. The new style of wild-fermented Riesling wines, long-aged on the lees, makes a great partner to the delicacies of modern cuisine."

—*Saskia Prüm, owner and winemaker, S. A. Prüm*

OTHER NOTABLE COUNTRIES

AUSTRALIA

Australia cultivated more Riesling than any other grape until the mid-1990s, when Chardonnay got the better of it. Made here in dry and sweet styles, Riesling grows in lots of Australian regions: Eden Valley, Barossa Valley, Clare Valley, Great Southern, Frankland River, King Valley, Great Western, Strathbogie Ranges, and Tasmania. Australian Riesling tends to have an unctuous mouthfeel with flavors of lemon-lime and peach backed by spice and floral notes. Versions from Clare and Eden valleys feature bright citrus flavors and clean acidity, while Tasmanian bottlings possess more florality and perfume. Producers also make it into "stickies," sweet dessert wines that taste of canned peaches, honeysuckle, and orange marmalade.

RECOMMENDED WINES: AUSTRALIA

BARGAIN
D'Arenberg The Dry Dam Riesling
Jim Barry Watervale Riesling
Robert Oatley Signature Series Riesling
Wakefield Estate Riesling

VALUE
Alkoomi Riesling
Kilikanoon Mort's Block Watervale Riesling
Mac Forbes RS10 Riesling
Ninth Island Riesling

SPECIAL OCCASION
Grosset Polish Hill Riesling
Henschke Julius Riesling
Penfolds Bin 51 Riesling
Pewsey Vale The Contours Museum Reserve Riesling

WINEMAKER WISDOM

"What's great about Riesling from Clare Valley is that you get two wines in one. They are imminently refreshing and drinkable in their youth, with lively and enjoyable flavors, and then they age so gracefully over the long term, developing into wines with layers of complexity and interest. In my cellar, I always have some for now and some for later. With young Rieslings, I always advise people to think about food that would benefit from a fresh squeeze of lemon or lime: oysters, prawns, any fresh seafood really, along with Thai food. Older Rieslings have more complexity; that fresh lemon-lime has evolved to delicious marmalade-on-toast characteristics, and the complexity of flavour will handle a more complex dish."

—*Mitchell Taylor, winemaker, Wakefield Wines (Taylors Wines in Australia)*

AUSTRIA

When it comes to white wine, the Eastern Realm may have a stronger reputation for Grüner Veltliner, but that doesn't stop wine lovers from raving about Austrian Riesling. The country has an ideal climate for the variety. Grapes grown on high terraces ripen to fullness under hot daytime sun, while cool nighttime breezes help the grapes retain acidity. Austrian Riesling almost always tastes dry, exhibiting fuller body and milder acidity than its German counterpart. The Wachau, Kamptal, Kremstal, and Traisental regions specialize in it, and Wachau uses two style designations: *federspiel*, a light, fresh wine, and *smaragd*, a richer, riper style. Don't confuse the latter style with the Riesling Smaragd grape variety, which comes from a cross between Riesling and Muscadelle. Expect flavors of peach, nectarine, orange blossom, and flint in Austrian Rieslings.

RECOMMENDED WINES: AUSTRIA

BARGAIN
Landhaus Mayer
Markus Huber Terrassen
Schlosskellerei Gobelsburg
Weingut Stadt Krems Riesling

VALUE
Brandl Ried Heiligenstein Reserve
Sepp Moser Ried Gebling Reserve
Steininger Ried Steinhaus Reserve
Zull Ried Innere Bergen

SPECIAL OCCASION
Bründlmayer Ried Heiligenstein Lyra Reisling
Domäne Wachau Ried Achleiten Smaragd
Jäger Ried Achleiten Smaragd
Prager Wachstum Bodenstein Riesling

SPLURGE
Emmerich Knoll Vinothekfüllung Smaragd
Nikolaihof Vinothek Riesling

WINEMAKER WISDOM

"As a child of Wachau, my love for Riesling was predetermined. It's the ability to age for decades that I love about this noble variety. If you taste aged Austrian Riesling, you enter another dimension of terroir expression. Austrian Rieslings have lower acidity and more body than Rieslings from Germany. Rieslings from Pfalz come closest in terms of ripeness to Rieslings from Austria. Alsatian Rieslings share their ripeness and fuller-bodied expression due to a warmer and drier climate, but the acidity and intensity are a little higher in Alsatian Rieslings than Rieslings from my country. New World Rieslings often have a perfumed expression of petrol and tropical fruits, and their residual sugar levels are higher as well. They are more distinctive in blind tastings than Old World Rieslings."

—*Fritz Miesbauer, winemaker, Weingut Stadt Krems*

ABOVE Riverfront vineyards at Prager Wachstum in Austria

FRANCE

Almost 1,000 producers make Riesling from 8,000 acres of Alsatian vineyards that border Germany on the Rhine River. Dry Alsatian Riesling features expressive minerality and vivid acidity with flavors of peach, green pear, lemon, and white flowers. If you want dry Riesling without risking a sweet bottle, Alsace is your best bet.

The 105-mile Alsace Wine Route winds through vineyards and villages straight from a fairytale. It divides into two sections: Bas-Rhin in the north and Haut-Rhin in the south. The names refer to altitude rather than compass direction, so the elevated Haut-Rhin hosts the majority of Alsace's Grand Cru vineyards. For much of its history, Alsace belonged to Germany, which explains why so many winemaking families have Germanic names.

WINEMAKER WISDOM

"Producing dry Riesling requires a combination of factors not often present in many places around the world. Riesling takes time to ripen, so if planted in a climate too hot, it often is harvested before physiological ripeness and will develop unpleasant petrol aromas. Leaving the grapes longer on the vines means too much richness (alcohol or unbalanced residual sugar). If planted in a place too cold, the acidity can be too high for a dry wine. Riesling also doesn't like excess water, so continental climates usually are suited better, as is soil with great drainage or slopes. Alsace has it all!"

—Olivier Humbrecht, owner and general manager,
Zind-Humbrecht

RECOMMENDED WINES: FRANCE

BARGAIN
Gustave Lorentz Riesling Reserve
Joseph Cattin Riesling

VALUE
Domaine Jean-Marc Bernard Riesling
Domaines Schlumberger Saering Riesling
Josmeyer Le Kottabe Riesling
Trimbach Reserve Riesling

SPECIAL OCCASION
Domaine Ostertag Muenchberg Riesling
Domaine Zind-Humbrecht Clos Hauserer Riesling
Hugel & Fils Grossi Laue Riesling
Josmeyer Hengst Riesling
Pierre Sparr Grand Cru Schoenenbourg Riesling
Trimbach Cuvée Frédéric Émile Riesling →

SPLURGE
Albert Boxler Sommerberg Riesling
Domaine Weinbach Cuvée Saint Catherine Riesling
Domaine Zind-Humbrecht Rangen de Thann Clos Saint Urbain Riesling
Hugel & Fils Riesling Schoelhammer

NEW ZEALAND

New Zealand Riesling amounts to just 3 percent of the country's plantings, but many winemakers love it. Styles run the gamut from bone dry to sticky sweet. Whatever the style, flavors of lemon, lime, apple, and spice shine. The best off-dry versions have bright acidity and crisp mineral notes that make it a perfect accompaniment for Pacific Rim cuisine. The North Island Hawke's Bay and Martinborough produce a fair share, while the cooler South Island regions of Marlborough, Central Otago, Nelson, and Waipara cultivate the majority of it.

SOUTH AFRICA

Produced in dry, off-dry, and sweet styles, Riesling in South Africa goes by Rhine Riesling and Weisser Riesling, both names a tip of the hat to Germany. (Don't confuse it with the Cape Riesling grape, used primarily in white blends, called Crouchen Blanc in its native France.) Riesling has decreased in popularity in the last 20 years, but it still grows throughout the country, doing especially well in cold-weather areas, such as the Elgin ward, where it balances fruit sweetness, minerality, and bold acidity. Fairview Riesling has tropical fruit and lemon-lime flavors with floral notes and touches of spice.

RECOMMENDED WINES: NEW ZEALAND

BARGAIN

Forrest Stonewall Riesling

Lawson's Dry Hills Riesling

Mount Edward Riesling

Spy Valley Riesling

TWR Te Whare Ra Riesling

Villa Maria Private Bin Dry Riesling

Zephyr Riesling

VALUE

Felton Road Bannockburn Riesling

Mount Beautiful Riesling

Pegasus Bay Riesling

Rippon Mature Vine Riesling

Two Paddocks Riesling

SPECIAL OCCASION

Dry River Craighall Vineyard Riesling

Mondillo Riesling

RECOMMENDED WINES: SOUTH AFRICA

BARGAIN

Lothian of Elgin Limited Release Riesling

Paul Cluver Clos Encounter Riesling

VALUE

Catherine Marshall Wines Riesling

Oak Valley Stone and Steel Riesling

Remhoogte Free To Be Weisser Riesling

Saurwein Chi Riesling

Thelema Mountain Vineyards Riesling

Vrede en Lust Early Mist Riesling

SPECIAL OCCASION

Paul Cluver Noble Late Harvest Weisser Riesling (sweet)

Spioenkop Riesling

USA

Riesling grows widely throughout America, with high concentrations in California, New York, and Washington and plantings in Oregon, Michigan, and Texas. When Prohibition ended, many states produced off-dry and sweet wines labeled "Riesling," though little to no Riesling likely made it into the bottles. Of total acres planted, the USA ranks second only to Germany.

California

German immigrants such as Charles Krug, Jacob and Frederick Beringer, and Jacob Gundlach originally planted the variety here, and it once reined as one of California's most popular wine grapes. That popularity waned as America's taste for sweet wines declined and consumers clamored for drier wines, such as Chardonnay and Pinot Grigio. Formally called White Riesling by the California Department of Food and Agriculture, Riesling grows on just shy of 4,000 acres in California, almost half of that in Monterey and the rest throughout the state. It comes in dry, off-dry, and sweet styles, but its high acidity here makes a nice foil for its fruit and floral flavors. As elsewhere, it does best in cool-weather regions. In recent years, it has regained some traction with American drinkers interested in dry, aromatic whites.

RECOMMENDED WINES: CALIFORNIA

BARGAIN

Firestone Vineyard Riesling

J. Lohr Estates Mist Riesling

Jekel Vineyards Riesling

Roku Riesling

San Antonio Winery Maddalena Riesling

Tobin James Cellars James Gang Reserve Riesling

VALUE

Bouchaine Bacchus Collection Riesling

Chateau Montelena Potter Valley Riesling

Fess Parker Dry Riesling

Pey-Marin Vineyards The Shell Mound Riesling

Smith Madrone Riesling

Stirm Wine Co. Wirz Vineyard Old Vine Riesling

V. Sattui Winery Early Harvest Dry Riesling

SPECIAL OCCASION

Cobb Vonarburg Vineyard Riesling

Lola Wines Dry Riesling

Navarro Vineyards Cluster Select Late Harvest Riesling (sweet)

Scribe Riesling

SPLURGE

Chateau St. Jean Late Harvest Riesling (sweet)

New York

In the 1950s, Ukrainian viticulturist Konstantin Frank first planted Riesling and other European varieties in upstate New York. Working with French native Charles Fournier, he proved that these varieties could thrive in the region's glacial soils. Years later, another immigrant, German-born Hermann Wiemer, founded a Riesling-focused nursery, vineyard, and winery that, alongside Frank's, remains one of the standard bearers of Finger Lakes Riesling. Just as New Zealand is known for its Sauvignon Blanc, New York's Finger Lakes region is becoming world famous for world-class Riesling. Some 130 wineries work their magic on lakefront vineyards. Of the 11 lakes, the highest concentration of vineyards lies near Cayuga, Seneca, Keuka, and Canandaigua lakes, which provide ideal climactic conditions for this German transplant. Around 10 percent of the state's Riesling also grows in the Hudson Valley and on Long Island.

WINEMAKER WISDOM

"Riesling is, next to Chardonnay, one of the greatest wines in the world. It's a late-ripening fruit that takes a lot of care and a special vineyard to become a great wine. That's what makes great Riesling so special. Our moderate climate on the East End of Long Island—the cooler Atlantic Ocean, great sun influence on the same latitude as Madrid or Naples (much farther south than Germany or Alsace!)—provides us with ripe but delicate fruit, lovely acidity, and moderate alcohol levels. The intensity of the fruit comes from low yields and well-exposed fruit. To give further depth and character to my wines, I like to leave them on the lees for a couple of months."

—Roman Roth, winemaker and partner,
Wölffer Estate Vineyard

RECOMMENDED WINES: NEW YORK

BARGAIN

Chateau LaFayette Reneau Semi-Dry Riesling
Fox Run Vineyards Dry Riesling
Hermann J. Wiemer Reserve Dry Riesling
Hosmer Estate Winery Semi-Dry Riesling
Lakewood Vineyards 3 Generations Riesling
Thirsty Owl Wine Company Dry Riesling
Wagner Caywood East Vineyard Dry Riesling

VALUE

Boundary Breaks Dry 230 Riesling
Dr. Konstantin Frank Margrit Dry Riesling →
Lamoreaux Landing Round Rock Riesling
Tierce Dry Riesling
Weis Vineyards Winzer Select A Riesling
Wölffer Estate The Grapes of Roth Dry Riesling

SPECIAL OCCASION

Red Newt Cellars The Knoll Riesling

LEFT Tractor between the vines at Wölffer Estate on Long Island, New York

Washington

With more than 5,000 acres planted, the Evergreen State is North America's largest producer of this variety. First cultivated here in 1967, Washington Riesling has become a favorite of winemakers and consumers alike. It thrives throughout Columbia Valley, including cool sites in Yakima Valley, warmer areas of Wahluke Slope, and high-altitude vineyards near the Cascade Mountains. That wide range of geography and temperatures leads to a diversity of styles, from bone dry to botrytized and everything between. Whichever style you like, Washington Riesling goes beautifully with the state's bounty of cold-water seafood and Pacific Rim cuisine.

WINEMAKER WISDOM

"Riesling shows a lively acidity, vibrant minerality, and stone fruit flavors and also offers great potential for aging. Rieslings from Nahe in Germany are similar to Columbia Valley Rieslings. Our wine has the same lively, vibrant mouthfeel, but the minerality and the intensity of the stone-fruit aromatics are more subdued in Washington."

—*Giles Nicault, director of winemaking and viticulture,*
Long Shadows Vintners

RECOMMENDED WINES: WASHINGTON

BARGAIN

Charles Smith Wines Kung Fu Girl Riesling

Chateau Ste. Michelle Dry Riesling

Côte Bonneville DuBrul Vineyard Riesling

Eroica Riesling

Poet's Leap Riesling

Pomum Cellars Riesling

Skyfall Vineyard Riesling

VALUE

Canvasback Royal Slope Riesling

Dunham Cellars Lewis Estate Vineyard Riesling

Efeste Evergreen Riesling

Palouse Winery Cloud Nine Riesling

Trailstone Riesling

SPECIAL OCCASION

Chateau Ste. Michelle & Dr. Loosen Eroica Gold Riesling

Figgins Riesling

RIGHT Riesling vineyard at Poet's Leap in Washington State

AROUND THE WORLD

Riesling grows in just about every winemaking country. Considered a cold-weather variety, it nevertheless thrives in small amounts in Israel and India, and it also grows in Italy's Langhe region. Elsewhere in Europe, you can find it in Bulgaria, Croatia, Moldova, Romania, and Slovenia. In the Southern Hemisphere, look for bottles from Argentina, Brazil, Chile, South Africa, Australia, and New Zealand.

RECOMMENDED WINES: AROUND THE WORLD

BARGAIN

A to Z Wineworks Riesling, USA: Oregon

Casas del Bosque Late Harvest Riesling, Chile

Sula Vineyards Riesling, India

Willamette Valley Vineyards Riesling, USA: Oregon

VALUE

G.D. Vajra Petracine Riesling, Italy

Golan Heights Winery Gilgal Riesling, Israel

Massolino Serralunga d'Alba Langhe Riesling, Italy

Penner-Ash Riesling, USA: Oregon

Reddy Vineyards Riesling, USA: Texas

ABOVE Riesling being bottled at Sula Vineyards in Nashik, India

RIGHT Sula vineyards and winery in Nashik, India

WINEMAKER WISDOM

"Rieslings from Oregon show floral aromas of honeysuckle and orange blossom with rich textured palates and clean acidity. When I think of European Rieslings, I think more of the petrol characteristics with layers of citrus. I love the range of character and expression a Riesling can take both in its young form and as the wine ages."

—*Kate Ayres, winemaker, Penner-Ash*

"An unmistakable grape, Riesling usually is associated with cooler or cold growing regions but is one of the varieties that show the diversity of the Texas High Plains. While it makes great wines when young, I particularly enjoy the characteristics that this variety develops with age."

—*Lood Kotze, executive winemaker and viticulturist, Reddy Vineyards & Winery*

"When I think of what I've tried in Austria, it's a bit different: more tension in the wine, a great minerality, with earthy aromas. It's all about subtlety, the slight sweetness and acidity of the wine playing together. A light-style Riesling—highly aromatic, with a low ABV—is perfect for the hot days that we can have here in India. You have this lemony flavour, with notes of grapefruit and honey. It's a really seductive wine."

—*Karan Vasani, chief winemaker, Sula Vineyards*

SAUVIGNON BLANC

(so-vin-YAHN BLAHNK)

IN THE GLASS

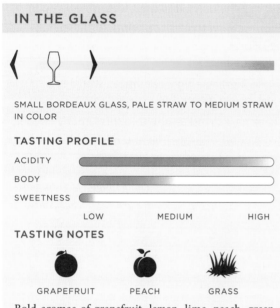

SMALL BORDEAUX GLASS, PALE STRAW TO MEDIUM STRAW IN COLOR

TASTING PROFILE

	LOW	MEDIUM	HIGH
ACIDITY			
BODY			
SWEETNESS			

TASTING NOTES

GRAPEFRUIT   PEACH   GRASS

Bold aromas of grapefruit, lemon, lime, peach, green apple, and melon join green herbs or cut grass. Those notes transition seamlessly to the same flavors with exotic fruit, such as gooseberry, lychee, and passion fruit, and even baking spices. Acidity and minerality run high, creating crisp, refreshing wines.

YOU SHOULD KNOW

Some Sauvignon Blancs have an aroma best described as cat pee, caused by pyrazines or thiols, both by-products of fermentation. Nodding to the grape's French origins and poking fun at wine snobs, we jokingly call this scent *pipi de chat*, which arises more often in cold-climate versions from New Zealand and France. It may not be to everyone's taste, but it's also not a flaw. If the scent doesn't put you off, you'll discover more and more pleasant fruit flavors in the wine.

FOOD PAIRINGS

SUSHI   CHEESE   SALAD

This crisp, bright, citrusy wine drinks well alongside many types of seafood, including shrimp, scallops, mussels, and sushi. It goes with tangy goat and sheep cheese, such as chèvre or feta. It also tastes terrific with tomato salads or green salads dressed with lemon vinaigrette.

RECOMMENDED WINES: FRANCE

BARGAIN
Domaine Cordaillat Tradition
Domaine Landrat-Guyollot La Rambarde
Francis Blanchet Kriotine
Paris Simoneau Domaine de la Rablais

VALUE
Domaine Delaporte Chavignol →
J. de Villebois Sancerre
Jean-Max Roger Le Petit Clos Blanc
Michel Redde et Fils La Moynerie
Saget La Perrière Sancerre

SPECIAL OCCASION
Château de Tracy 101 Ranges
Domaine Fouassier Mélodie
Henri Bourgeois Les Ruchons
Jonathan Didier Pabiot Prédilection

SPLURGE
Château Margaux Pavillon Blanc
Domaine Delaporte Les Monts Damnés
Domaine Vacheron Le Pavé

From *SAUVAGE AND BLANC*, the French words for "wild" and "white," Sauvignon Blanc grows in every wine-growing country in the world. "Sauvage" originally referred to the vine's unkempt appearance when untrained, but at this point it nods to the variety's wild success in the global marketplace.

Experts long surmised that it originated Bordeaux or the surrounding area and migrated to the Loire Valley, but historical documentation and DNA evidence both reverse that trajectory. French writer and thinker François Rabelais referred to it as Fiers, an old synonym, in *Gargantua and Pantagruel*, his 1534 satiric magnum opus. In the early 1700s, texts written in Margaux mention "the white wine in which the grape is for the most part Sauvignon." Before the advent of DNA testing, people often confused Sauvignon Blanc with Savagnin, an older, lesser-known variety that happens to be one of its parents—and a prolific one at that. Sauvignon Blanc's half siblings include Chenin Blanc, Grüner Veltliner, Petit Manseng, Silvaner, and Verdelho. In turn, Sauvignon Blanc gave rise to Cabernet Sauvignon, sharing parental duty with Cabernet Franc.

Sauvignon Blanc achieved truly international popularity after its success in New Zealand. A clear divide separates Old World and New World styles. The former style, from France in particular, specializes in restrained elegance. The latter style boasts a bolder, brasher side. Part of its popularity derives from the ABC movement (Anything But Chardonnay) of the last 15 years, as wine lovers moved away from heavily oaked whites to aromatic, fruit-forward varieties. The market already had plenty of Sauvignon Blanc on hand, capitalizing quickly on the migration in taste preferences.

RIGHT Harvested Sauvignon Blanc grapes at Saget La Perrière in Sancerre, France

You'll see lots of traditional, positive adjectives such as bright, crisp, elegant, and refreshing describing Sauvignon Blanc, but asparagus, canned peas, cat pee, and cut grass also feature in many tasting notes. The majority of Sauvignon Blanc ages in stainless steel, rather than oak, making it harder for winemakers to mask potentially unpleasant aromas. The compounds that translate in the glass as cat pee and cut grass come from the winemaking process itself, while canned peas and asparagus occur as the wine ages in the bottle. Some drinkers love these aromas, seeking brands exhibiting these characteristics, but others eschew the entire variety after just one glass. If you fall into the latter category, we suggest you give Sauvignon Blanc another try from producers more aligned with your taste.

In the Loire, the most famous appellations for Sauvignon Blanc include Sancerre and Pouilly-Fumé, but you can find fine versions from Quincy, Reuilly, Touraine, and Menetou-Salon. From on the area centering on Pouilly-sur-Loire, Pouilly-Fumé takes its name from the gray color that the ripe grapes develop when ready for harvest; *fumé* means "smoke" in French. Sancerre and Pouilly-Fumé have many characteristics in common—including bold acidity, strong minerality, and flavors of grapefruit, peach, and cut grass—but Sancerre drinks better when young, whereas Pouilly-Fumé ages well.

Sauvignon Blanc forms the foundation white Bordeaux (page 184). By law, winemakers here can blend it with Sémillon and Muscadelle, though many fresh, young versions now contain predominantly Sauvignon Blanc. Bordelaise Sauvignon Blanc may have a more perfumed nose than its counterparts from the Loire, with flavors of grapefruit, lemon, cut grass, and honeysuckle. Even Burgundy, the ancestral home of Chardonnay and Pinot Noir, features a small appellation, Saint-Bris, near Chablis, that produces luscious Sauvignon Blancs.

ABOVE Sauvignon Blanc harvest at Saget La Perrière in Sancerre

RIGHT Stainless steel tanks in open air cave at Saget La Perrière

WINEMAKER WISDOM

"Sauvignon Blanc is an invitation to enjoy discovering new aromatic expressions, new terroirs and climates. Its capacity to make the best of its growing location while maintaining a typical aromatic profile really brings something unique to the table. The best example is how it perfectly adapts to the various Loire Valley climates and terroirs, too! Exploring the multiple appellations along the river, you truly can taste the different expressions. Where I work, in Touraine, you can taste notes going from citrus to exotic fruits. In Sancerre and Pouilly-Fumé, you can taste a more flinty and complex expression of the variety on well-known terroirs."

—*Patrice Merceron, technical director,*
Domaine J. de Villebois

"Sauvignon Blanc can reveal different aromas, depending on vintage, soil, and winemaker's choice on when to begin harvest. When below maturity, we find herbal notes. When maturing, it can vary from fresh, with notes of citrus, to sunny, with notes of white-flesh fruit to exotic fruit notes. When above maturity, we have honeyed and candied notes. Plus, the terroir gives different mineralities and substance to the wines. Kimmeridgian marls bring a lot of fullness and sweetness with a salty finish. Limestones bring a lot of purity, minerality, wet chalk, and salinity. Flint brings a specific minerality, the taste of gunflint, spice, salinity, and persistence."

—*Sébastien and Romain Redde, winemakers,*
Michel Redde et Fils

"Sauvignon Blanc is known for giving wines with nice balance, combining richness and elegance. What is not as widely known is that it also has great potential for aging, especially when grown on flint soils and partly vinified in oak barrels."

—*Laurent Saget and Philippe Reculet, winemakers,*
Saget La Perrière

OTHER NOTABLE COUNTRIES

ITALY

Sauvignon Blanc grows throughout Italy, and plantings here have more than doubled in the last 50 years. Called just Sauvignon in Italy, the best-known examples hail from Friuli–Venezia Giulia and Trentino–Alto Adige. In Friuli–Venezia Giulia and the Veneto, the cooling effects of the Adriatic and Lake Garda preserve acidity and fresh flavors. In these areas, winemakers usually vinify it only in stainless steel, though some producers use a judicious amount of oak to produce a rounder, more elegant style. Trentino–Alto Adige Sauvignon Blanc benefits from the area's high elevation. Lower nighttime temperatures at high altitude have the same effect as nearby bodies of water would.

The warm climate of Marche leads to a riper style, while versions from Abruzzo have fuller body and distinct minerality and salinity. Small amounts grow in Tuscany, where winemakers may age the wines in oak to tame qualities induced by warmer weather. Sicilian producers recently introduced plantings of Sauvignon Blanc, and the best versions here come from high-altitude mountainside vineyards.

RECOMMENDED WINES: ITALY

BARGAIN
Cantina Puiatti Sauvignon Blanc →
Castelvecchio Sauvignon Blanc
Conti Formentini Caligo
Pighin Sauvignon Blanc

VALUE
Attems Cicinis Sauvignon Blanc
Bollini Sauvignon Blanc
Erste + Neue Puntay
Girlan Flora
Jermann Sauvignon Blanc
Schiopetto Sauvignon Blanc

SPECIAL OCCASION
Gump Hof Markus Prackwieser Praesulis
Pfitscher Mathias Sauvignon Blanc

WINEMAKER WISDOM

"Flavor profiles depend on whether the grape grows in a cool or warm climate and run the spectrum from citrus or orchard fruit to full-on tropical fruit. Cool-climate Sauvignon Blanc from France, Chile, and New Zealand will have high acidity along with green flavors of grass and green pepper, along with passion fruit and elderflower. Sauvignon Blanc from France includes a hint of minerality, smoke, or even gunflint. Sauvignon Blanc from Australia and California will have more superripe grapefruit, along with other bold tropical fruit flavors and grassiness."

—*Andrea Lonardi, COO, Cantina Puiatti*

RIGHT Sauvignon Blanc vineyard at Cantina Pulatti in Italy

NEW ZEALAND

Sauvignon Blanc singlehandedly brought global attention to New Zealand winemaking, and it reigns as the country's most planted variety. It accounts for a whopping 65 percent of all vineyard acreage. Growers first planted the variety in Auckland, on the North Island, in the early 1970s, and it made its way to Marlborough, on the South Island, shortly thereafter, taking the world by storm from there. The first vintage of viable quantity came in 1980, and since then it has become a global phenomenon. Today, 90 percent of the variety grows in Marlborough, with small amounts cultivated in Hawke's Bay, Nelson, and the rest of the nation. New Zealand Sauvignon Blanc has full-on flavors of passion fruit, mango, lemon-lime, and grapefruit joined by pungent notes of green pepper, cut grass, green herbs, and *pipi de chat*.

ABOVE Nobilo Sauvignon Blanc vineyard in New Zealand

WINEMAKER WISDOM

"If you pick up a glass of Marlborough Sauvignon, you know what it is. It has a lot of personality, too. It really doesn't need a huge amount of winemaker intervention. We nurture and support it, and it really is a pure expression of a vineyard site and all the factors that influence that terroir. Some Sauvignon Blancs also have a mineral quality. Think of it a bit like visiting a pebble or rocky beach after it's rained. French ones taste less fruity than the Marlborough style. However, they can be more textural and have an elegance about them. South African and Chilean Sauvignons generally have a softer acidity. The wines from these countries all have their own story to tell."

—*Natalie Christensen, chief winemaker, Yealands*

"It's a crowd-pleaser in that everyone will enjoy it and a 'wow wine' because many will smell and taste it and immediately comment 'Wow!' Acid balance and clear flavors with distinctive passion fruit notes separate Marlborough Sauvignon Blancs from other regions of the world. From some subregions, such as Dillons Point, you also will find hints of refreshing salinity at the finish. Due to the excellent acid balance, the finish is long, lingering, clean, and refreshing. This is what entices you to have another sip!"

—*Julie Ibbotson, director, Saint Clair Family Estate*

"Sixty years ago, no one could have predicted the worldwide attention, scale, and growth we have garnered over the last decade or so. All Sauvignon Blancs are beautiful in their own way. They all tell different origin stories. On a trip to Bordeaux a few years ago, I was inspired by their Sauvignon Blanc and Sémillon blends and how they're crafting such age-worthy wines, which led in part to the creation of our own iconic Marlborough Sauvignon Blanc fermented gracefully in classic French oak barriques."

—*Helen Morrison, winemaker, Villa Maria Winery*

"Sauvignon Blanc delivers appealingly high acidity seemingly no matter where it grows, but from there the wines can differ significantly. French Sauvignon Blanc can be mineral driven while also delivering subtle herbaceous notes. Notes of lemongrass, fresh green herbs, cut grass, or jalapeño connect Marlborough Sauvignon Blancs together. Napa and Sonoma Sauvignon Blancs are riper and richer, with more tree fruit characteristics than other regions."

—*Tony Vlcek, senior director of winemaking, Nobilo*

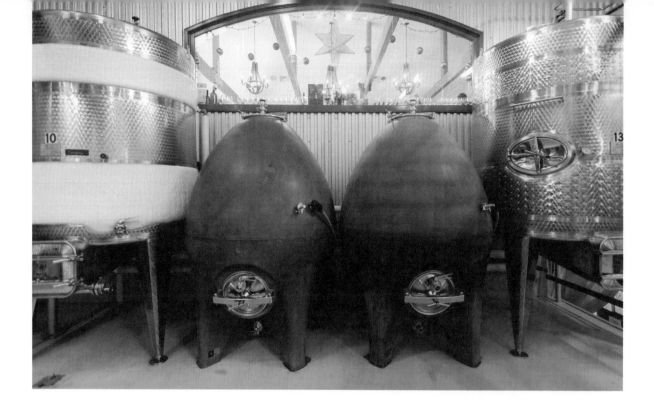

USA

Conventional wisdom holds that older wine lovers drink regions, while younger ones drink varieties. We owe that shift to the late Robert Mondavi. In the 1960s—when Americans drank generic blends of domestic wine called Hearty Burgundy and Mountain Chablis—Mondavi began bottling single-varietal wines at his Napa Valley winery, changing the way America drinks. Nodding to Pouilly-Fumé, he gave his Sauvignon Blanc the name Fumé Blanc. The name caught on, as did the variety, which has become the second-most-popular white grape in America (after Chardonnay). Sauvignon Blanc's popularity here certainly owes a debt to drinkers who prefer fresh, high-acid wines rather than the oaky, buttery whites made en masse 20 years ago.

Washington may have a more robust reputation for its Riesling, Chardonnay, and Pinot Gris, but don't overlook the state's crisp Sauvignon Blancs that taste perfect with Pacific Northwest seafood. The variety also does well in New York, where it thrives in the cool Finger Lakes and Long Island regions. Small amounts grow in the Lone Star State's Texas High Plains, Escondido Valley, and Texas Hill Country AVAs, as well as in Ohio near the Ohio River and Lake Erie.

RECOMMENDED WINES: USA

BARGAIN

Billsboro Winery Sauvignon Blanc, New York
Dr. Konstantin Frank Sauvignon Blanc, New York
Glenora Wine Cellars Sauvignon Blanc, New York
Leonard Oakes Estate Winery Sauvignon Blanc, New York
Ryan William Vineyard Sauvignon Blanc, New York

VALUE

Damiani Wine Cellars Sauvignon Blanc, New York
Gaslighter Sauvignon Blanc, Sonoma, California
Macari Vineyards Katherine's Field Sauvignon Blanc, New York
Palmer Sauvignon Blanc, New York
Paumanok Sauvignon Blanc, New York
Reddy Vineyards Petals and Clay Sauvignon Blanc, Texas
Sagemoor Without Rehearsal, Washington
Suhru Sauvignon Blanc, New York
Wölffer Estate Antonov Sauvignon Blanc, New York

ABOVE Steel tanks and concrete eggs at Macari Vineyards on Long Island

WINEMAKER WISDOM

"Cooler-climate areas drive a lot of the greener style of aromatics and flavors, such as gooseberry and lemongrass. At times, however, it can go too far and taste skunky like lager. Warmer-climate Sauvignon Blancs drive great tropical and citrus notes but lack acidity on the palate. California can maximize the best of both climates to produce a balanced and beautiful Sauvignon Blanc because of our diverse AVAs and viticulture practices."

—Steven DeCosta, winemaker, Line 39
(O'Neill Vintners & Distillers)

"We always have approached Sauvignon Blanc production to increase the layers of flavors, structure, and texture by harvesting the same block over a number of weeks. I learned this when working in New Zealand with Adrian Baker and Doug Wisor at Craggy Range. The first pick always would drive an electric acidity and a lean, green focus. As the days and picks went by, we would see green apple and firm mango. Toward the end of the picks, the entire flavor profile had changed to more rich and hedonistic contributions from pineapple to candied ginger. The density changed and grew, and the freshness took a backseat to ripe fruit. At the end of the fermentation, we put all these separate picks back together to make a far more complex, layered, and complete Sauvignon Blanc."

—Matt Dees, winemaker, Jonata

"Sauvignon Blanc opens the conversation at a party. It changes with the light in the vineyard, the interaction with oxygen, fermentation temperatures, and yeast, so a winemaker can choose to do different styles, and it's always fun. Sauvignon Blanc from Sancerre has tension, and it focuses not on thiols but more on palate flavors. 'Sauvies' from New Zealand have greener thiols, such as lemongrass and basil notes. Their natural acidity runs higher since the climate is cooler. Sonoma County Sauvignon Blanc vineyards receive the maritime influence, and temperatures are higher during the growing season, compared to other parts of the world. Depending on the producer's style, vineyard location, clones, and harvest times, the winemaker could pursue a style similar to Sancerre or a Fumé Blanc style, which is riper with almond and toast flavors coming from newer oak barrels."

—Marcia Torres Forno, winemaker, Matanzas Creek

"We take a slice of Brie and top it with a honeycomb from our estate beehives and a freshly picked rosemary flower. The tanginess of the young Brie compliments the freshness of the wine, while the crunchy sweet honeycomb accentuates the acidity of the wine. The rosemary flower makes the pairing look beautiful and highlights the herbaceousness of the fruit."

—Alex McGregor, director of winemaking, Saracina Vineyards

California

Sauvignon Blanc grows in every winemaking region of California. The highest concentrations center in Napa and Sonoma, and you can find significant plantings in San Joaquin, Lake, Monterey, Mendocino, San Luis Obispo, and Santa Barbara counties. Styles range from lean and racy to plump and fruity.

ABOVE Fermenting Sauvignon Blanc at Ryan William Vineyard in New York

WINEMAKER WISDOM

"Sauvignon Blanc can light up a glass and stir the imagination of the drinker with its outpouring of flavors and aromas. Sauvignon Blanc from the North Fork does a wonderful job of striking a delicate balance. Many of the hallmark aromas are present, but it never feels like they're competing for your attention: fruity without being bombastic, herbaceous without the austerity. With low alcohol and great acid, it's an easy wine to go back to, an absolute natural for warm Long Island summer days spent by the beach."

—Byron Elmendorf, winemaker, Macari Vineyards

"Sauvignon Blanc produces bright, crisp, aromatic, dry white wines on the High Plains of Texas with the regional fingerprint evident in the richness and balanced acidity. I enjoy different styles from all producing regions, however I am biased to South African examples, my biggest influence, where the brightness and pyrazine varietal character balanced with tropical fruit is often the leading characteristic in these cold-fermented wines."

—Lood Kotze, executive winemaker and viticulturist, Reddy Vineyards & Winery

"I love the way this variety demands attention from harvest to bottling. It's a thin-skinned grape that doesn't like much oxygen exposure. Our sites and style lend themselves to a more Bordeaux style of Sauvignon Blanc. We also influence that style by fermenting in mostly oak barrels and softening the blend with Sémillon, the difference being that white Bordeaux tends to be more citrus and floral, rarely grassy or herbal."

—Ali Mayfield, winemaker, Sagemoor

"The great thing about Sauvignon Blanc is that, no matter where it's produced, it retains its varietal characteristics and is clearly identifiable. It's instantly recognizable to our guests, whether novice or experienced."

—Ryan William, winemaking team, Ryan William Vineyard

AROUND THE WORLD

Called "Sauvy" in South Africa, Sauvignon Blanc benefits from the cooling effects of the Atlantic and Indian oceans and accounts for about 10 percent of all grapes grown in the country. You'll find it, content on valley floors and hillsides alike, in Bot River, Cape Agulhas, Cape Point, Constantia, Darling, Durbanville, Olifants River, Overberg, Plattenberg Bay, Robertson, Swartland, and Walker Bay. Its propensity for cooler climates means that it thrives at higher elevations, where plunging nighttime temperatures preserve freshness and acidity.

South African Sauvignon Blanc has a crisp, clean profile with bold citrus and tropical fruit flavors joined by notes of green bell pepper, cut grass, and asparagus.

Recently edging out Chardonnay, it's Chile's most widely grown white grape. It grows in the cool-weather regions of Limari, Casablanca, San Antonio, Biobío, and Itata. Chilean Sauvignon Blanc has a profile more of pear, Granny Smith apple, and tropical fruit than strong citrus overtones. Colder areas here sometimes impart grassiness in the glass but much less *pipi de gato*. In past years, much Chilean Sauvignon Blanc turned out to be a "field blend" of the variety and Sauvignon Vert, which lacks the same acidity and aromatic brightness.

Sauvignon Blanc grows in small amounts in almost every other wine country around the globe. In Argentina, Sauvignon Blanc often plays third wheel to Chardonnay and Torrontés, but growers in high-elevation regions in the north or in the frigid wilds of Patagonia are planting it in significant numbers. From 1999 to 2020, Austria's Sauvignon Blanc vineyards tripled in size, and they continue to increase in Steiermark, Burgenland, and Niederösterreich. Austrian Sauvignon Blanc made with malolactic fermentation and/or barrel maturation has excellent aging potential. Larger retailers have discovered Bulgarian Sauvignon Blanc, inexpensive and refreshing. In India, it grows in Nashik and Bangalore, and producers do quite well with it, despite the country's heat and humidity. Israeli producers grow it at the higher elevations of Upper Galilee in the north. Spanish regulations allow it in Rueda, either as a single-varietal wine or as a secondary blending variety with Verdejo.

RECOMMENDED WINES: AROUND THE WORLD

BARGAIN

Bodega Norton Barrel Select Britto Sauvignon Blanc, Argentina

Cederberg Sauvignon Blanc, South Africa

Lapostolle Grand Selection Sauvignon Blanc, Chile →

Marqués de Cáceres Sauvignon Blanc, Spain

Montes Classic Sauvignon Blanc, Chile

Las Mulas Sauvignon Blanc, Chile

Mulderbosch Sauvignon Blanc, South Africa

Recanati Sauvignon Blanc, Israel

Septima Sauvignon Blanc, Argentina

Sula Vineyards Sauvignon Blanc, India

Tokara Sauvignon Blanc, South Africa

VALUE

Luigi Bosca Sauvignon Blanc, Argentina

Saints Hills Frenchie, Croatia

Sattlerhof Sauvignon Blanc, Austria

Garzon Sauvignon Blanc, Garzon, Uruguay

ABOVE Sauvignon Blanc harvest at Sula Vineyards in India
LEFT Vineyards at Sattlerhoff in Austria

WINEMAKER WISDOM

"I really like its different expressions in every different terroir, and I love the uniqueness of its character, which always stays true to the grape variety. Upper Galilee is one of the finest growing regions in Israel. The soil and climate here express fresh, sharp, crispy fruit flavors of white peach, grapefruit, and lime, with hints of cut grass and tarragon."

—Kobi Arviv, chief winemaker, Recanati

"Sauvignon Blanc from Rueda typically delivers tropical flavors such as passion fruit and vegetables such as fig or tomato leaf. It achieves a structured mouthfeel and a minerality that the gravelly soils of the area give it. It definitely can appeal to fans of both Old and New World styles."

—Carmen Blanco Martín, technical agricultural engineer, Marqués de Cáceres

"Fine examples abound from around the globe, from edgy, nervous examples from the Loire Valley in France to aromatically explosive examples of sunshine in a glass from South Africa and New Zealand. The best have an instantly recognizable, unique signature. The variety is incredibly versatile and probably the most researched in terms of aromatic components and their expression and preservation. It's truly a winemaker's wine."

—Stuart Botha, winemaker, Tokara

"Sauvignon Blancs from Mendoza can be very diverse, depending on the specific area they come from. From cold and high-elevation areas, the flavors are more intense, on the fresh citric and grapefruit side. In the lowest areas, the expression has more white fruit, herbal, and floral characteristics. But the common factor in Mendoza Sauvignon Blanc is the roundness and sweet balance on the palate. Some of my favorites are from New Zealand, Chile, and of course the Loire region in France. I love all of them!"

—Pablo Cúneo, winemaking and vineyard director, Luigi Bosca

"The Loire Valley offers Sauvignon Blancs that are more mineral with good structure and freshness. New Zealand Sauvignon Blancs are easier to recognize by the herbal, floral, juicy citrus notes. Sauvignon Blanc from Friuli–Venezia Giulia offers a richer body and some herbaceous notes meshed with passion fruit. I like Sauvignon Blancs from cooler climates, such as the Andes or Coastal Range. It's important that the acidity remains as natural as possible, and, on the nose, I like to find a mix of citric, herbaceous, and slightly tropical aromas."

—Eduardo Jordan, chief winemaker, Sociedad Vinícola Miguel Torres Chile

WINEMAKER WISDOM

"It always carries the shade of herbs and grass around, in some more intense, in others just a hint. Most coastal areas, such as New Zealand and Leyda Valley in Chile, produce very herbaceous, sharp wine, more of an aperitif. Then you have Sancerre with its amazing minerality and Bordeaux, more fruity and rich and often blended with Sémillon. Napa Sauvis are more fruit driven, typically showing melon and nectarine with a richer palate, also sometimes fermented in oak barrels to create a Fumé style. South Africa has some interesting ones, notably in the Cape region, carrying a more grassy nose with a round palate. Mendoza in Argentina also offers an array of styles playing with high-altitude vineyards that have cooler conditions."

—Andrea Léon, winemaker, Viña Lapostolle

"Our Sauvignon Blancs fall between the two classic styles of New Zealand and Sancerre. New Zealand tastes extreme and intense, and with Sancerre you have more elegance and complexity but more subtle flavors. It invites you to drink a second glass from the moment you smell the first."

—Aurelio Montes Jr., chief winemaker, Montes

"I love that it's a white wine variety meant for aging if harvested at full ripeness on great terroir. Our style of Sauvignon Blanc in Steiermark is smoky and mineralic. By harvesting organic grapes at high ripeness, the wines can last in the bottle for decades. In our case, no green-and-grassy stuff! New Zealand focuses on primary green aromas, and Bordeaux usually plays rich yellow aromas with small oak barrels. The Sancerre style comes closer to Steiermark. Both can taste flinty and mineralic, though Steiermark offers a fresher texture and Sancerre feels silky on the palate."

—Alex Sattler, winemaker, Sattlerhoff

"One of my favorite styles of Sauvignon Blanc comes from Sancerre. The length of those wines, their subtlety, and the balanced aromatics make them superb wines—and really different in style than ours. Two different worlds, two different styles! Green apple, guava, and bell pepper flavors dominate our Sauvignon Blanc. It's quite close to a New Zealand Sauvignon Blanc in style, but our terroir gives it a personality that I don't find anywhere else. It's a super fresh, crisp, zingy wine with a great, approachable personality."

—Karan Vasani, chief winemaker, Sula Vineyards

SÉMILLON

(seh-mee-YOHN)

IN THE GLASS

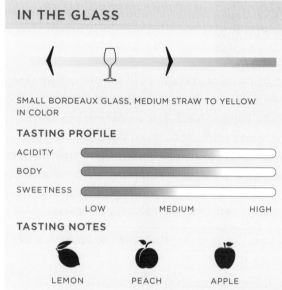

SMALL BORDEAUX GLASS, MEDIUM STRAW TO YELLOW IN COLOR

TASTING PROFILE

ACIDITY

BODY

SWEETNESS

LOW   MEDIUM   HIGH

TASTING NOTES

LEMON   PEACH   APPLE

Sweetness ranges from low to high. Dry Sémillon has aromas of lemon and grapefruit and maybe some light floral notes as well, with flavors of Granny Smith apple, Bartlett pear, and lemon. If oaked, expect soft vanilla and butter notes. Sweet versions smell of peach, apricot, and honey, with flavors of orchard fruit joined by bold acidity and a waxy texture.

FOOD PAIRINGS

PASTA   CHEESE   ICE CREAM

The strong acidity of dry Sémillon pairs with rich pasta dishes, including spaghetti carbonara and fettuccine Alfredo. Off-dry or sweet Sémillon tastes terrific with blue cheese, either solo or in dishes such as pizza with blue cheese and figs or pasta tossed with Roquefort or Gorgonzola. Drink sweet Sémillon with rum raisin, butter pecan, or vanilla ice cream.

RECOMMENDED WINES: AROUND THE WORLD

BARGAIN

Brokenwood Semillon, Australia
L'École No 41 Semillon, USA: Washington
Tyrrell's Wines Hunter Valley Semillon, Australia

VALUE

Amavi Cellars Sémillon, USA: Washington
Bodega Aleanna El Enemigo Semillón, Argentina
Chateau Suau Sauternes, France (sweet)
Wölffer Estate Sémillon, USA: New York

SPECIAL OCCASION

Boekenhoutskloof Semillon, South Africa →
The Sadie Family Die Ouwingerdreeks Kokerboom,
  South Africa
Yellowhawk Sparkling Sémillon, USA: Washington

SPLURGE

Château Climens Sauternes, France (sweet)
Château Rieussec Sauternes, France (sweet)
Château d'Yquem Sauternes, France (sweet)

YOU SHOULD KNOW

Relatively easy to cultivate, Sémillon reportedly used to be the most widely grown grape in the world. In the 1800s, Chile and South Africa grew tons of it. Even as recently as the 1960s, it ranked as the most planted variety in Bordeaux, where it served primarily as a blending grape in dry white Bordeaux and sweet Sauternes and Barsac. It's not always easy to find single-varietal bottlings of Sémillon, but your taste buds will thank you for making the effort. Various producers spell the variety's name with and without the accent.

IN A WINE-WORLD RICHES TO RAGS STORY, Sémillon has gone, in the span of about 150 years, from one of the most widely planted grapes in the world to growing in a few places mainly as a blending variety. From its birthplace in Sauternes, Bordeaux, it spread far and wide in the 1800s and found new homes around the globe.

Sémillon seems to have come into its name from a contraction of Saint-Émilion, one of Bordeaux's best-known communes. If you hunt around, you can find excellent bottles of single-varietal Sémillon from its birthplace, but at home it primarily functions as a blending grape. DNA testing shows a close genetic relationship between Sémillon and Sauvignon Blanc, though exactly how remains unclear. Dry Graves and Pessac-Léognan often contain 100 percent Sémillon, not immediately apparent because French labels privilege appellation names over varietal names. Its susceptibility to botrytis makes it the perfect grape for Sauternes and Barsac. Producers in the nearby Cérons, Sainte-Croix-du-Mont, and Loupiac appellations also make sweet single-varietal bottles and Sémillon-dominant blends. Because of its long history of use in a four-to-one ratio with Sauvignon Blanc for both dry and sweet wines here, it will surprise few wine enthusiasts that Sémillon remains the most widely planted white grape in Bordeaux and southwest France.

But it may surprise many wine lovers to learn that it once grew so prolifically in South Africa that its names in Afrikaans are *groendruif*, which means "green grape," and *wijndruif*, "wine grape." In the early 1800s, so much of it grew in South Africa that Sémillon Rose, a red mutation, spontaneously emerged. First noted in the 1820s, little of this pink-skinned Sémillon remains. Other vines have supplanted the main variety, but Sémillon still grows throughout Stellenbosch, Franschhoek, and Swartland, where producers bottle it solo and use it in blends.

Handpicked Semillon grapes at Amavi Cellars in Washington

Chilean winemakers often adhere to French varieties, and in the first half of the 1900s, they extensively planted Sémillon throughout the country, pushing it to prominence as the number one white variety by the 1950s. As global tastes changed, they replaced their Sémillon vineyards with Sauvignon Blanc and other increasingly popular varieties. That said, small amounts still grow in Chile, and several wineries produce stellar versions. Elsewhere in South America, you can find plantings in Argentina and Uruguay.

In the Southern Hemisphere, Semillon also found an adoptive home on the coasts of Australia, where, you will notice, the name doesn't take the accent. For many years, it went by the name of Hunter Valley Riesling, but producers now use the correct name, making it into dry wines with high acidity, low alcohol, and the ability to age well in the bottle. On the other side of the country, vintners in Margaret River took notice and began working with Sémillon, too, which adapted well to that region's cool climate. Between the two areas, in South Australia, it grows in Adelaide Hills and the Barossa and Clare valleys,

where winemakers often create a fuller-bodied, barrel-aged style. Sweet Australia Sémillons, like their French forebears, are highly prized.

In America, the variety name appears with or without the accent, depending on producer preference. Since the late 1800s, it has grown in California on its own and for blends. It appears to have arrived in Washington around 100 years later, with quite a few single-varietal examples hailing from Walla Walla and the Columbia Valley. It also grows in New York and Texas. Elsewhere in the world, you can find Sémillon in Hungary, Turkey, Italy, and Israel.

WINEMAKER WISDOM

"It's so delicate but complex, elegant but so rich. Due to our major diurnal temperature shift during the ripening season, we preserve a great amount of natural acidity, which keeps the wine so mouthwatering and balanced. Sémillon is so food-friendly, but my favorite pairing is with scallops."

—*Jean-François Pellet, director of winemaking, Amavi Cellars*

"Washington Sémillons are more concentrated, weightier wines, while those from France have excellent acidity and residual sugars. Acidity plays a secondary role in Australian Sémillons, which also are more structured. South African Sémillon more closely resembles our high-altitude Sémillons from Argentina. Sémillon has held an important place in the history of Argentine wine, a variety often planted alongside Malbec, in lesser quantities, on centenarian vineyards."

—*Alejandro Vigil, head winemaker and co-owner, El Enemigo*

"We provide a lot of extra care in the vineyard, ensuring the fruit homogeneously ripens, and we pick it quite late to ensure the maximum sun exposure on leaves and fruit. I ferment this wine on the skin. The result is a lot of extra structure, texture, depth, and weight. But I don't want to make an orange wine, so we avoid oxygen contact during the winemaking process. For example, I don't do any pump-overs or punch-downs during skin fermentation. Instead, I use the Pulsair system, where you shoot big nitrogen gas bubbles into the tank, and the bubbles, rising to the surface, break the skin cap, ensuring a good and healthy fermentation at a consistent temperature. We also ferment at 64°F to preserve the fruit. The result is a wine that will age for many years."

—*Roman Roth, winemaker and partner, Wölffer Estate Vineyard*

LEFT Egg-shaped fermenting tanks at Bodega Aleanna in Argentina

TORRONTÉS

(toh-rohn-TESS)

IN THE GLASS

AROMATIC GLASS, PALE STRAW TO MEDIUM STRAW IN COLOR

TASTING PROFILE

ACIDITY

BODY

SWEETNESS

LOW　　　　MEDIUM　　　　HIGH

TASTING NOTES

WHITE FLOWERS　　　APPLE　　　HERBS

Torrontés wines have heady floral aromas, including jasmine and honeysuckle. They also have aromas of green apple, lemon zest, and mandarin orange peel. On the palate come flavors of zesty citrus fruits, white peach, apricot, and fresh green herbs.

YOU SHOULD KNOW

Consume even the best Torrontés within two years of release. Its moderate acidity means it doesn't age as well as other whites.

FOOD PAIRINGS

CURRY　　　SALAD　　　CHEESE

Torrontés pairs well with spicy food, especially Szechuan chicken and Thai curries, and it also goes well with salads and grilled fish. Its moderate acidity aligns with soft cheeses, such as Brie and chèvre.

RECOMMENDED WINES: ARGENTINA

BARGAIN

Alta Vista Premium Torrontés

Bodega Norton Finca la Colonia Torrontés

Callia Torrontés

Catena Alamos Torrontés

Colomé Torrontés

Dominio del Plata Crios de Susana Balbo Torrontés

Familia Zuccardi Serie A Torrontés

Luigi Bosca Finca La Linda Torrontés

San Pedro de Yacochuya Torrontés

Susana Balbo Crios Torrontés →

Terrazas de los Andes Torrontés

Tilia Torrontés

Trivento Reserve Torrontés

VALUE

Bodega Monteviejo Lindaflor Petite Fleur Torrontés

Chakana Estate Selection Torrontés de Maceración Prolongada

Finca Quara Vina La Esperanza Single Vineyard Torrontés

Passionate Wine Ineditos Via Revolucionaria Torrontés Brutal

Santa Julia Plus Torrontés

SPECIAL OCCASION

François Lurton Torrontés

Matias Riccitelli Old Vines from Patagonia Torrontés

I N 1557, Spanish priests and conquistadores brought Muscat of Alexandria and Criolla (called Pais in Chile and Mission in California) to Argentina. They planted the vines in areas crisscrossed with irrigation canals built by the Huarpe people to catch snowmelt flowing from the Andes. Had the two peoples not collaborated in this way, many parts of Argentina would have no viticulture.

As confirmed by DNA testing, Argentina Torrontés isn't the same grape as grown in Spain's Ribeiro region, a common misconception. Misled by the name, many historians incorrectly assumed that the grape originated in the Spain's Rioja wine region, but the Torrontés Riojano subvariety takes its name from Argentina's La Rioja area, one of the best growing regions for the grape, along with Salta. Three different Torrontés varieties grow in Argentina: Torrontés Riojano, Torrontés Sanjuanino, and Torrontés Mendocino. Their genetic profiles, while not identical, have similarities. Experts consider each a

spontaneous field crossing between Mission and Muscat of Alexandria. Most winemakers and critics think Torrontés Riojano, the most prevalent, makes the best wines.

The vines thrive in Argentina's high-altitude growing regions, especially Cafayate at 1,700 meters (approximately 5,600 feet) above sea level. Torrontés also does well with the extremely dry climate and huge temperature swings between hot days and cold nights. Cafayate receives only about 8 inches of rainfall per year, so growers trellis the vines into 6-foot-high pergolas that shield the grapes from excessive sun, allowing them to develop the best expression of flavors.

The most widely grown white grape in Argentina, Torrontés has many ardent fans in America, Britain, and the rest of the world, as it should. The wines taste floral, slightly spicy, herbaceous, and fruity with moderate acidity. That profile makes for easy-drinking bottles available at reasonable prices.

ABOVE Susana Balbo vineyards in front of snowcapped Andes Mountains in Mendoza
LEFT Harvested Torrontés at Susana Balbo in Argentina

WINEMAKER WISDOM

"According to UC Davis, this variety is approximately 120 years old. This means it is relatively young, especially if we consider that Syrah is thousands of years old, as confirmed by the discovery of Syrah seeds in the pyramids in Egypt. What I like the most about the Torrontés grape is the versatility of styles that you can achieve: naturally sweet, young, fresh, and fruit-forward; a more complex Torrontés, fermented in 500-liter oak barrels; and a late-harvest version pleasant for dessert. It can become even more interesting and complex when grown in high-elevation terroirs. Calcareous soils let the variety develop a more citric, herbaceous, and wilder profile."

—Susana Balbo, founder and winemaker,
Susana Balbo

"Mendoza Torrontés has a well-defined aromatic profile, with a fruity character and intense aromas. In Argentina, beef empanadas and *humita* go great with it. You can compare it with Gewürztraminer or Moscatel, the main difference being the fruity character with medium acidity making it easy to drink. A great balance in the mouth makes our Torrontés extremely special."

—David Bonomi, chief winemaker, Bodega Norton

"The most interesting characteristic of Torrontés is the complex aromatic richness, which varies depending on the maturity at which it's harvested: at first citrus and acid notes, then floral profiles, and finally ripe fruits. It's a very versatile wine, ideal for fatty fish, such as sushi, although it also can be enjoyed as an aperitif."

—Gustavo Daroni and Eduardo Alvarez Griffouliere,
winemakers, Bodegas Callia

RIGHT Net-protected vineyard at Susana Balbo in Mendoza

TREBBIANO

(trehb-YAH-no)

IN THE GLASS

⟨ 🍷 ⟩

SMALL BORDEAUX GLASS, YELLOW TO GOLDEN IN COLOR

TASTING PROFILE

ACIDITY

BODY

SWEETNESS

LOW   MEDIUM   HIGH

TASTING NOTES

LEMON   GRAPEFRUIT   FLINT

Trebbiano has aromas of lemon rind, grapefruit pith, and salt. Flavors include citrus, white peach, Granny Smith apple, and fresh green herbs. It has a strong mineral backbone with nuances of river rock and seashells.

YOU SHOULD KNOW

Trebbiano encompasses a group of grapes indigenous to Italy, the most popular being Trebbiano d'Abruzzo and Trebbiano Toscano. Others include Trebbiano Giallo, Trebbiano di Lugana, Trebbiano Romagnolo, Trebbiano Spoletino, and Trebbiano Modenese, the last used mostly in Modena for high-quality balsamic vinegar production.

RIGHT Old Trebbiano vine at Zenato Winery in Italy

FOOD PAIRINGS

FISH   PASTA   CHEESE

Freshly caught, simply prepared seafood—grilled fish or mussels and clams sautéed with garlic and white wine—makes a great match. Pastas with a simple pesto or a light tomato seafood sauce also go well with Trebbiano.

RECOMMENDED WINES: ITALY

BARGAIN

La Chiamata Trebbiano

Cirelli Trebbiano

Contesa Trebbiano

Masciarelli Trebbiano

Umani Ronchi Montipagano Trebbiano

Umani Ronchi Trebbiano

Valle Reale Trebbiano

VALUE

Amorotti Trebbiano

Ciavolich Fosso Cancelli Trebbiano

Faraone Le Vigne di Faraone Trebbiano

Lugana Riserva Sergio Zenato

Masciarelli Marina Cvetic Riserva Trebbiano

Natale Verga Il Poggio dei Vigneti Trebbiano

Valle Reale Trebbiano

SPECIAL OCCASION

Azienda Vitivinicola Tiberio Fonte Canale Trebbiano

Emidio Pepe Trebbiano

Valle Reale Vigna del Convento di Capestrano Trebbiano

SPLURGE

Azienda Agricola Valentini Trebbiano

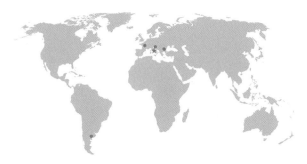

IN *NATURAL HISTORY*, published in 77 CE, Pliny the Elder referred to a grape called *trebulanum*, which historians believe took its name from Trebula, the Roman town around which it grew (now called Treglia in Campania, southern Italy). Ampelographers have identified numerous grape varieties as Trebbiano, but we'll concentrate on the two most widely available in wine shops: Trebbiano d'Abruzzo and Trebbiano Toscano, related but genetically distinct. The first subvariety grows unsurprisingly in Abruzzo, in central Italy, and the latter, also called Ugni Blanc, grows widely around the world. Trebbiano d'Abruzzo may bear some relation to Bombino Bianco, which also grows in Abruzzo, and quite a few Italian winemakers use the two names interchangeably.

Italian wine law requires Trebbiano d'Abruzzo to contain a minimum of 85 percent Trebbiano d'Abruzzo (or Bombino Bianco) or Trebbiano Toscano. The DOC also allows a few other blending varieties, including Malvasia and Passerina, but many of the wines available in export markets give just the predominant grape.

Italian wine regulations allow Trebbiano Toscano in more than a quarter of Italy's DOCs. At one time, Italian producers commonly used it in bolder red wines to lighten them and give them more florality in the bouquet. When grown in other countries, the variety more often goes by Ugni Blanc, which many spirit lovers know as the base wine for Cognac and Armagnac in France. Other countries, including Croatia, Bulgaria, and Argentina, also grow it for still white wine.

Abruzzo, flanked by the Apennine Mountains in the west and the Adriatic Sea to the east, has a cuisine con-

sisting of pork, beef, pasta, and seafood, distinct from other Italian regions. If you visit, make time for a meal in one of the ancient *trabocchi* along the Costa dei Trabocchi between Ortona and Vasto. Many locals compare the trabocchi, most built more than 100 years ago, to giant spiders sitting on the surface of the sea. These wooden, overwater fishing shacks have long "legs" extending outward in four directions, from which fishermen hung and cast their nets. No longer used for fishing, they have become restaurants serving freshly caught seafood. When you sit down, you won't receive a menu, but expect to stay for four hours, having eaten no fewer than seven courses—a culinary experience not to be missed.

WINEMAKER WISDOM

"Trebbiano di Lugana, formerly known as Turbiana, has ancient origins. Distinguishing the various clones of Trebbiano, present in various parts of Italy, isn't easy. Trebbiano di Lugana has its own characteristics that make it a unique grape variety, thanks to the clay soil and mild climate influenced by Lake Garda. Sensing its great potential, we invested in it in the early 1960s. From still to sparkling, Lugana is a versatile wine, long-lived, suitable for refinement and aging. It represents the highest expression of the value we give, then as now, to the land, to the respect of nature's time, to the work in the vineyard and in the cellar. It's our first great love."

—*Alberto Zenato, co-owner, Zenato Winery*

Manual Trebbiano harvest at Zenato Winery

VERDEJO

(vehr-DAY-ho)

IN THE GLASS

⟨ 🍷 ⟩

SMALL BORDEAUX GLASS, MEDIUM STRAW TO LIGHT
YELLOW IN COLOR

TASTING PROFILE

ACIDITY

BODY

SWEETNESS

LOW   MEDIUM   HIGH

TASTING NOTES

CITRUS   GRASS   MELON

Expect beautiful citrus aromas of grapefruit, lemon
pith, and lime zest. Other aromas include cut grass and
ripe cantaloupe. Flavors include white peach and fennel
before a crisp, zesty finish.

YOU SHOULD KNOW

By smell, people often mistake Verdejo for Sauvignon
Blanc. They have similarities but are completely distinct grapes. Before the 1980s, producers in Rueda,
Spain, grew Verdejo to make Sherry-style wines, very
different than the fresh, citrus-driven bottles enjoyed
globally. These fortified wines, locally consumed, often
contained a blend of Verdejo and Palomino, and winemakers aged them in large wooden barrels with ample
airspace for oxidation to impart a nutty character popular at the time.

RIGHT Verdejo being bottled in Rueda, Spain

FOOD PAIRINGS

SALAD

AVOCADO

CHEESE

Young, crisp, acidic Verdejos pair well with strong vegetables, such as asparagus and tomatoes. They also go
with salads dressed with vinegar and play well other
hard-to-pair vegetables, including avocado and arti-
choke. For something different, try Verdejo with smoked
or cured salmon on a bagel with cream cheese or with
piquillo peppers stuffed with goat cheese.

RECOMMENDED WINES: SPAIN

BARGAIN

Bodegas José Pariente Verdejo

Bodegas Naia Verdejo

Bodegas Protos Verdejo

Bodegas Ramón Bilbao Monte Blanco Verdejo

Cantos Blancos Rueda

Marqués de Cáceres Verdejo

Monteabellon Verdejo

VALUE

Bodega Martinsancho Verdejo

Bodegas Ordóñez Nisia Las Suertes Old Vines Verdejo

La Capilla Verdejo

Familia Zuccardi Poligonos del Valle de Uco San Pablo Verdejo,
    Argentina

Marqués de Riscal Barón de Chirel Verdejo

Protos Verdejo Reserva

SPECIAL OCCASION

Bodega Belondrade y Lurton Verdejo

Ossian "Capitel" Blanco

Vina El Principal Kine Verdejo, Chile

THE NAME OF THIS VARIETY comes from *verde*, Spanish for "green," because the fruit on the vine has a vibrant green color that glistens in the sun. Historians believe that the vines came from North Africa to Spain in the early 1100s. In the late 1400s, vintners used Verdejo grapes to make Dorado ("golden"), a favorite wine of King Fernando II of Aragon and Queen Isabel of Castile.

Today, in a Spanish tapas bar, a glass of *vino blanco* generally contains Verdejo. If you ask for Rueda, it always will be Verdejo. For most Spanish bartenders, the Rueda region and Verdejo grape are almost interchangeable—no small coincidence because Verdejo wine put Rueda on the wine lovers' map. Until the 1970s, Rueda winemakers grew Palomino and Verdejo to make fortified wines. In that transitional decade, Marqués de Riscal planted Verdejo expansively, and Rueda received DO status in 1980.

Verdejo vines in Rueda grow at high altitudes, in strong sun, and with cooling nighttime breezes, giving the wines strong acidity. Rueda wines must contain at least 85 percent Verdejo, but many of the better producers use it exclusively. Other authorized grapes include Palomino Fino (as of the 1930s), Macabeo/Viura (1950s), Sauvignon Blanc (1970s), Chardonnay (2019), and Viognier (2019). In 2022, Spanish wine regulations created Gran Vino de Rueda, an exciting new category that focuses on fine wine production. Designed for aging and fine dining, these wines must come from vines more than 30 years old, and producers must limit grape production to 6,500 kilograms per hectare. In addition, Gran Vino de Rueda must age for at least a year prior to release.

About a two-hour drive from Madrid, Rueda stands surrounded by Valladolid, Segovia, Ávila, and Salamanca. If you visit, stay in Valladolid, which lies near five amazing wine regions: Rueda, Ribera del Duero, Toro, Tierra de León, and Cigales. Sample wines from each of them paired with the imaginative tapas of Valladolid. If you can, visit during the Concurso de Tapas, Valladolid's famous tapas competition.

Verdejo also grows in other Spanish regions, especially Castile and León, and in small quantities in Chile and Argentina.

WINEMAKER WISDOM

"You can find fruit-driven wines but also intense and medium- to full-bodied wines balanced by fine acidity and interesting cellaring potential. The best examples display ripe notes of stone fruits and herbal hints. In oak-fermented Verdejos, you'll find creamy and toasty flavors with interesting texture."

—Laura Sanz, winemaker, Bodegas Naia

VERDICCHIO

(vehr-DEE-kee-o)

IN THE GLASS

SMALL BORDEAUX GLASS, PALE STRAW TO MEDIUM STRAW IN COLOR

TASTING PROFILE

	LOW	MEDIUM	HIGH
ACIDITY			
BODY			
SWEETNESS			

TASTING NOTES

LEMON   APPLE   ALMONDS

Verdicchio wines have aromas of citrus blossom, lemon zest, and green apple. Citrus fruit flavors include pink grapefruit and lemon-lime. Sometimes you can taste a little bitter almond in the otherwise zesty finish.

YOU SHOULD KNOW

Italian wine law allows Verdicchio in more than a dozen DOCs but usually only in small amounts. Verdicchio dei Castelli di Jesi and Verdicchio di Matelica, both in Marche, require a minimum of 85 percent Verdicchio, and many producers use 100 percent.

FOOD PAIRINGS

SALAD   OYSTERS   LOBSTER

Verdicchio pairs well with acidic foods, such as salads with lemon vinaigrette dressing; fried shrimp or calamari with lemon juice; and raw clams and oysters on the half shell. They also taste great with lobster, sushi, and sashimi.

RECOMMENDED WINES: ITALY

BARGAIN

Allegrini Oasi Mantellina Lugan

Andrea Felici Verdicchio dei Castelli di Jesi Classico Superiore

Bisci Verdicchio di Matelica

Garofoli Serra Del Conte Verdicchio dei Castelli di Jesi Classico

Lucchetti Verdicchio dei Castelli di Jesi Classico

Pievalta Verdicchio dei Castelli di Jesi

Sartarelli Verdicchio dei Castelli di Jesi Classico

Umani Ronchi Verdicchio dei Castelli di Jesi Classico

VALUE

Montonale Orestilla Lugana

Otella Le Creete Lugana

Sartarelli Balciana Verdicchio dei Castelli di Jesi Classico Superiore

Umani Ronchi Plenio, Castelli di Jesi

Umani Ronchi Verdicchio Vecchie Vigne dei Castelli di Jesi Classico →

SPECIAL OCCASION

Bisci Senex Verdicchio di Matelica

La Staffa Selva di Sotto Verdicchio dei Castelli di Jesi Classico Riserva

Villa Bucci Verdicchio dei Castelli di Jesi Classico Riserva

MOST EXPERTS CONSIDER Verdicchio indigenous to Marche, and most agree that the name ultimately derives from *viridis*, Latin for "green," likely because of the wine's greenish hue. Historical documents record Verdicchio's presence in this part of Italy since the 1300s, and many of today's best wines come from Verdicchio dei Castelli di Jesi and Verdicchio di Matelica in the Ancona and Macerata provinces.

One of Italy's best white wine grapes, Verdicchio grows widely and makes delicious wines, but it has a reputation for being temperamental. From year to year, vines produce varying yields of varying quality. As such, viticulturists play an important role in limiting the vineyard yields to produce full-flavor grapes with proper acidity. Winemakers then adjust their techniques, taking harvest conditions into consideration, to make the best possible wines.

Verdicchio wines tend to have high acid levels, which makes them an excellent aperitif while relaxing and enjoying *far niente*, the Italian concept of "doing nothing." Drink entry-level Verdicchios within two years of bottling, but note that high acidity means that well-made wines from excellent producers age well. Five-year-old Verdicchios aren't uncommon in Italy, and some people cellar them for up to 10. Over time, the youthful wine's lemon-lime and bitter almond flavors transform to lemon curd and marzipan, making it great on its own or paired with more substantial foods.

WINEMAKER WISDOM

"Verdicchio is an incredibly versatile grape, from which you can produce excellent *méthode champenoise* sparkling wines, serious white wines with surprising aging capacity, and pleasant, easy-to-drink whites. The aging capacity is the dimension I like most. It's a very 'Mediterranean' variety in the sense that it's normally not very aromatic, but it's incredibly charming on the palate, combining acidity and freshness with incredible strength and personality."

—Michele Bernetti, owner and CEO,
Azienda Vinicola Umani Ronchi

"The greatest difference between Matelica and Jesi is the terroir: Jesi is very rich in clay and fossil deposits, while Matelica is richer in minerals. In the spring, following the harvest, Verdicchio can be enjoyed as an aromatic young wine. When the wine matures for a longer period in the cellar, it is bottled only at the end of summer and at this point achieves good balance, thanks to the extra maturation in steel tanks or sometimes even in large wooden casks."

—Andrea Lonardi, operations director, Fazi Battaglia

VERMENTINO

(vehr-mehn-TEE-no)

IN THE GLASS

SMALL BORDEAUX GLASS, MEDIUM STRAW IN COLOR

TASTING PROFILE

	LOW	MEDIUM	HIGH
ACIDITY			
BODY			
SWEETNESS			

TASTING NOTES

CITRUS   APPLE   ALMONDS

This light, crisp, refreshing wine has aromas of white flowers, Granny Smith apple, and citrus peel. Zesty on the palate, it features flavors of grapefruit, lemon-lime, and a touch of almond in the clean finish.

YOU SHOULD KNOW

Winemakers in the South of France call it Rolle, generally blending it with other white varieties to make an easy drinking *vin blanc*, but some use it to make interesting rosé wines. In Italy, most producers make it as a single-varietal wine, but some also blend it with other grapes to make sweet, late-harvest wines and Vin Santo. When young, some Vermentino wines have a slight effervescence.

FOOD PAIRINGS

FISH   CRAB   CURRY

Extremely versatile, Vermentino pairs nicely with seafood and fish, but pour a glass the next time you have a bagel with cream cheese and smoked salmon. It works well with Italian stuffed clams and Maryland crab cakes, and the crisp acidity cuts deliciously through the spice of green curries and hot chile peppers.

RECOMMENDED WINES: ITALY

BARGAIN
Aia Vecchia Vermentino
Argiolas Costamolino Vermentino
Bibi Graetz Casamatta Vermentino
Campo al Mare Vermentino
Mazzei Tenuta Belguardo Vermentino
Poggio al Tesoro Solosole Vermentino
Sella & Mosca La Cala Vermentino

VALUE
Antonella Corda Vermentino
Capichera Vign'angena Vermentino
Château Miraval Côtes de Provence Blanc, France
Clos Canarelli Corse Figari Blanc, France
Marchesi Antinori Tenuta Guado al Tasso
    Vermentino
Sella & Mosca Monteoro Vermentino →
Surrau Branu Vermentino

SPECIAL OCCASION
Podere Grattamacco Vermentino
Massa Vecchia Ariento Maremma
Domaine Giudicelli Patrimonio Blanc, France

Vermentino also has become popular in the American market thirsty for crisp, clean, zesty white wines available at reasonable prices. A few vineyards in California, Texas, Virginia, and North Carolina now produce it. It also grows in small amounts in Australia and Lebanon.

S OME SARDINIAN WINEMAKERS emphatically believe that Vermentino came to their island from Spain in the 1300s, but recent evidence disproves this claim. Most wine writers agree that the name likely comes from the Italian *fermentino*, a conjugation of the verb meaning "to ferment."

The variety grows on Corsica, Sardinia, and in other parts of Italy, such as Liguria, Piedmont, and Cinque Terre. Many winemakers in Bolgheri, Tuscany, make excellent examples. The grape likes the long, sunny, warm days of the Tuscan climate. Many Bolgheri producers also use skin contact and barrel aging to create voluptuous, fuller-bodied wines.

Vermentino di Sardegna received DOC status in 1988 and can include wines made from Vermentino grapes grown anywhere on the island. Here the vines enjoy hot summer days and mild, rainy winters. Grapes grow on rolling hillsides containing limestone and clay soils that add minerality to the finished wines. The clay in particular importantly helps the ground retain water from the winter rains. In 1996, Vermentino di Gallura earned DOCG status, Italy's highest classification and the only one on Sardinia. This region lies on the northeastern part of the island, where vines, exposed to cooling sea breezes, grow in deep granitic soils.

In the last 15 years, plantings in coastal Tuscany have more than sextupled, and Italians across the country drink it in trendy restaurants, wine bars, and sidewalk cafés alike. The Maremma Toscana DOC, which protects and promotes the region's wines, holds an annual Vermentino Grand Prix judged by Italian sommeliers and wine journalists. The contest showcases both the fresh and fruity style and the more recent trend toward complex, aged versions.

WINEMAKER WISDOM

"Vermentino is the most important white grape in the region, and I love this wine as it reflects the radiance of the Vermentino grape and embodies the colors, fragrances, and flavors of these lands that lie so close to the sea."

—*Marilisa Allegrini, winemaker, Poggio al Tesoro*

"Vermentino cultivated in Sardinia has a strong Mediterranean aromatic character, which traces back to the spiciness of herbs typical of our region, such as rosemary, helichrysum, and thyme, almost always accompanied by a captivating tropical fruit note. The Alghero area stands out as particularly suited for this variety. The predominantly calcareous soils, strong salty wind, and excellent exposure to the sun give our Vermentino its fresh aroma, taste, and great flavor. Meticulous care in the vineyard, low yields per hectare, and a rigorous manual harvest give the cellar the precious treasure of golden September grapes."

—*Giovanni Pinna, chief winemaker, Sella & Mosca*

NEXT PAGE Vermentino vineyard at Poggio al Tesoro in Italy

VIOGNIER

(vee-ohn-YAY)

IN THE GLASS

⟨ 🍷 ⟩

AROMATIC GLASS, MEDIUM STRAW TO LIGHT YELLOW IN COLOR

TASTING PROFILE

ACIDITY

BODY

SWEETNESS

LOW   MEDIUM   HIGH

TASTING NOTES

PEACH   MELON   FLOWERS

Viognier offers aromas of peach, apricot, honeydew, and apricot with pronounced floral notes. Flavors include tropical fruits, such as pineapple, mango, and passion fruit, and orchard fruits, such as peach and apple. It has strong minerality and soft spice notes as well. The combination of tropical fruit and floral flavors can give even the driest Viognier a sense of sweetness on the tongue.

YOU SHOULD KNOW

When describing Viognier, an entire perfume garden comes to mind: rose, geranium, petunia, honeysuckle, orange blossom, jasmine, chamomile, zinnia, and 'Stargazer' lily. These flowers imbue the nose more than the taste buds, but a moderate amount of florality translates to the palate as well.

FOOD PAIRINGS

CHEESE   CURRY   SAUSAGE

It tastes terrific alongside runny cheeses, especially baked Brie or Camembert with fruit toppings or cheese fondue with a touch of nutmeg. It pairs nicely with basil curry and Thai red curry, especially when made with coconut milk. Viognier complements Italian fennel sausage or any meat dish seasoned with fennel or aniseed.

RECOMMENDED WINES: FRANCE

BARGAIN

Jean-Luc Colombo Viognier La Violette

Maison Les Alexandrins Viognier

Paul Jaboulet Aîné Viognier

VALUE

Caves Yves Cuilleron Condrieu La Petite Côte

Domaine Georges Vernay Le Pied de Samson Viognier

Michel & Stephane Ogier Condrieu

Les Vins de Vienne Condrieu La Chambée

SPECIAL OCCASION

André Perret Condrieu Chery

Domain Jamet Condrieu Vernillon

François Villard Condrieu De Poncins

Jean-Michel Gerin Condrieu Les Eguets

M. Chapoutier Condrieu Invitare

SPLURGE

Château de Saint Cosme Condrieu

Château Grillet Condrieu La Carthery

E. Guigal Condrieu Luminescence

M. Chapoutier Condrieu Coteaux de Chery

IF ENJOYING A GLASS OF WINE is how you like to stop and smell the flowers, then the floral aromas and flavors of Viognier are for you. Some think that it has grown in the northern Rhône Valley since the Roman era, but the first written evidence of the grape's cultivation here dates from the late 1700s. One possible source for the grape's name points to the nearby city of Vienne, colonized by Julius Caesar in the 1st century BCE as Vienna (not the Austrian settlement, called Vindobona then). Another theory holds that the word derives from *via Gehennae*, Latin for "the way to Hell." It's not the easiest grape to cultivate, but that possible etymology overstates the difficulty of growing this finicky grape on the Rhône's steep slopes.

At the start of the 1970s, this aromatic variety almost had gone extinct. It suffers from many diseases, especially in wetter seasons, and offers low yields, making cultivation complex. Once growers in Condrieu rehabilitated their vineyards and increased production, Viognier's fame spread, prompting winemakers around the globe to experiment with it on their home turf. By the 1990s, it was growing just about everywhere that wine grapes grow.

The vineyards of Condrieu—meaning "corner of the stream"—line a 9-mile stretch of the Rhône River. In the northern Rhône Valley, Condrieu and Château-Grillet, an 8.6-acre single-vineyard appellation within Condrieu, are the world's only appellations that require their wines to contain 100 percent Viognier. Most vineyards here grow on granite hillsides facing south and southeast and climb up from the river. Flint, chalk, and mica soils add mineral notes to the ample-bodied wine made here. In the early 1980s, just a few acres of Viognier grew in the region. Condrieu now boasts about 400 acres. In addition to the popular dry style, Condrieu also produces a sweet style, Condrieu Sélection de Grains Nobles.

Elsewhere in the Rhône Valley, producers use Viognier mainly as a blending grape, and French regulations allow it in Côtes du Rhône, Côtes du Rhône-Villages, and Lirac wines. In Côte-Rôtie and some New World locations, it coferments with Syrah to add perfume to the nose and soften the deep color of that red wine. Growers also cultivate Viognier widely throughout southern France, with a concentration of plantings in Languedoc-Roussillon.

When handling this low-acid grape with a high sugar content, viticulturists must take care to keep alcohol levels low while focusing on freshness. Viognier does well in warm climates and on granite and limestone soils similar to those in the Rhône Valley, and planting it facing south or southeast maximizes ripeness. It has full body and good mouthfeel, which *bâtonnage* and malolactic fermentation can bolster. It usually ferments entirely in stainless steel, but some producers age it partially in oak for a short time, which adds body and spice notes to the mix. A judicious amount of oak best suits Viognier's delicate flavors. Producers usually make it in a dry style, though you can find off-dry, sweet, and even orange (long skin contact) versions. Its lower acidity doesn't stand up to long aging, however. Most Viognier tastes best within two to three years of release. Some well-made bottles, especially from Condrieu or higher-acid expressions from California's Central Coast, will hold for a decade or longer.

WINEMAKER WISDOM

"We have had some Viognier from the USA, Australia, and South Africa. Usually, they taste richer and have less acidity. We really love the complexity and balance that we can achieve between the opulence of the grape and the freshness of the terroir here in the Condrieu Appellation. My favorite food paring is white asparagus with a homemade mayonnaise mousseline."

—*Michael and Alexis Gerin, winemakers, Jean-Michel Gerin*

OTHER NOTABLE COUNTRIES

USA

In America, Viognier grows primarily in Virginia, California, and Washington, with smaller amounts in Oregon, Texas, New York, Georgia, North Carolina, Michigan, Missouri, Colorado, New Mexico, Arizona, Idaho, New Jersey, Maryland, and Pennsylvania. In the late 1980s, growers first planted it in California, and today it thrives there. The Central Coast, in particular Paso Robles, San Luis Obispo, and Santa Barbara, hosts large plantings vinified either solo or in a blend with Roussanne and Marsanne. It also grows in San Joaquin, Sonoma, and Yolo counties. The Rhône Rangers, American winemakers who promote white and red Rhône varieties, have attracted a lot of the attention lavished on Viognier and its hometown companions.

In 2011, the Virginia State Wine Board named Viognier the Old Dominion's signature grape. As in California, winemakers first planted it here in the 1980s, and today a wide range of wineries produce it. It does well in Virginia's hot, humid climate, where growers can harvest it early in the season, rather than leaving the fruit on the vine into the fall, causing imbalances in sugar and alcohol levels. In Washington, producers make it in a variety of styles, from austere, bone-dry versions made in stainless steel to creamy styles that have undergone malolactic fermentation.

WINEMAKER WISDOM

"Viognier is similar in weight to Chardonnay but much more aromatic. I love that it can be rich and spicy along with light floral and fruit aromas. Our region, Santa Maria Valley, has a huge ocean influence. We have foggy mornings and windy afternoons, so the grapes can ripen slowly. The California sunshine helps with exuberant flavors, while the fog and wind help retain acidity. Our sandy soils also impact the flavor of our Viognier. A savory element is pronounced, and I love the balance that it brings to this typically very perfumed wine."

—*Jill Russell, winemaker, Cambria Estate Winery*

RIGHT Vine nursery at Yalumba in Barossa Valley, Australia

AROUND THE WORLD

Elsewhere in North America, Viognier also grows in Mexico and Canada. In the Southern Hemisphere, it debuted in Australia's Eden Valley in 1980. It constitutes just 1 percent of the country's total plantings, but it still grows in 25 regions. Plantings in Argentina represent half of 1 percent of vineyards, concentrated mainly in Mendoza, but Argentine winemakers enjoy working with it. Very little of the variety grows in New Zealand, but restaurants here love to showcase it on wine lists alongside Riesling and Pinot Blanc. South Africa grows small amounts, and Viognier has become a cult favorite among winemakers and consumers alike. These riper New World versions have more pronounced notes of tropical fruit rather than orchard fruit. Even more modest amounts also grow in Spain, Portugal, Austria, Germany, Hungary, Italy, Israel, India, Greece, and Turkey.

RECOMMENDED WINES: AROUND THE WORLD

BARGAIN
Bisquertt Family Vineyards La Joya Gran Reserva Viognier, Chile
Galil Mountain Winery Viognier, Israel
Grover Zampa Vineyards Art Collection Viognier, India
Ktima Gerovassiliou Viognier, Greece
Millton Riverpoint Viognier, New Zealand
Sula Vineyards Dindori Reserve Viognier, India

VALUE
Yalumba Samuel's Collection Viognier, Australia

SPECIAL OCCASION
Clonakilla Viognier, Australia
Lismore Viognier Estate Reserve, South Africa

SPLURGE
Yarra Yering Carrodus Viognier, Australia

STYLES & BLENDS

BORDEAUX

(bor-DOH)

IN THE GLASS

SMALL BORDEAUX GLASS, MEDIUM STRAW TO LIGHT YELLOW IN COLOR

TASTING PROFILE

	LOW	MEDIUM	HIGH
ACIDITY			
BODY			
SWEETNESS			

TASTING NOTES

LEMON   GRAPEFRUIT   FLOWERS

Crisp, unoaked white Bordeaux has aromas of lemon, grapefruit, passion fruit, honeysuckle, and grass. Bold acidity emphasizes citrus flavors underpinned by light floral notes. More complex versions have an elegant citrus nose with notes of vanilla and spice. Flavors include lemon curd, green fig, baked apple, and chamomile tea, and the liquid offers a creamy, almost waxy texture.

YOU SHOULD KNOW

Long before the current demand for Cabernet Sauvignon, Bordeaux had an international reputation for its elegant white wines. Good white Bordeaux in the bargain range usually contains more Sauvignon Blanc. More complex and more expensive versions, mainly from Pessac-Léognan, generally have a higher proportion of Sémillon. Depending on producer preference and label, we spell the word *château* with and without the accent.

FOOD PAIRINGS

SUSHI   SALAD   VEAL

White Bordeaux pairs naturally with sushi and sashimi, nicely holding up to the saltiness of soy sauce and the heat of wasabi. Have a glass with your next salad of strong greens, such as arugula, kale, or spinach, particularly with a citrus dressing or goat cheese. Richly textured versions, especially from Pessac-Léognan, go excellently with veal: saltimbocca, veal Française, Wiener schnitzel, or a truffle-studded veal roast.

RECOMMENDED WINES: BORDEAUX

BARGAIN
Baron Philippe de Rothschild Mouton Cadet Blanc
Chateau Bonnet Blanc
Château Marjosse Blanc

VALUE
Château Rieussec R de Rieussec Bordeaux Blanc Sec →
Clarendelle Blanc
Denis Dubourdieu Clos Floridène Graves Blanc
Domaine de la Solitude Blanc

SPECIAL OCCASION
Château Climens Asphodèle Grand Vin Blanc Sec
Château Lynch-Bages Blanc de Lynch-Bages
Vignobles André Lurton Château La Louvière Blanc

SPLURGE
Aile d'Argent Blanc de Château Mouton Rothschild
Château Haut-Brion Blanc
Château Pape Clément Blanc
Pavillon Blanc du Château Margaux

RIEUSSEC

Grapes destined for Bordeaux Blanc
at Château Rieussec

For centuries, this region of southwest France has made high-quality white wine. In 1137, when Eleanor, Duchess of Aquitaine, married King Henry II of England, wine from Bordeaux travelled across the English Channel to supply the royal court. Once upon a time, more white grapes than red grew in Bordeaux, but today just 8 percent of the region's vineyards host white varieties. About 60 percent of that harvest becomes white Bordeaux, meaning that the grapes can come from anywhere within the Bordeaux appellation.

French wine law allows seven grapes in the blend, but winemakers largely stick to Sauvignon Blanc and Sémillon. For many years, Sémillon filled the blends in higher proportions than Sauvignon Blanc, but the latter variety has surged in popularity, so many winemakers have shifted the balance in its favor. Muscadelle normally accounts for no more than 10 percent. The other allowed varieties are Sauvignon Gris, Colombard, Ugni Blanc (Trebbiano), and Merlot Blanc. Each grape brings its own qualities to the mix. Sauvignon Blanc has high acidity and bold flavors of lemon, grapefruit, and lychee with notes of green herbs, honeysuckle, and cut grass. Sémillon has strong citrus flavors but also an orchard-fruit profile, adding Granny Smith apple, green pear, and peach to the blend. With lower acidity than Sauvignon Blanc, Sémillon has fuller body and more texture, which explains why many higher-quality white Bordeaux have a mouthfeel often described as waxy or oily. Muscadelle boosts the wine's spice and floral elements.

The Entre-Deux-Mers ("between two tides") appellation sits between the region's two major tidal rivers, the Garonne and Dordogne. Entre-Deux-Mers wines must contain a blend of the allowed grapes, no single-varietal wines allowed. Around 20 percent of dry white Bordeaux comes from here.

Graves, on the left (west) bank of the Garonne, stretches for about 30 miles southeast of Bordeaux. This AOC, which produces white, red, and sweet wine, takes its name from its primarily gravel soils, which add minerality to the wines. Only one Graves location, Château Haut-Brion, had a place in the famous Bordeaux classification of 1855. In 1953, Graves created a classification system for its red wine producers, and dry white wine producers joined the club in a 1959 update. Graves produces about 6 percent of the white wines made in Bordeaux.

Pessac-Léognan, a subregion of Graves, received recognition in 1987. Named for two communes near Bordeaux, praised for the best and most expensive wines within Graves, Pessac-Léognan produces complex wines with potential for long aging. Pessac-Léognan makes around 3 percent of white Bordeaux. Blaye Côtes de Bordeaux, a small region on the northern edge of the right (east) bank of the Gironde/Dordogne, makes roughly the same quantity.

White Bordeaux falls into two style categories. The first, generally made entirely in stainless steel, tastes light and fruity. These wines have citrus and tropical fruit flavors and bright acidity. Many bottles have screw caps and approachable price levels. The second genre, more complex, ages partially or completely in oak barrels and may have a higher percentage of Sémillon. Most of these more sophisticated wines come from Pessac-Léognan.

. . . .

WINEMAKER WISDOM

"I love the aromatic freshness of white Bordeaux, the finesse of its fruit and its tangy balance. I like the subtle elegance of its wood, the structuring and floral side of its Sémillon, as well as the mineral and exotic side of its Sauvignon Blanc."

—*Olivier Trégoat, technical director DBR (Lafite),*
Château Rieussec

. . . .

RIGHT Barrel cellar at Château Rieussec in Bordeaux

CAVA

(KAH-vah)

IN THE GLASS

FLUTE GLASS, PALE STRAW TO MEDIUM STRAW IN COLOR

TASTING PROFILE

	LOW	MEDIUM	HIGH
ACIDITY			
BODY			
SWEETNESS			

TASTING NOTES

APPLE   FLOWERS   ALMONDS

Young Cava has aromas and flavors of apple, apple blossom, and acacia flowers. Cava Reserva can have notes of fresh bread and anise seed, while Cava Gran Reserva will have more smoky notes, such as dried apricots, toasted walnuts, and toasted bread. All Cavas have persistent, fine bubbles that tickle the tongue and pleasant acidity on the palate.

YOU SHOULD KNOW

This Spanish sparkling wine comes from a designated region, using the traditional method and specific grapes, mainly Parellada, Macabeo, and Xarel·lo. All Cava sparkles, but not every Spanish sparkling wine is Cava. Given its flavor profile and complexity, Cava could command the retail prices of other, better known sparkling wines, but it remains an under-the-radar bargain.

RIGHT Ancient Macabeo vines at Pere Ventura in Spain

FOOD PAIRINGS

AVOCADO   EGGS   PORK

Young Cava de Guarda pairs nicely with raw seafood, including oysters, ceviche, poke bowl, and sushi. It also goes well with guacamole and chips. Cava Reserva, which has a little more intensity, matches well with tortilla española, crab cakes, or chicken tacos. Drink Cava Gran Reserva with more complex foods, such as jamón ibérico, paella, or smoked meats.

RECOMMENDED WINES: CAVA

BARGAIN

Anna de Codorníu Blanc de Blancs Cava

Los Dos Cava Brut

Freixenet Cordon Negro Brut Cava

Freixenet Carta Nevada Brut Cava

Marqués de Cáceres Brut Cava

Mas Fi Brut Cava

Mercat Brut Nature Cava

Mirame Brut Selección Cava

Pere Ventura Tresor Brut Reserva Cava

Segura Viudas Organic Brut Cava

VALUE

Lola Brut Cava by Paco and Lola

Segura Viudas Reserva Heredad

Vara Silverhead Brut Reserva

SPECIAL OCCASION

Agusti Torello Mata Kripta Gran Reserva Cava

Llopart Original 1887 Gran Reserva Brut Nature Cava

Pere Ventura Gran Vintage Cava

MANY SPANIARDS STILL REFER to Cava as Champaña or Champan, its name for the first century of its existence. In 1872, Josep Raventós i Fatjó brought the traditional method of making sparkling wine from Champagne to Catalonia, and his new wine quickly caught on with Catalan society. His son, Manuel Raventós i Domènech, receives credit for establishing, in 1888, the standard blend of three native varieties: Macabeo, Xarel·lo, and Parellada.

In the 1970s, Champagne producers won a court battle to the exclusive rights to the name "Champagne" and any derivation thereof, so Champaña became Cava. The Catalans chose "Cava" because their wines spend so much time aging in wine cellar caves, or *cava*. All Cava must age on the lees for at least nine months, with longer requirements for Reserva and Gran Reserva bottles.

Most Cava blends Macabeo, Xarel·lo, and Parellada, all white grapes. Xarel·lo adds body, Parellada adds fruit flavors, and Macabeo adds a floral bouquet to the wine. In 1986, Spanish regulations admitted Chardonnay, which winemakers like to use for its exotic fruit aromas. The DO also allows for Subirat Parent. Pinot Noir, Monastrell, Trepat, and Garnacha may join the party for Cava rosado.

Cava production centers on Sant Sadurni d'Anoia and surrounding areas, but Spanish law allows for Cava production in four DOs across the kingdom. Sant Sadurni

d'Anoia falls within the Comtats de Barcelona DO, which lies near Barcelona and accounts for more than 95 percent of Cava production. In 2020, the Cava regulatory board authorized subzones for more distinct wines. Comtats de Barcelona contains five subzones: Serra de Mar, Valls d'Anoia-Foix, Conca del Gaia, Serra de Prades, and Pla de Ponent. The Ebro Valley, in the north, covers areas influenced by the Ebro River. It divides into two subzones: Alto Ebro, near Logroño in Rioja, and Valle del Cierzo, farther south along the river. In Badajoz province, the Viñedos de Almendralejo DO lies close to the Portuguese border. It has a drier climate than the other two DOs, and its vines grow in higher-altitude vineyards. The fourth area, called the Levante Zone, meaning highlands, encompasses the town of Requena, about an hour's drive west of Valencia.

In 2020, some 200 producers made more than 200 million bottles of Cava; 70 percent of it sold to the export market—mostly America, Japan, and Switzerland—and Spaniards consumed the remaining 30 percent. Also in 2020, the Cava Regulatory Board added Cava de Guarda to the mix, emphasizing the "capacity of a wine with the appropriate characteristics for aging correctly." Cava de Guarda covers regular Cava. Cava de Guarda Superior includes Cava Reserva, Cava Gran Reserva, and Cava de Paraje Calificado. The first two designations refer to the time in the bottle, and the last denotes grapes grown in a qualified place.

Cava de Guarda must age for 9 months, Cava Reserva for 18 months, Cava Gran Reserva for 30 months, and Cavas de Paraje Calificado for 36 months. Cava Brut Nature must have fewer than 3 grams of sugar per liter. Extra Brut can have fewer than 6, and regular Brut may contain 12 grams maximum per liter. Extra Seco falls between 12 and 17 grams, Seco between 17 and 32, Semi Seco between 32 and 50, and Dulce tops the chart with more than 50 grams per liter.

A handful of producers has broken away from the Cava DO. They produce a sparkling wine called Corpinnat, and they have formed an association named AVEC, which translates to the Association of Corpinnat Winemakers and Winegrowers. They require 100 percent organic vineyards, manual harvesting, and their Reserva wines must age at least 18 months prior to release.

WINEMAKER WISDOM

"We work mainly with five different varieties. Macabeu and Xarel·lo provide golden and green apple flavours; Parellada conveys jasmine aromas; Chardonnay provides density and a peach flavour; and Pinot Noir, cherry. I particularly like opening a big meal with a young Cava and then pairing the food with a more aged one. Let's not forget the need to toast and celebrate with Cava at any special occasion."

—*Bruno Colomer, head winemaker, Codorníu*

ABOVE Undergound Cava cellar at Pere Ventura
LEFT Xarel-lo vineyard at Pere Ventura in Spain

CHAMPAGNE & CRÉMANTS

(sham-PAYN, kreh-MAHNTS)

IN THE GLASS

FLUTE GLASS, PALE STRAW TO MEDIUM STRAW IN COLOR

TASTING PROFILE

ACIDITY

BODY

SWEETNESS

LOW   MEDIUM   HIGH

TASTING NOTES

APPLE   BREAD   ALMONDS

Sweetness ranges from low to high. When poured, all French sparkling wines should have *perlage* (fine bubbles), and *mousse* (a layer of foam). The bubbles should tickle your nose before the bouquet becomes apparent. Aromas and flavors differ, but young nonvintage French sparkling wines usually smell and taste of apple, white flowers, and citrus, whereas aged versions normally have added notes of baked bread and toasted almonds or hazelnuts.

YOU SHOULD KNOW

All that sparkles isn't Champagne, which legally denotes sparkling wine made from specific grape varieties, using the méthode champenoise, in the Champagne region of France. Sparkling wines made with the traditional method in other parts of France fall under the banner of crémant ("creamy"), which describes their mouthfeel.

FOOD PAIRINGS

OYSTERS   POPCORN   CHICKEN

Young, nonvintage French sparkling wines stand alone as excellent aperitif wines. They also make an excellent match for raw oysters, sushi, crudo, ceviche, or vodka-cured salmon. For something (perhaps) unexpected, try them with truffled Parmesan popcorn. Older, vintage sparklers pair well with oven-baked chicken or fish in a cream sauce. Some sweeter sparkling wines complement such desserts as crème brûlée, flan, or sponge cake with macerated strawberries. There's really no wrong pairing!

RECOMMENDED WINES: CHAMPAGNE

SPECIAL OCCASION

Champagne André Jacquart Vertus Blanc de Blancs

Champagne Boizel Ultime Extra Brut NV

Champagne Delamotte Blanc de Blancs NV Champagne

Charles Heidsieck Brut Reserve

Gosset Grande Reserve Champagne

JCB No. 44 Champagne by Jean-Charles Boisset →

Leclerc Briant Reserve Brut NV Champagne

Pommery Royal Brut Champagne

Vollereaux Blanc de Blancs Champagne

SPLURGE

Alfred Gratien Cuvée Paradis Vintage Brut

Dom Pérignon Brut Champagne

Louis Roederer Cristal Vintage Champagne

Rare Millésime by Champagne Piper-Heidsieck

Taittinger Comtes de Champagne Blanc de Blancs

M OST CHAMPAGNE MAKERS AGREE that the production of the first sparkling wine occurred in the late 1600s in Champagne, when a blind Benedictine monk named Pierre Pérignon accidentally created the first effervescent wine. The story goes that he tasted a wine that had refermented in the bottle and called out to his fellow monks, "Come quickly! I am drinking the stars!" An impressive bronze statue in front of the Moët & Chandon cellars captures this magical moment. It makes a great story—that likely isn't true.

At that time, wine made or cellared in cold weather commonly refermented in the bottle when warmer summer temperatures reactivated dormant yeast. Most historians don't know whether Dom Pérignon was blind or was tasting "blind," but he accurately receives credit for advancing the technique to make white wine from red grapes. He maintained that the best wines came from darker-skinned varieties, which other winemakers had been trying to achieve for years. He also apparently spent much effort trying to prevent wines from refermenting in the bottle, the exact opposite process for making Champagne. Separating fantasy from fact, Dom Pérignon produced high-quality grapes, developed meticulous winemaking skills, and advocated a rational approach to blending.

Other important moments in Champagne production include the development, in the 1700s, of manufacturing processes to produce stronger glass bottles and the invention of "riddling" frames to allow bottles to age upside down. In 1837, French pharmacist Jean-Baptiste François invented a process to measure the optimal amount of sugar to add to the still wine to obtain the best bubbles. In 1844, the wire cage to hold the cork in place came along. Louis Pasteur began studying fermentation in 1857, and many of his discoveries remain in use by makers of still and sparkling wines.

Chardonnay grapes at Champagne Boizel

The Champagne AOC came into being in 1936 with a strictly defined geographical area. Champagne wines can come only from the Champagne AOC, east of Paris. Some 34,000 hectares of vineyards encompass 320 villages, with 42 ranked as Premier Cru and 17 designated Grand Cru. Roughly 15,000 growers tend 278,000 individual vineyard plots, each around 18 acres. Most of the vines grow at altitudes of 90 to 300 meters (300 to 1,000 feet) above sea level. The AOC allows seven grape varieties, the most common being Chardonnay (white, 30 percent), Pinot Meunier (red, 32 percent), and Pinot Noir (red, 38 percent). The other allowed varieties, all white grapes, consist of Arbane, Petit Meslier, Pinot Blanc, and Pinot Gris (called Fromenteau locally), but together they constitute less than 1 percent of the vines planted in the region. Even if pressed from red grapes, Champagne is still a white wine. For purists, Blanc de Blancs Champagne usually consists entirely of Chardonnay. Regulations even limit pruning techniques to a specific four: the Chablis system,

Cordon system, Guyot system, and Marne Valley system, the last used only for Pinot Meunier.

In Champagne, most producers hold true to their house "style." If you open a bottle of Champagne today and another bottle of the same brand in five years, they will taste the same. To achieve their styles, Champagne winemakers keep multiple vintages of base wine to blend together. Champagne containing multiple vintages of base wine bears the designation "NV" (nonvintage). When a bottle of Champagne has a year on the label, all the grapes in the base wine came from that year's harvest.

All sparkling wines undergo two fermentations, the first to create the base wine and the second to create the bubbles. With Champagne, secondary fermentation must occur in the bottle. They cannot make use of other techniques, including the Charmat-Martinotti method used in Prosecco. The traditional method, known as the méthode champenoise, involves quite a few steps. Producers press the grapes, allowing alcoholic and malolactic fermentation to occur. The still wines go into bottles (if vintage Champagne) or into blends and then into bottles (if NV). Champagne wines can't be bottled until the January following the harvest. A specified amount of *liqueur de tirage* (yeast and sugar) goes into the bottles for the *prise de mousse* (second fermentation; literally, "capturing

the sparkle"). As the yeasts die and settle, the wine ages on riddling frames, which keep bottles at a 45-degree angle, allowing for easy rotation to coax the lees downward to the bottle's neck. Producers disgorge the lees, replace it with sweet *liqueur de dosage* (a sugar solution), and fit the cork and cage into place. Different styles of Champagne have varying final sweetness levels:

STYLE	SWEETNESS (grams of sugar per liter)
Brut Nature, Pas Dosé, Dosage Zero	0–3
Extra Brut	0–6
Brut	6–12
Extra Dry	12–17
Sec	17–32
Demi-Sec	32–50
Doux (sweet)	50+

ABOVE Grape harvest at Taittinger
RIGHT Taittinger's vaulted Champagne cellar

NV bottles must age for a minimum of 15 months, and vintages 36 months, but most houses cellar their wines for much longer. Many NV wines hit the market after two or three years of aging, and vintage Champagnes regularly see between 4 and 10 years of aging before release.

Many people drink sparkling wines from a Champagne flute, but sommeliers and other wine experts usually drink older, more complex sparklers from a small Bordeaux glass or tulip glass to release the aromatics and flavors. Don't toss your flutes, but use them for younger, less complicated sparkling wines and a small Bordeaux glass for older, more complex wines.

WINEMAKER WISDOM

"I have enjoyed sparkling wines from Tasmania and England a lot; they both offer a similar balance as Champagne, yet they don't achieve the same depth and complexity. I love the diversity and complexity Champagne can offer. It can be a very complex blend or a single-varietal from a single year. The bubbles create a unique sensation combining texture and freshness together, just irresistible! You can never get bored of drinking Champagne."

—Cyril Brun, cellar master, Charles Heidsieck

"What I love about Champagne is the notion of pleasure and sharing. Drinking or tasting Champagne is always a synonym for a special moment."

—Marie Doyard, owner and winemaker, Champagne André Jacquart

"We believe Champagne should be 'created' and not 'manufactured.' We use a handcrafted approach. Our creative process begins in the vineyards, thanks to our winegrower partners, with whom we have had links for many years, some of them for more than 100 years. We use the finest grapes from three main Champagne regions: Côte des Blancs for Chardonnay, Montagne de Reims for Pinot Noir, and Marne Valley for Pinot Meunier. We are one of the last remaining houses that carries out the entire vinification process using wood. All of our cuvées vinify in oak barrels."

—Nicolas Jaeger, winemaker and cellar master, Alfred Gratien

"Champagne is a wine with finesse, elegance, but also character. Champagne is a symbol of joyful moments and shared pleasure around the world and, at the same time, a fine wine produced from a unique terroir."

—Florent Roques-Boizel, CEO and cellar master, Champagne Boizel

CRÉMANTS

Sparkling wine made with the traditional method but outside the designated Champagne region falls into a category called crémants. They consist of 10 specific types, 8 of them within France: Alsace, Bordeaux, Bourgogne, Die, Jura, Limoux, Loire, and Savoie. Two crémant designations fall outside France: Luxembourg and Wallonia (Belgium). Aging rules differ slightly from region to region. Generally speaking, they must age on the lees for at least nine months before release. Most of them, with the exception of Bourgogne, use different grapes, which depend on the specific region. For example, you might find Auxerrois Blanc or Riesling in Crémant d'Alsace; Savagnin in Crémant du Jura, and Chenin Blanc in Crémant de Loire. Many crémant producers follow the same system of maintaining a house style and making NV or vintage wines. Most crémants can age for a few years, but vintage Champagne can age for decades. Crémants also offer quality sparkling wine at lower prices than Champagne.

CRÉMANT D'ALSACE

In northeastern France, near the German border, Alsace specializes in mineral-driven white wines made from Pinot Gris and Riesling. It also makes interesting sparkling wines called Crémant d'Alsace (*kreh-MAHN dahl-ZAHSS*). In addition to the two varieties just mentioned, you can find Auxerrois Blanc, Chardonnay, Pinot Blanc, and Pinot Noir in the mix. The next time you want a quality French sparkler at a reasonable price, look for Crémant d'Alsace.

WINEMAKER WISDOM

"Crémant d'Alsace knows how to remain simple and affordable and brings everyone around the table. A simple, fruity crémant will accompany a platter of salmon and dill toasts or a sampling of sushi. A fuller-bodied crémant better suits a more sophisticated dish, such as creamed chicken or salt-baked salmon."

—*Corinne Perez, head winemaker, Pierre Sparr*

CRÉMANT DE BOURGOGNE

Champagne lovers looking for a less expensive sparkling wine need look no further. Crémant de Bourgogne (*kreh-MAHN duh boor-GO-nyuh*) holds closer to Champagne than many other crémants because it uses the same grapes, Chardonnay and Pinot Noir. Regulations allow other grapes, including Aligoté, Gamay, Pinot Blanc, and Pinot Gris, but many quality producers stick to the classics for their sparklers. Many also age the wines on the lees longer than the minimum nine months. In 2013, Burgundy created two new categories for this wine: Éminent, which requires 24 months' aging on the lees, and Grand Éminent, which requires 36 months. Vintage Crémant de Bourgogne also ages for 36 months before release.

WINEMAKER WISDOM

"We have a very elegant and complex style in Burgundy. We have the chance to use the noble varieties, Pinot Noir and Chardonnay, as the messengers of this terroir without making any compromises on blending and respecting the time needed for long aging, combined with a precise dosage to highlight the quality and precision of the wine. It can be described as classic and posh, particularly with bottles that have had long aging. If the producer brings energy and attention to these wines, it will be a crémant to remember."

—*Alexandre Graffard, owner and winemaker,*
Henri Champliau

LEFT Walled vineyard at Albert Bichot Domaine du Pavilion in Burgundy

CRÉMANT DE LIMOUX

The Limoux (*lee-MOO*) appellation has the highest altitude in France's Languedoc region. It's also the coldest area, and the cold nights help preserve necessary acidity. Allowed grapes in the blend include up to 90 percent Chardonnay and Chenin Blanc, a maximum of 40 percent Pinot Noir, and 20 percent Mauzac. The wines age at least nine months on the lees and an additional two after disgorging before heading to market.

RECOMMENDED WINES: CRÉMANT DE LIMOUX

BARGAIN

Calmel & Joseph Crémant de Limoux Brut

Château Beausoleil Crémant de Limoux Brut

Côté Mas Crémant de Limoux Brut

Domaine Collin Crémant de Limoux Brut

Domaine J. Laurents Crémant de Limoux Brut

Domaine Rosier Crémant de Limoux Brut

Gerard Bertrand Crémant de Limoux Brut

VALUE

Aguila Crémant de Limoux Brut

Antech Crémant de Limoux Cuvée Saint-Laurent Brut

Étienne Fort Crémant de Limoux Brut Nature

Faire La Fête Crémant de Limoux Brut

Michele Capdepon Crémant de Limoux Brut

Roche Lacour Crémant de Limoux Brut

Sieur d'Arques Toques et Clochers Crémant de Limoux Brut

WINEMAKER WISDOM

"I love the tiny bubbles and the freshness as well as Crémant de Limoux's fruitiness and crispness. It's delicious before lunch and dinner but also will taste great with fish for a very refined meal."

—*Bastien Lalauze, winemaker and estate manager,*
Château Martinolles

ABOVE Bottles resting at Côté Mas

RIGHT Underground cellars at Bouvet Ladubay

CRÉMANT DE LOIRE

In export markets, the most common bottles of Crémant de Loire (*kreh-MAHN duh LWAHR*) come from the Vouvray and Saumur appellations. Regulations allow many grape varieties in the blend, including Cabernet Franc, Cabernet Sauvignon, Chardonnay, Chenin Blanc, Grolleau Gris, Grolleau Noir, Orbois, Pineaud'Aunis, and Pinot Noir.

WINEMAKER WISDOM

"I love the celebration and delicacy, the sound of a cork popping announcing both the pleasures of a fine tasting and a moment of friendliness. Crémant de Loire has both in the bottle!"

—*Jérôme Loisy, cellar master, Château de Montfort*

RECOMMENDED WINES: CRÉMANT DE LOIRE

BARGAIN

Amirault Crémant de Loire

Bouvet Ladubay Crémant de Loire

Château de Montfor Crémant de Loire Brut

Domaine Pré Baron Crémant de Loire Brut

Gratien & Meyer Crémant de Loire

Paul Buisse Crémant de Loire Brut

Robert et Marcel de Chanceny Crémant de Loire Brut

VALUE

Abbesse de Loire Crémant de Loire Brut

Château de l'Éperonniere Crémant de Loire

Château Pierre-Bise Crémant de Loire Brut

Château Soucherie Crémant de Loire Brut

Domaine des Baumard Crémant de Loire Carte Turquoise

Domaine Ogereau Brut de Schistes Crémant de Loire Brut

Langlois-Chateau Crémant de Loire Reserve

Marquis de Goulaine Crémant de Loire Brut

GAVI

(GAH-vee)

IN THE GLASS

SMALL BORDEAUX GLASS, PALE STRAW TO MEDIUM STRAW IN COLOR

TASTING PROFILE

ACIDITY

BODY

SWEETNESS

LOW · MEDIUM · HIGH

TASTING NOTES

WHITE FLOWERS · CITRUS · ALMONDS

Wines from Cortese grapes grown in the Gavi DOCG have delicate aromas of white flowers, citrus blossoms, fresh apple, and white peach along with flavors of citrus peel, peach, and a touch of bitter almond in the finish. They feature a strong mineral backbone and generous mouthfeel.

YOU SHOULD KNOW

The people of Gavi maintain that the local Raviolo family invented ravioli here. The original ravioli contained meat, cheese, and escarole, but the Knights of Raviolo and Gavi fiercely guard the exact recipe and proportions. In this region, you can find ravioli served three ways: *a culo nudo* (without any sauce), *al tocco* (with a red meat sauce); or with a simple sauce made from Gavi wine.

FOOD PAIRINGS

PASTA · SAUSAGE · SALAD

Crisp, clean, mineral-driven Cortese di Gavi wines pair with local specialties, such as ravioli, or *testa in cassetta*, a local sausage. The wine also pairs with fire-roasted meats and grilled seafood. Its delicate aromas and moderate acidity also nicely compliment salads, grilled vegetables, sushi, and sashimi.

RECOMMENDED WINES: GAVI

BARGAIN

Banfi Vigne Regali Principessa Gavia Gavi

Beni di Batasiolo Gavi

La Doria San Cristoforo Gavi

Michele Chiarlo Le Marne Gavi →

Picollo Ernesto Gavi

Stafano Massone Masera Gavi

VALUE

Broglia Bruno Gavi

Broglia La Meirana Gavi

Coppo La Rocca Gavi

Fontanafredda Gavi

Marchesi di Barolo Gavi

Pio Cesare Gavi

SPECIAL OCCASION

La Scolca Gavi dei Gavi d'Antan

Villa Sparina Monte Rotondo Gavi

Broglia Vecchia Annata Gavi

RIGHT Gavi harvest at Fontanafredda

NEXT PAGE Fontanafredda vineyards in Gavi, Piedmont

LOCAL LEGEND HAS IT that in 528 CE, Princess Gavia, who loved a commoner, escaped the wrath of King Chlodomer of Orléans, her father, by hiding in the hills of Piedmont. The pope, hearing of this brave young woman's plight, interceded on her behalf. As the fairy tales say, the couple lived happily ever after. The story goes that the locals renamed their village "Gavi" in her honor, and the grape's name derives from her "courteous" manner. The Cortese grape and Gavi region practically have become synonymous. Most consumers, even in the New World, know the wines by the region rather than by grape, so we'll write about Cortese di Gavi by using "Gavi" for short.

In the region's microclimate, wind from the Ligurian Sea meets cold air from the Apennines. After cold winters, the summers run warm, with a long growing season for the grapes. The region has three distinct soils: alluvial deposits and gravels, sandstone, and clay and marine fossils. Grapes grown on each band have different aromatic and flavor characteristics.

Historical documentation suggests that the marchese di Cambiaso first planted Cortese grapevines on his Cen-

turiona and Toledana estates in 1856. Italian law established the DOCG rules for Gavi in 1974, requiring that wines properly labeled "Gavi" or "Cortese di Gavi" must consist entirely of Cortese grapes grown in the specified region in Italy's Piedmont. The DOCG authorizes five styles: Tranquillo (still), Frizzante (fizzy), Spumante (sparkling), Riserva (reserve), and Riserva Spumante Metodo Classico (reserve traditional-method sparkling wines). Most of the wines on the export market are still.

The Piemonte DOC allows Cortese as a single-varietal, and the variety constitutes the wines of Colli Tortonesi and Cortese dell'Alto Monferrato. Cortese also grows in Lake Garda, Brescia, Mantova, and Verona in Italy and in small numbers in California.

WINEMAKER WISDOM

"Gavi shows freshness and mineral complexity, features typical of the Cortese variety that this wine aims to highlight as much as possible. I recommend Gavi to those who drink young and fresh white wines but also look for character. Pinot Grigio lovers would be surprised by the taste of this white wine, a fresh and elegant benchmark for all Italian whites."

—*Luigi Coppo, CEO, Coppo*

MADEIRA

(ma-DAY-ra, ma-DEE-ra)

IN THE GLASS

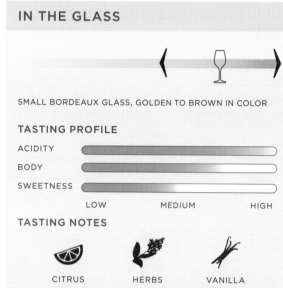

SMALL BORDEAUX GLASS, GOLDEN TO BROWN IN COLOR

TASTING PROFILE

ACIDITY

BODY

SWEETNESS

LOW   MEDIUM   HIGH

TASTING NOTES

CITRUS   HERBS   VANILLA

Sweetness ranges from low to high. Madeiras made from the traditional white varieties have different aroma and flavor profiles, depending on the variety used. Sercial runs driest, with aromas and flavors of walnut, peach, and citrus. Verdelho tastes medium-dry, with aromas and flavors of lemon and herbs. Bual creates medium-sweet wines with flavors of vanilla, cinnamon, and baked goods. Malvasia (Malmsey) tastes sweetest, with aromas and flavors of caramel, toffee, prunes, and vanilla.

YOU SHOULD KNOW

In the rest of the world, barrel rooms usually lie at or below ground level to maintain cool temperatures. Creating Madeira requires heating wines stored in oak barrels by exposing them to the sun and then cooling them. Madeira is the only place in the world where we had to walk *up* three flights of stairs to see a barrel room.

FOOD PAIRINGS

OLIVES   CHEESE   CHOCOLATE

Dry Madeira wines pair with salty nuts, olives, sushi, sashimi, and smoked salmon. Medium-dry wines taste great with goat cheese, Havarti, Gruyère, or Gouda. Serving sweeter Madeira with berries, chocolate, creamy desserts, cakes, or a pungent blue cheese, such as Stilton. When made into a sweet, passito-style wine, Malvasia pairs with hard cheeses, such as Parmigiano-Reggiano and aged Gouda, and sweet, fruity desserts, including apple pie and raspberry tart.

RECOMMENDED WINES: MADEIRA

BARGAIN

NV Barbeito 5 Year Old Malvasia Reserva

NV Barbeito Bual Reserva Velha

VALUE

Blandy's 10 Year Old Malmsey

NV Blandy's 10 Year Old Verdelho

NV H.M. Borges 15 Years Old Malmsey

SPECIAL OCCASION

Blandy's Colheita Harvest Malmsey

Cossart Gordon 10 Year Old Bual →

NV Cossart Gordon 10 Year Old Verdelho Medium Dry

NV Henriques & Henriques 15 Years Old Verdelho

SPLURGE

Blandy's Vintage Bual

Blandy's Vintage Malmsey

Cossart Gordon Solera Bual

D'Oliveiras Verdelho Vintage Madeira

I F YOU WANT A WINE that will age for the next 200 years, buy a bottle of vintage Madeira. We have enjoyed century-old Madeira while visiting this Portuguese island, and it tasted amazingly young and fresh. Serious collectors regularly buy and sell much older bottles. Most well-made, hand-crafted Madeira wines come from four white varieties, in increasing order of sweetness: Sercial, Verdelho, Bual, and Malvasia. The wine will look amber, sometimes even brown, in the glass, but the color comes from the barrel, aging, and oxidation.

On Madeira, vines planted in volcanic soil cover hillside slopes, giving the resulting wines strong minerality. Wine production here dates to the Age of Exploration at the end of the 1400s. The island had strategic importance for European ships before they sailed west or east. The Dutch East India Company, founded in 1602, purchased vast amounts of Madeira wine for sale in the American colonies, Brazil, Britain, and Africa. Madeira makes several appearances in the plays of William Shakespeare. In *Henry IV*, Part 1, John Falstaff sells his soul to the Devil for a glass of Madeira and a cold piece of chicken. In *Richard III*, George Plantagenet, Duke of Clarence, chooses drowning in a butt of Malmsey—meaning a cask of Madeira—after being sentenced to death for attempting to kill his brother King Edward IV. In the 1800s, men and women of the nobility used Madeira rather less dramatically as aftershave or perfume.

To preserve the wines for a long sea voyage, a neutral spirit, usually rum, went into to the barrels. In the hold of the ship, the barrels withstood the rocking motion of the sea, cold nights, and blistering daytime heat. This unique process resulted in a unique style of wine much loved by American colonists. Any wine not sold in the New World made the return voyage to Madeira, where wine merchants discovered that the wines tasted even better than

BELOW Seaside vineyards at Cossart Gordon in Madeira

when they left. They called the wines that had crossed the Atlantic and come back again *vinho da roda* (round-trip wine), which discerning consumers sought.

Ingenious vintners developed a technique to create wines with similar flavor profiles without the expense or risk of sending their barrels to sea. The Canteiro method, still used today, places full barrels in hot attics. There they bear exposure to full sun and cool nighttime sea breezes. This process, used only for more expensive bottles, can take from 20 to 100 years. Estufagem, a less expensive method, entails heating wines in concrete or stainless-steel tanks using heat coils. This process takes about three months.

Some producers use red grapes, especially Tinta Negra, to make low-priced Madeira wines, but traditional Madeira made from the white varieties is well worth the additional cost.

. . . .

WINEMAKER WISDOM

"It's a round wine, if described in a geometric shape, and very rich. Wines of the Bual variety develop bouquets rich in pastry elements, such as candied fruits, brown sugars, and vanilla-like spice. With aging, they sometimes acquire aromas reminiscent of ripe tropical fruits."

—*Francisco Albuquerque, winemaker, Cossart Gordon*

. . . .

RIGHT Madeira barrels in aging attic at Blandy's

MARSALA

(mahr-SAH-lah)

IN THE GLASS

SMALL BORDEAUX GLASS, AMBER TO BROWN IN COLOR

TASTING PROFILE

ACIDITY		
BODY		
SWEETNESS		
	LOW MEDIUM HIGH	

TASTING NOTES

BAKING SPICES   VANILLA   ALMONDS

Sweet Marsala wines smell of roasted hazelnuts, cinnamon, nutmeg, and licorice root. On the palate, they taste sweet, with flavors of vanilla, baking spices, toasted almonds and hazelnuts, and a nutty finish. Dry Marsalas taste crisp, with flavors of toasted nuts.

YOU SHOULD KNOW

In the 1800s and early 1900s, Marsala's enormous popularity sowed the seeds of its downfall. Producers concentrated on quantity rather than quality. Today's younger vintners have reverted to making high-quality Marsala wines.

FOOD PAIRINGS

CHEESE   ALMONDS   PORK

Sweet Marsala tastes great as an aperitif and pairs well with charcuterie plates and such cheeses as Gouda or Havarti. Enjoy it with roasted almonds, oven-roasted meat dishes, such as porchetta, or intense cheeses, such as Stilton and Cabrales blue cheese.

RECOMMENDED WINES: MARSALA

BARGAIN
Baglio Baiata Alagna Marsala
Cantine Pellegrino Marsala Superiore Dry
Florio Vecchioflorio Marsala Superiore
Paolo Lazzaroni & Figli Marsala Fine Ambra Dry

VALUE
Cantine Florio Targa Riserva 1840 Marsala Superiore Semisecco
Cantine Florio Terre Arse Marsala Vergine
Cantine Pellegrino Marsala Vergine Riserva
Curatolo Arini Marsala Superiore Riserva Storica 1988
Martinez Marsala Vergine Riserva

SPECIAL OCCASION
Cantine Intorcia 3 Gen Marsala Superiore Riserva Ambra Dolce
Francesco Intorcia Heritage Vintage Marsala Vergine Secco
Marco de Bartoli Vigna La Miccia 5 Anni Marsala Superiore Oro
Rallo Soleras Vergine Riserva 20 Anni Marsala

SPLURGE
Ingham Whitaker & Co. Marsala Superiore Riserva
Jacona della Motta Ora da Re Marsala
Marco De Bartoli Marsala Superiore Riserva

IN THE EARLY 1770S, British wine merchant John Woodhouse—who specialized in selling Madeira, Port, and Sherry—saw an opportunity to mass-produce oxidated, fortified, sweet wines in Sicily and introduced the technique to Italian winemakers. His contacts in the British Navy allowed him to sell thousands of barrels for their consumption alone, and Marsala quickly gained popularity in English society. Even Thomas Jefferson purchased a barrel in the early 1800s.

Winemakers can use up to 10 different varieties of white grapes, but most use a majority of Grillo, for its high acidity, blended with Inzolia and Catarratto. The wines must contain at least 18 percent alcohol, and the grapes can grow only in Sicily's Trapani province. In 1950, more than 200 producers made Marsala, but they didn't achieve DOC status until 1969. The damage already had been done, however. By 2010, fewer than 10 percent of those 200 producers continued making Marsala wine.

Marsala suffer from the stigma of being mass-produced, sweet, cooking wines, but look past those $5 grocery-store brands. Marsala Vergine, best in class, must age for at least five years in oak barrels. After another five years, they become Vergine Riserva or Vergine Stravecchio. If they make use of the solera method, producers can label their wine Vergine Sol-

eras. If you like your wine sweet, look for "*dolce*" on the label, which means the liquid contains more than 100 grams of residual sugar per liter. For the middle of the road, *semisecco* has 40 to 100 g/L, and *secco* fewer than 40 g/L.

WINEMAKER WISDOM

"Grillo vineyards find their perfect habitat in a unique and wild land made of sun, wind, and sea. Marsala flavors range, depending on the barrel's proximity to the sea and the aging process. The Marsala we are vinifying today will tell the story of our present to future generations, many years from now."

—*Tommaso Maggio, head winemaker, Cantine Florio*

ABOVE Marsala aging in large barrels
RIGHT Tasting Marsala in the barrel room

PROSECCO &
ITALIAN SPARKLING

(pro-SEH-ko)

IN THE GLASS

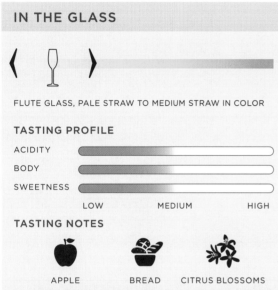

FLUTE GLASS, PALE STRAW TO MEDIUM STRAW IN COLOR

TASTING PROFILE

ACIDITY

BODY

SWEETNESS

LOW   MEDIUM   HIGH

TASTING NOTES

APPLE   BREAD   CITRUS BLOSSOMS

Sweetness ranges from low to high. Italian sparkling wine comes in a variety of styles, from bone dry to fruity sweet, but some aromatic and flavor characteristics run in the family. A fruit note in the bouquet suggests Granny Smith or Winesap apples and citrus blossoms along with a fresh brioche note, especially in sparkling wine that undergoes secondary fermentation in the bottle.

YOU SHOULD KNOW

Just as Champagne comes only from Champagne, the same holds true for Prosecco, Franciacorta, and Trentodoc. They come only from their designated regions in Italy, nowhere else. For sparkling Moscato d'Asti, see the Muscat chapter (page 104).

FOOD PAIRINGS

OYSTERS   CHICKEN   CHOCOLATE

Bone-dry Italian sparkling wines make a great pairing partner with briny, raw oysters, clams, sushi, and sashimi. Prosecco, Franciacorta, or Trentodocs with a little residual sugar pair nicely with white meats such as chicken and pork or grilled salmon and swordfish. Wines with higher residual sugar match with creamy desserts, cakes, fruit tarts, and chocolate.

RECOMMENDED WINES: PROSECCO

BARGAIN

Brilla Prosecco

Caposaldo Prosecco

Gran Passione Prosecco

Mionetto Prosecco Brut Treviso

Tiamo Prosecco di Valdobbiadene

Valdo Marca Oro Brut

Villa Sandi Il Fresco Brut

Zardetto Brut

VALUE

Adami Vigneto Giardino Valdobbiadene

Bisol Cartizze Valdobbiadene →

Bottega Venetian Gold Prosecco

La Marca Luminore Prosecco Superiore

Mionetto Luxury Cartizze

Valdo Cuvée 1926 Prosecco Superiore

IN HIS WRITINGS, Roman scholar Pliny the Elder indicates that Livia, wife of Emperor Augustus, lived a healthy life and reached old age by drinking Pucino wine. Galen, a Greek physician and writer who lived a century later, also told his patients to drink Pucino wine to maintain their health. That wine came from the area we know as Prosecco today.

Prosecco lies in the northeastern corner of Italy, and the Prosecco DOC covers nine provinces in the Friuli–Venezia Giulia and Veneto regions. More than 11,000 growers farm more than 60,000 acres that supply grapes to roughly 1,200 wineries. Sales, measured in *hundreds of millions* of bottles, quadrupled between 2009 and 2019.

By law, Prosecco wines contain at least 85 percent of the Glera grape, but many producers use it exclusively. Regulations allow Verdiso, Perera, and Bianchetta Trevgiana, all white, for the remaining 15 percent, and new rules in 2020 permitted up to 15 percent Pinot Noir for Prosecco rosato (pink). Prosecco Conegliano Valdobbiadene wines can come only from the smaller DOCG areas between the towns of Conegliano and Valdobbiadene.

Producers make the still wine as any other: harvesting, destemming, pressing, and primary fermentation in stainless-steel tanks. Then, following the Charmat-Martinotti method, they transfer it to a pressurized stainless-steel tank, into which they add grape juice, sugar, and yeast. In those massive tanks, the wine undergoes its secondary fermentation for at least 30 days (60 for rosato). When bottled, these spumante (sparkling) wines have more than three bars of pressure and usually more than 11 percent ABV. Prosecco ranges in sweetness from Brut Nature (dry) to Demi-Sec (sweet). About a quarter of production stays in Italy, with the lion's share going to the export market, which prefers the extra-dry style. Britain is the number one importer, followed by the USA, Germany, and France.

WINEMAKER WISDOM

"I love sparkling wines made from Glera because they are easy to drink, light, low in ABV, with an overall balanced aroma. They have delicate floral and fruity notes and are known for their fresh minerality."

—*Gianfranco Zanon, chief winemaker, Valdo*

FRANCIACORTA

Historical documents show that, as far back as the 11th century, winemaking formed an important part of daily life in Lombardy, but the "invention" of Franciacorta (*FRAHN-cha-KOR-tah*) occurred relatively recently. In the late 1950s, young winemaker Franco Ziliani convinced established producer Guido Berlucchi to work together to make a traditional method Italian sparkling wine. They produced their first vintage of Franciacorta in 1961. Its popularity grew fast and steadily. The Italians hold Franciacorta wines, shining stars of the Lombardy region, in high esteem. About 10 percent of the wines make it to the export market.

During the last ice age, ancient glaciers carved the specified production area, delineated by Lake Iseo to the north, the Oglio River to the west, and alpine foothills to the northwest. The name derives from *franchae curtes*, meaning "tax-free." The DOC Consortium formed in 1990 to establish the rules by which the roughly 120 winemakers must abide. Allowed grapes include Chardonnay (more than 80 percent), Pinot Noir, Pinot Bianco, and Erbamat, and secondary fermentation must occur in the bottle. Styles range from very dry Zero Dosage (no added sugar) to sweet Demi-Sec, which can have up to 12 grams of sugar per liter.

TRENTODOC

Archaeologists have confirmed that, by 3000 BCE, people were making wine in what is now the Trentino region. In 1902, Giulio Ferrari began making sparkling Trentino wine, and the Trento DOC received official recognition in 1993. In this high-altitude region, more than 70 percent of the vineyards sit at 1,000 meters (3,300 feet) above sea level, with 20 percent sitting at more than 2,000 meters (6,500 feet). These elegant sparklers must come from within Trento province; contain only Chardonnay, Pinot Bianco, Pinot Noir, or Pinot Meunier grapes; and have their secondary fermentation in the bottle. About three-quarters of the vineyards here grow the two permitted white varieties, and the remaining quarter grow the two reds.

Made white or rosato, Trentodoc (*TREHN-toh-dahk*) wines fall into three categories: Brut, aged on its lees for a minimum of 15 months; Millesimato, lees-aged for at least 24 months; and Riserva, aged on its lees for a minimum of 36 months. Many producers age their wines much longer to add more complexity. Added-sugar sweetness varies from Extra Brut (0–6 g/L) to Demi-Sec (32–50 g/L). The wines export mainly to America, Germany, and Britain.

RECOMMENDED WINES: FRANCIACORTA

VALUE
Berlucchi 61 Brut
Bosio Girolamo Bosio Riserva
Contadi Castaldi Saten
Marchese Antinori Montenisa Cuvée Royale

SPECIAL OCCASION
Bellavista Saten Millesimato
Cavalleri Giovanni Cavalleri
La Marchesine Secolo Novo Riserva Dosage Zero

SPLURGE
Bella Vista Riserva Vittorio Moretti Extra Brut
Ca' del Bosco Cuvée Annamaria Clementi

RECOMMENDED WINES: TRENTODOC

VALUE
Altemasi Brut
Cesarini Sforza Spumante Metodo Classico Brut
Ferrari Brut
Rotari Flavio Riserva Brut

SPECIAL OCCASION
Abate Nero Riserva Cuvée dell'Abate
Endrizzo Masetto Prive Millesimato Riserva
Ferrari Perle Nero
Letrari 976 Riserva del Fondatore
Maso Martis Madame Martis Brut Riserva

SPLURGE
Fratelli Lunelli, Giulio Ferrari, Riserva del Fondatore

WINEMAKER WISDOM

"The Trentino region offers high-quality grapes that give us the opportunity to produce long-aging, classic method wines. Trentodoc wines have good acidity and freshness but are softer and more structured than Champagne."

—*Matteo Ferrari, enotechnician, Maso Martis*

"As a mountain sparkling wine, Trentodoc is unique among Italian sparkling wines: an optimal expression of the rapport between a unique climate and the altitude of the foothills of the Italian Alps. I love the elegance, finesse, harmony, complexity, and longevity that result from this union."

—*Marcello Lunelli, owner, Ferrari Trento*

ABOVE Bottle aging cellar at Cantine Ferrari
RIGHT Resting bottles at Cantine Ferrari

RHÔNE VALLEY

(ROHN VAL-ee)

IN THE GLASS

SMALL BORDEAUX GLASS, MEDIUM STRAW IN COLOR

TASTING PROFILE

	LOW	MEDIUM	HIGH
ACIDITY			
BODY			
SWEETNESS			

TASTING NOTES

PEAR · PEACH · FLOWERS

Appellations vary, but white Rhône Valley wines generally have flavors of pear, peach, orange, and apple with notes of spice, dried herbs, and flowers. Viognier specializes in bold floral aromas and flavors, and Marsanne or Roussanne wines also offer floral touches.

FOOD PAIRINGS

CHICKEN · PORK · SHRIMP

The classic pairing with a white Rhône is roast chicken with herbes de Provence. White Rhônes also taste terrific with pork or veal in cream sauce. Order a white Rhône for a cold shellfish platter and impress your tablemates by pairing Condrieu with fennel bulb, either braised or in a salad.

RECOMMENDED WINES

See regional recommendations throughout the chapter.

YOU SHOULD KNOW

Most Rhône producers label their wines by appellation, not variety. In the northern part, Condrieu exclusively consists of Viognier, while Saint Joseph, Hermitage, and Crozes-Hermitage whites blend Marsanne and Roussanne. Châteauneuf-du-Pape Blanc, in the southern stretch, contains Grenache Blanc, Roussanne, Clairette, and other grapes.

RIGHT Vineyards at Domaine de Beaurenard in the Rhône Valley

GRAPES HAVE GROWN on the Rhône River's precipitous slopes since the Roman era, but modern winemaking here began rather more recently. In 1737, barrels from the region featured the initials "CDR," for Côte du Rhône, but that designation referred to wines only from the right bank of the river. It took almost a century for the left bank to receive official recognition for its fine wine production. The same initials took on expanded meaning to include the *Côtes* du Rhône, plural. The AOC/AOP system didn't exist yet, but the very first AOC gave official status to Châteauneuf-du-Pape in 1936. Côtes du Rhône followed the next year, with revisions in 1996 and 2001.

The Rhône divides into two regions. The Northern Rhône extends from Vienne to Valence, south of Avignon. The main white grapes here include Marsanne, Roussanne, Viognier, and Clairette. In the Southern Rhône, white Châteauneuf-du-Pape comes from Grenache Blanc, Roussanne, Clairette, and other lesser-known grapes. Here, producers make white Côtes du Rhône and Côtes du Rhône Villages wines with Grenache Blanc, Roussanne, Marsanne, Viognier, Clairette, and Bourboulenc. Some Côtes du Rhône Villages appellations, called Rhône Crus, follow stricter regulations.

The white grapes from this region grow around the world and become single-varietal bottlings or blends, usually appearing on wine lists as Rhône-style whites. The best examples hail from warmer, Mediterranean-style climates. The Rhône Rangers, a not-for-profit group, promotes Rhône-variety wines throughout America. The varieties grow throughout California, with excellent expressions coming from the Central Coast, especially Paso Robles. You also can find wonderful versions from Australia, Spain, Morocco, South Africa, and Israel.

NORTHERN RHÔNE APPELLATIONS

CONDRIEU

The name of this appellation comes from a French phrase meaning "corner of the stream," describing the winding 9-mile stretch of the Rhône here. Condrieu allows only the Viognier grape, known for its ample body and exquisite floral aromas. Chalk, flint, and mica soils add mineral notes. Growing on granite hillsides, most vineyards here face south and southeast. Most Condrieu tastes dry, but producers make a sweet style called Condrieu Sélection de Grains Nobles. Condrieu wines feature flavors of peach, apricot, orange, and honeydew melon with bold floral notes that include rose petal, orange blossom, and violet.

RECOMMENDED WINES: CONDRIEU

VALUE

Brotte Condrieu Versant Dore

Paul Jaboulet Aîné Condrieu Les Cassines

Xavier Gerard Condrieu Côte Chatillon

SPECIAL OCCASION

Domaine Chirat Condrieu Les Chays

Ferraton Père & Fils Condrieu Les Mandouls

François Villard Les Terrasses du Palat Condrieu

Jean-Luc Colombo Amour de Dieu Condrieu

Maison Les Alexandrins Condrieu

SPLURGE

Delas Frères Condrieu Clos Boucher

E. Guigal Condrieu La Doriane

Georges Vernay Condrieu Chaillées de l'Enfer

Château-Grillet

One of the smallest appellations in France at just 8.6 acres, Château-Grillet, a single vineyard, lies within the borders of Condrieu on the Rhône's right bank. The appellation allows only Viognier.

SAINT-JOSEPH

Mainly a red-wine region, Saint-Joseph produces a few whites made from Marsanne and Roussanne. King Louis XII of France owned the Clos de Tournon vineyard here. Saint-Joseph can benefit from aging, but the saying goes that you drink Saint-Joseph while waiting for Hermitage and Côtes-Rôtie wines to age to perfection. Expect richly textured wines with flavors of apricot, peach, nectarine, pear, and touches of spice and flowers.

RECOMMENDED WINES: SAINT-JOSEPH

VALUE

Aurelian Chatagnier Saint-Joseph Blanc

Domaine Coursodon Saint-Joseph Blanc Silic

Domaine Garon Saint-Joseph Blanc

Domaine Guy Farge Saint-Joseph Blanc Vania

SPECIAL OCCASION

Domaine Bernard Gripa Saint-Joseph Blanc

Domaine Faury Saint-Joseph Blanc

Domaine Monier Perréol Saint-Joseph Blanc

Yves Cuilleron Saint-Joseph Blanc

SPLURGE

Chapoutier Saint-Joseph Les Granits Blanc

HERMITAGE

This region reportedly received its name from Gaspard de Stérimberg, a wounded crusader who came here in 1224, planted Syrah vines, and received permission from Queen Blanche of France to build a hermitage. (Today, Paul Jaboulet Aîné owns the chapel atop that structure.) Syrah is still the big news in town, but Marsanne and Roussanne proliferate here, constituting almost a third of the area's production. Most white Hermitages contain a majority of Marsanne. Properly stored, they can mature in the bottle for up to 15 years. Expect flavors of pineapple, papaya, pear, and orange blossom with bold mineral notes. A sweet white, Hermitage Vins de Pailles comes from grapes raisinated on straw mats.

RECOMMENDED WINES: HERMITAGE

SPECIAL OCCASION

E. Guigal Hermitage Blanc

Jean-Louis Chaves Selection Hermitage Blanche

Maison Les Alexandrins Hermitage Blanc

Paul Jaboulet Aîné Hermitage Chevalier de Sterimberg

SPLURGE

Bernard Faurie Hermitage Blanc

E. Guigal Hermitage Ex Voto Blanc

Jean-Louis Chaves Hermitage Blanc

M. Chapoutier Ermitage L'Ermite Blanc

Viognier cluster at Domaine Gerin

CROZES-HERMITAGE

This appellation is larger than its neighboring Hermitage AOC, both in size and production. Just 10 percent of the area's wine are whites, from Marsanne and Roussanne. Many of the wines age in oak, so expect a full body, creamy mouthfeel, and flavors of apple and peach with notes of honeysuckle and toasted brioche.

RECOMMENDED WINES: CROZES-HERMITAGE

VALUE

Alain Graillot Crozes-Hermitage Blanc

Cave de Tain Nobles Rives Crozes-Hermitage Blanc

Chapoutier Crozes-Hermitage La Petite Ruche Blanc

J. Vidal-Fleury Crozes-Hermitage Blanc

SPECIAL OCCASION

Dard et Ribo Crozes-Hermitage Blanc

Jean-Baptiste Souillard Crozes-Hermitage Blanc

SAINT-PÉRAY

Many lovers of white wine often overlook this small appellation in favor of better-known wines from Condrieu or Saint-Joseph. But this area has a rich history, and Napoléon Bonaparte claimed that the first wine that ever passed his lips came from Saint-Péray. Wines here can blend Marsanne and Roussanne or contain 100 percent of either aromatic variety. Expect ripe fruit flavors of peach, pear, and grapefruit alongside floral notes, vanilla, and touches of bitter almond. Saint-Péray also produces sparkling wine made with Roussanne and Marsanne.

. . . .

WINEMAKER WISDOM

"Roussanne gives a slight, pleasant bitterness to the wine. Marsanne reinforces the blend, bringing structure but also freshness. You'll find aromas of hawthorn, acacia, and wild plum tree flowers, the species around the vineyards of Saint-Péray."

—*Laure Colombo, winemaker, Jean-Luc Colombo*

. . . .

RECOMMENDED WINES: SAINT-PÉRAY

VALUE

Domaine Guy Farge Grain de Silex Saint-Péray Blanc

Julien Pilon Saint-Péray Blanc

Jean-Luc Colombo Saint-Peray La Belle de Mai →

Paul Jaboulet Aîné Saint-Péray Blanc Les Sauvageres

SPECIAL OCCASION

Domaine Auguste Clape Saint-Péray Blanc

ABOVE Jean-Luc Colombo vineyard in Saint-Péray

LEFT Barrel cellar at Domaine de Beaurenard

SOUTHERN RHÔNE APPELLATIONS

CÔTES DU RHÔNE

Established in 1937, the Côtes du Rhône AOC covers almost 75,000 acres of vines spread across 171 villages, mainly in the southern valley. Allowed white grapes include Grenache Blanc, Roussanne, Marsanne, Viognier, Clairette, and Bourboulenc. The region runs about 125 miles along the Rhône River and boasts wildly diverse terrain, from broad alluvial plains with clay and sandy soils to steep terraced hillsides of granite and limestone. These entry-level whites have flavors of white peach, nectarine, and white flowers, with many offering strong minerality.

Côtes du Rhône Villages

More specific than the Côtes du Rhône AOC, Côtes du Rhône Villages encompasses 95 villages near Avignon and Orange that can add their names to wine labels. Many of the villages aren't well known, though, so the Côtes du Rhône Villages appellation can help familiarize consumers with the wines made here. Just 3 percent of Côtes du Rhône Villages are white. Permitted grapes include Grenache Blanc, Roussanne, Marsanne, Viognier, Clairette, and Bourboulenc, creating wines with flavors of apple, peach, and citrus with floral and spice notes, strong minerality, and good body.

RECOMMENDED WINES: CÔTES DU RHÔNE

BARGAIN

Chapoutier Belleruche Côtes du Rhône Blanc

Famille Perrin Côtes du Rhône Blanc Réserve

Ferraton Père & Fils Côtes du Rhône Samorëns

Jean-Luc Colombo Les Abeilles Côtes du Rhône

Vignerons de l'Enclave La Resistance Made with Organic Grapes Côtes du Rhône

VALUE

Domaine Charvin Côtes du Rhône Blanc

Domaine de la Solitude Côtes du Rhône Blanc

E. Guigal Côtes du Rhône Blanc

JV Fleury Côtes du Rhône Blanc

SPECIAL OCCASION

Château de Saint Cosme Côtes du Rhône Blanc Le Poste

Domaine Gramenon Côtes du Rhône Blanc La Vie On Y Est

Jean-Paul, Corinne & Loïc Jamet Côtes du Rhône Blanc

RECOMMENDED WINES: CÔTES DU RHÔNE VILLAGES

BARGAIN

Domaine du Couron Côtes du Rhône Villages Blanc

Domaine Galuval Le Coq Volant Côtes du Rhône Villages Blanc

Domaine Pélaquié Côtes du Rhône Villages Laudun Blanc

Piaugier Côtes du Rhône Villages Blanc

Pierre Henri Morel Côtes du Rhône Villages Laudun Blanc

VALUE

Domaine Chaume-Arnaud La Cadène Blanc

Malmont Côtes du Rhône Villages Seguret Blanc

Rotem & Mounir Saouma Inopia Blanc Côtes du Rhône Villages

RIGHT Tree-lined entrance to Famille Perrin vineyard

CHÂTEAUNEUF-DU-PAPE

In French, this appellation means "the pope's new castle," referring to the Western Schism, in which the head of the Catholic Church moved from Rome to Avignon in the Middle Ages. In the early 1930s, Baron Pierre Le Roy, owner of several wine estates, advocated for the creation of the AOC system. Châteauneuf-du-Pape received the very first AOC designation in 1936. Only 5 percent of wines made here are white, but collectors and drinkers covet them. In addition to the usual grapes, Picpoul, Picardan, Grenache Gris, and Clairette Rose may join the blend as well. Richly textured white Châteauneuf-du-Pape has luscious flavors of pineapple, apple, lemon, orange, honeysuckle, and spice. The wines age well, and producers here also make a small amount of sweet vin de paille.

RECOMMENDED WINES: CHÂTEAUNEUF-DU-PAPE

VALUE

Brotte Châteauneuf-du-Pape Blanc Hautes de Barville

Domaine Chante Cigale Châteauneuf-du-Pape Blanc

Domaine des Pères de l'Église Le Calice de Saint Pierre Châteauneuf-du-Pape Blanc

Famille Perrin Châteauneuf-du-Pape Les Sinards Blanc

SPECIAL OCCASION

Château de la Font du Loup Châteauneuf-du-Pape Blanc

Château La Nerthe Châteauneuf-du-Pape Blanc

Domaine de Beaurenard Châteauneuf-du-Pape Blanc →

Domaine de la Solitude Châteauneuf-du-Pape Blanc

Domaine du Vieux Lazeret Châteauneuf-du-Pape Blanc

Famille Perrin Châteauneuf-du-Pape Blanc

SPLURGE

Château de Beaucastel Châteauneuf-du-Pape Blanc

Domaine de la Janasse Châteauneuf-du-Pape Blanc

Domaine Pegau Cuvée A Tempo Blanc Châteauneuf-du-Pape

LIRAC

On the right bank of the Rhône, nine miles northwest of Avignon, Lirac received AOC status in 1947. It's one of the southernmost crus in the Rhône Valley and one of the least familiar to international drinkers. Around 10 percent of the wine made here is white, mainly Grenache Blanc, with small amounts of Roussanne, Marsanne, Viognier, Clairette, and Bourboulenc. This low-profile appellation offers lots of good examples in the value range.

VACQUEYRAS

Written evidence documents viticulture in Vacqueyras in 1414, but the area didn't receive official status until 1990. Just 5 percent of this appellation's wines are white. Grown in sandy clay alluvial soils, Grenache Blanc and other varieties benefit from the cooling mistral wind that preserves their acidity while they ripen under the hot summer sun. You'll taste tropical fruit flavors with soft floral notes and touches of minerality.

RECOMMENDED WINES: LIRAC

VALUE

Château Mont-Redon Lirac Blanc
Domaine de la Mordorée Lirac Blanc La Reine des Bois
Domaine Lafond Roc-Épine Lirac Blanc
Famille Brechet Plateau des Chênes Lirac Blanc

RECOMMENDED WINES: VACQUEYRAS

VALUE

Domaine de la Verde Vacqueyras Odyssey Blanc
Domaine La Fourmone Vacqueyras Blanc Le Fleurantine
Montirius Vacqueyras Blanc
Tardieu-Laurent Vacqueyras Blanc

SPECIAL OCCASION

Domaine Le Clos des Cazaux Vacqueyras Blanc Vieilles Vignes
Domaine Le Sang des Cailloux Vacqueyras Un Sang Blanc

BELOW Grape press at Jean-Luc Colombo

MUSCAT DE BEAUMES DE VENISE

We saved the sweet stuff for last. In the foothills of the Dentelles de Montmirail, vineyards face south and southeast, producing grapes with high sugar content. Producers here make this wine from Muscat Blanc à Petit Grains (locally called Muscat de Frontignan), fortifying it with 190-proof spirit to stop fermentation and preserve sweetness. Muscat de Beaumes de Venise ranges in color from golden to amber and features luscious flavors of honeycomb, dried apricot, canned peaches, orange marmalade, jasmine, and honeysuckle. Enjoy a demi (375 milliliters) with blue cheese, foie gras, or custard-based desserts.

RECOMMENDED WINES: MUSCAT DE BEAUMES DE VENISE

BARGAIN

Domaine de Durban Muscat de Beaumes de Venise

J Vidal-Fleury Muscat de Beaumes de Venise

Trésor de Clocher Muscat de Beaumes de Venise

VALUE

Château du Trignon Muscat de Beaumes de Venise

Domaine de Fenouillet Muscat de Beaumes de Venise

Famille Perrin Muscat de Beaumes de Venise

Pesquié Muscat de Beaumes de Venise

ABOVE Horsepower at Domaine de Beaurenard

RIOJA

(ree-OH-hah)

IN THE GLASS

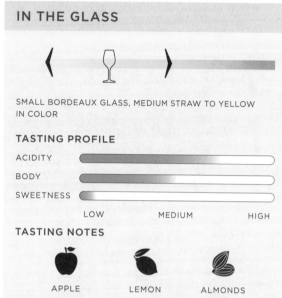

SMALL BORDEAUX GLASS, MEDIUM STRAW TO YELLOW IN COLOR

TASTING PROFILE

ACIDITY

BODY

SWEETNESS

LOW   MEDIUM   HIGH

TASTING NOTES

APPLE   LEMON   ALMONDS

Fresh and zesty versions have aromas of green apple and citrus with notes of flint or river rock. Flavors include Granny Smith apple, lemon zest, oyster shell, and a hint of white flowers. Barrel-aged Rioja Blanco features aromas of apple, hazelnut, almond, and toffee, with flavors of green pear, toasted nuts, and caramel.

YOU SHOULD KNOW

White Rioja comes in two styles. The traditional version contains mostly or entirely Viura (Macabeo in the Rioja region) and ages in barrels, creating full-bodied wines not unlike buttery, oaky Chardonnays. The more recent trend produces easy-drinking wines with a high percentage of Tempranillo Blanco and other varieties, with little or no time in oak, that taste light and fresh.

RIGHT Grapes on the vine at Viña Bujanda in Rioja

FOOD PAIRINGS

HAM   EGGS   SHRIMP

The time-honored pairing for aged Rioja Blanco is jamón ibérico, cured Spanish ham, hand cut into razor-thin slices. It also tastes terrific with tortilla española or any egg dish. Try it with mushroom risotto, too. Fresh, unoaked bottlings make a wonderful match with asparagus risotto or light seafood dishes, such as shrimp scampi or flounder Française.

RECOMMENDED WINES: RIOJA

BARGAIN

Bodegas Faustino Art Collection Viura-Chardonnay
Bodegas Lacort Mariano J. Lacort
Marqués de Cáceres Antea →
Viña Cerrada Rioja Blanco

VALUE

Baron de Ley Tres Viñas Blanco Reserva
Bodegas Franco-Españolas Bórdon Viña Sole
  Selección Tête de Cuvée
CVNE Monopole Clássico
Muga Rioja Blanco
Sierra Cantabria Organza

SPECIAL OCCASION

Muga Flor de Muga Blanco
Remírez de Ganuza Blanco Reserva
Viña Leizaola Paloma de Sacramento

SPLURGE

Marqués de Murrietta Castillo Ygay Blanco Reserva Especial
R. López de Heredia Viña Tondonia Reserva Blanco

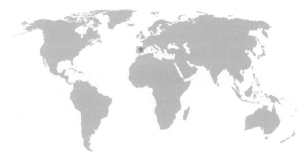

Y ES, SPAIN'S RIOJA REGION produces white wines as well as red. Until the end of the 1800s, more vineyards here grew white varieties than red. At the end of that century, when the phylloxera blight hit France, winemakers from Bordeaux headed south to ply their trade, shifting the area's focus from white to red for the export market. Their plan worked—until the vine-killing louse migrated to Spain and destroyed the vineyards here, too, upending the region's winemaking capability for decades.

Today, 10 percent of Rioja's vineyards grow white varieties. Not only that, but they produce two totally different styles: lusty, round, barrel-aged bottles; and fresh, unoaked expressions to quench your warm-weather wine cravings. For years, growers here planted Viura (called Macabeo elsewhere in the kingdom), Garnacha Blanca,

and Malvasía Riojana. Producers made classic white Rioja from the three permitted varieties, aging it in barrels and bottles prior to release, creating deliciously oxidized wines that taste perfect with Manchego cheese and other Spanish delicacies. Backed by brilliant acidity, these golden, full-bodied wines have notes of lemon curd, honeycomb, baking spices, and toasted nuts. The best-known producers of this style include López de Heredia, Marqués de Murrieta, and Bodegas Franco-Españolas.

Modern tastes have drifted away from this style of winemaking, however. As a result, Rioja now offers lighter, fresher bottlings. The game-changer came in the 1970s when Marqués de Cáceres introduced fermentation in stainless-steel tanks, aided by cold-fermentation practices to maintain freshness and acidity. In 2007, the DOCa allowed six other white grapes in the blend: Chardonnay, Maturana Blanca, Sauvignon Blanc, Tempranillo Blanco, Turruntés, and Verdejo, each bringing specific characteristics to the mix. Allowing for maximum flexibility in the future, Rioja Blanco may contain any of these grapes exclusively or blend them.

The prolific Viura vine grows a lot of grapes, but in winemaking quantity rarely equates with quality. The more grapes on the vine, the less flavorful the finished

wine. With proper yield control, it offers fresh, floral aromas to the wine along with flavors of apple, pear, and citrus. Tempranillo Blanco evolved from the red Tempranillo grape first discovered in Rioja in 1988. It adds acidity and soft herbal notes to the blend. Malvasía Riojana has low acidity and oxidizes easily, an important characteristic for the traditionalist style. In modern versions, it imparts body and weight to the finished wine. Garnacha Blanca brings body, alcohol, and citrus notes, while Maturana Blanca also brings alcohol, acidity and notes of tropical fruit. Turruntés—not to be confused with Torrentés from Argentina—has high acidity and flavors of apple and bitter almond. Verdejo adds notes of chopped herbs and cut grass and also brings zesty acidity to the party.

Fewer than 15 months old, Rioja Blanco *joven* (young) may ferment and age completely in stainless steel or have light touches of oak, with no minimum oak requirements. Crianza wines must age for at least 12 months, 6 of those in oak. Reserva and Gran Reserva wines also require a minimum of six months in oak. Producers can't release Reservas until two years after harvest and Gran Reservas four years. That additional bottle aging of Crianza, Reserva, and Gran Reserva wines allows the oak tannins to soften, making the wines ready to drink on release. But many winemakers create their Rioja Blanco Reserva and Gran Reserva to age further. Under proper storage conditions, they will last for at least 10 years and beyond.

WINEMAKER WISDOM

"Rioja Blanco balances the difficult combination of the freshness and fruitiness with the complexity and elegance of the fermentation and aging in new oak barrels. Ideal for drinking by the glass as a starter or with a small appetizer on a terrace."

—*Isaac Muga, technical director, Bodegas Muga*

RIGHT Barrel-making at Bodegas Muga in Haro, Rioja

SAUTERNES

(so-TURN)

IN THE GLASS

SMALL BORDEAUX GLASS, GOLDEN TO AMBER IN COLOR

TASTING PROFILE

	LOW	MEDIUM	HIGH
ACIDITY			
BODY			
SWEETNESS			

TASTING NOTES

CITRUS   BAKING SPICES   HONEY

Sauternes and Barsac wines have enticing aromas of orange, grapefruit blossoms, and exotic fruits, such as lychee and mango. On the palate, they taste smooth, with flavors of candied fruits including orange peel, caramelized pineapple, and baking spices. The full-bodied mouthfeel offers gorgeous sensations of beeswax and acacia honey in its sweet finish.

YOU SHOULD KNOW

Most Sauternes are sold in demi bottles (375 milliliters). This half size takes into account their expense and that people normally drink smaller amounts of sweet wines.

FOOD PAIRINGS

CHOCOLATE   CHEESE   APPLE PIE

Try the classic pairings of chocolate desserts, pungent cheeses, fruit pies and tarts, or crème brûlée. If you're feeling more adventurous, go for pasta with roasted butternut squash, curried pumpkin soup, and Korean fried chicken.

RECOMMENDED WINES: SAUTERNES

VALUE
Château Bastor-Lamontagne Les Remparts de Bastor-Lamontagne
Chateau Rieussec Les Carmes de Rieussec

SPECIAL OCCASION
Chateau Bechereau
Château Coutet
Château Mauras
Château Raymond-Lafon
Chateau Sigalas Rabaud

SPLURGE
Chateau Caillou
Château Climens
Château Coutet Cuvée Madame
Château d'Yquem
Chateau de Fargues, Sauternes, France
Château Rieussec

RIGHT Harvesting noble-rot grapes and barrels at Château Rieussec

THOMAS JEFFERSON enjoyed Château d'Yquem, one of Sauternes's most famous sweet-wine producers, so much that he ordered 250 bottles for himself and even more for George Washington. Experts agree that their wines have amazing aging potential. In 1996, wine critic Robert Parker scored an 1811 vintage with 100 points. In 2018, we had the good fortune to taste a 1983 vintage with managing director Pierre Lurton. After 35 years, the wine showed amazing balance and youthfulness, with many more years left to enjoy. A bottle of 1929 Château Rieussec that we enjoyed in 2010 had turned almost mahogany in color, but the wine still tasted young, with alluring flavors of toasted hazelnut, acacia honey, yellow peach, and canned apricots with bold acidity in the finish.

Southeast of the city of Bordeaux, within the Graves region and Sauternes subregion, Château d'Yquem has one of the largest footprints with 126 hectares (half a square mile). Most of its neighbors have much smaller vineyards, many with fewer than 5 hectares (12 acres) each. The appellations of Sauternes and Barsac represent only 2 percent of the total vine acreage of Bordeaux, but local residents quickly note that they garnered 27 Grand Crus, almost a third of the total number, in the famous 1855 classification of Bordeaux producers.

Sauternes and Barsac owe their success to temperature differences and proximity to the Garonne and Ciron Rivers. At their confluence, morning fog and mist encourage the development of *Botrytis cinerea*, the "noble rot" needed to concentrate the grapes' sugars. Botrytis doesn't form uniformly, however, so winemakers must pass through their vineyards multiple times to pick only the most botrytized grapes each time. This labor-intensive process makes the finished wines more expensive than other styles of sweet wines.

French regulations authorize the use of Sémillon, Sauvignon Blanc, and Muscadelle for these special wines. The finished wines generally contain 80 percent Sémillon, 20 percent Sauvignon Blanc, and very little Muscadelle. But small amounts of that last grape impart powerful aromas. Almost a third of the wines go to the export market, and Barsac winemakers can label their wines Barsac or Sauternes.

WINEMAKER WISDOM

"I love their richness and their incredible aromatic complexity, their finely tuned balance between freshness and candied, as well as their elegance."

—Olivier Trégoat, technical director
DBR (Lafite), Château Rieussec

ABOVE Smelling botrytized grapes at Château Rieussec
RIGHT Ivy-covered walls at Château Rieussec

SHERRY

(SHEH-ree)

IN THE GLASS

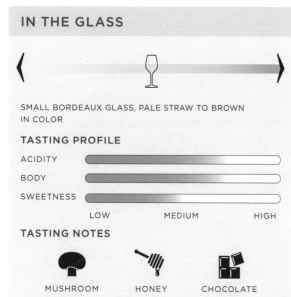

SMALL BORDEAUX GLASS, PALE STRAW TO BROWN IN COLOR

TASTING PROFILE

	LOW	MEDIUM	HIGH
ACIDITY			
BODY			
SWEETNESS			

TASTING NOTES

MUSHROOM   HONEY   CHOCOLATE

Sweetness ranges from low to high. Palomino Fino can produce dry wines with enticing savory and saline characteristics. The same grapes also produce semi-sweet or sweet wines, depending on the amount and timing of the added spirit. The finished wines have aromas and flavors ranging from mushroom, forest floor, and truffle to candied fruit, honey, raisins, figs, and dark chocolate. Sherry has a style for every wine lover.

YOU SHOULD KNOW

"Sherry" is the phonetic transcription of the English pronunciation of "Xeres," an old spelling of the city today called Jerez de la Frontera, the center of Sherry production. The various styles include Amontillado, from the Montilla region; Cream, describing mouthfeel, like crémants, no dairy inside; Dulce (sweet); Fino (fine); Manzanilla, meaning "chamomile," describing the color and bouquet; Oloroso (scented); and Pedro Ximénez, the name of the grape variety.

FOOD PAIRINGS

ALMONDS   CHEESE   CHOCOLATE

Fino and Manzanilla (dry) go beautifully with briny seafood, such as shrimp or langoustines, and salty almonds or olives. Palo Cortoado, Amontillado, and Oloroso pair well with prosciutto or jamón ibérico and hard cheeses, such as Manchego, Parmesan, or aged Gouda. Cream Sherry drinks well with creamy desserts, such as flan, crème brûlée, apple pie, and vanilla ice cream. Enjoy Pedro Ximénez with brownies, chocolate cake, and rum raisin ice cream.

RECOMMENDED WINES: SHERRY

BARGAIN

Emilio Hidalgo Pedro Ximénez

Napoleon Amontillado

Williams & Humbert Pando Fino

VALUE

Bodegas Yuste Aurora Oloroso

Don Zoilo Amontillado →

González Byass Néctar Pedro Ximénez

Lustau Almacenista Manzanilla Pasada de Sanlúcar

SPECIAL OCCASION

Bodegas Alonso Velo Flor Manzanilla Sherry

Bodegas Ximénez Spinola Pedro Ximénez Sherry

Fernando de Castilla Antique Oloroso Sherry

SPLURGE

A.R. Valdespino Toneles Moscatel Sherry

González Byass Anada Palo Cortado Sherry

Osborne Venerable VORS 30 Year Old Pedro Ximénez Sherry

Raisinated grapes at González-Byass

T O APPRECIATE AUTHENTIC Sherry culture, picture the Feria de Jerez, the local horse fair. A cadre of well-dressed riders balance short-stemmed glasses of Sherry while astride immaculately groomed steeds. The locals go all out with traditional clothing, decorated horse-drawn carriages, and impromptu displays of horsemanship. If you visit, don't miss the Royal Andalusian School of Equestrian Art here, which stages equally memorable performances.

More than 3,000 years ago, the Phoenicians planted grapevines here in the area they named Xera. During the Muslim conquest of Spain, the city took the Arabic-inflected name of Sherish, as confirmed on an 1150 map commissioned by King Roger II of Sicily and designed by cartographer Muhammad al-Idrisi. To avoid confusion among all the different spellings and pronunciations, many wine producers conveniently label their bottles with all three words: Jerez, Xerez, Sherry.

For centuries, producers made Sherry from three predominant grape varieties: Palomino Fino, Pedro Ximénez, and Moscatel de Alejandría (Muscat of Alexandria). In 2021, six additional white varieties legally entered the mix: Mantúo Castellano, Mantúo de Pilas, Vejeriego, Perruno, Cañocazo, and Beba. Recognized in Spain in 1933, Jerez-Xérès-Sherry and Manzanilla Sanlúcar de Barrameda—separate DOs—share the same vineyards and regulatory council. All Sherries released prior to 2021 must come from the Sherry Triangle, the area among three towns: Jerez de la Frontera, Sanlúcar de Barrameda, and Puerto de Santa Maria. Wines made in the Manzanilla style and labeled "Manzanilla Sanlúcar de Barrameda" can come only from a small area around that one place. The Fino style can come only from Jerez de la Frontera and Puerto de Santa Maria. Also in 2021, the DO ruled

that the Fino and Manzanilla styles don't require fortification, but they must have a minimum 15 percent ABV and can come from a larger geographical area, effectively ending the exclusivity of the Sherry Triangle. Some older wines, aged more than 20 or 30 years, now can carry the certification of Vino de Jerez con Vejez Calificada, which applies to the Amontillado, Oloroso, Palo Cortado, and Pedro Ximénez styles.

Not all Sherry tastes sweet! Fino and Manzanilla, not fortified or lightly fortified (15 to 17 percent ABV), drink dry. They come from Palomino Fino grapes and age under a layer of yeast called *flor* or *veil de flor*. The flavors and aromas of Fino and Manzanilla include raw almonds and chamomile flowers. The finish tends to taste a bit astringent, with flavors of bitter almonds and bitter herbs. Amontillado also starts under a veil of flor. Then the flor disappears, and the wine oxidizes, creating flavors such as toasted hazelnut, dried herbs, and tobacco leaf.

Oloroso also comes from Palomino Fino grapes, but it doesn't age under flor. Instead, winemakers add a neutral spirit to raise the alcohol level to 17 percent. This wine also oxidizes during the aging process. It generally appears amber to brown and has aromas and flavors of wood, nuts, and even mushrooms or truffles.

For Palo Cortado wines, producers fortifying the grape must to 15 percent ABV and allow the wine to age under flor until the cellarmaster adds a second dose of alcohol (to more than 17 percent) that will allow the wine to oxidize and age perfectly. Flavors include toasted hazelnuts, mushrooms, and truffles.

Dulce Sherries include Pale Cream, Medium, and Cream subcategories. Pale Cream Sherry ages under flor, but a dose of "rectified" must goes into to the wine to lessen the dryness. The resulting wine somehow tastes both dry *and* sweet at the same time. Medium Sherry has a bit more sugar added, and Cream Sherry blends oxidized Oloroso and sweet Pedro Ximénez, resulting in a caramel-colored wine with more than 115 grams of sugar per liter.

Naturally sweet Sherries generally come from the Pedro Ximénez or Muscat grape varieties. To increase their sugar content, the grapes raisinate in the sun. During fermentation, the addition of a neutral spirit halts fermentation, resulting in a delightfully sweet, thick wine. Sweet wines made from Muscat grapes have aromas of white flowers, jasmine, and orange blossoms and flavors of honeysuckle and raisins. Sweet wines made from Pedro Ximénez have aromas of figs, dates, and raisins and flavors of candied fruit, toasted coffee beans, dark chocolate, and licorice. Pedro Ximénez Sherry can look mahogany in color, but remember that it comes from white grapes!

It's rare to see a single-vintage Sherry. Most producers use the solera system. They stack numerous tiers of barrels in gigantic wooden warehouses, some as large as a football field. Wine for bottling comes from the lowest barrels, but no more than 25 percent leaves the lowest barrel at a given time. Wine from the tier above fills that lowest barrel, the tier above that one goes into the second lowest, and so on. Many Sherry bottles display the creation date of the solera, which can stretch many decades in the past. The bottle will contain only a small portion of wine from that date, but it still will taste delicious.

WINEMAKER WISDOM

"I love the unique and artisanal vinification process via the solera method, which concentrates the PX variety's aromas and flavors. PX grows mostly in the south of Spain and Portugal (Jerez, Montilla, Huelva, Málaga, Valencia, Algarve); some South American countries, Peru and Chile, for making Pisco; and in Barossa in Australia. The whitish soil that we have in Jerez transmits a saline character that balances the sensation of sweetness."

—*Antonio Flores, winemaker, González Byass*

"What I really love about these incredible wines is their capacity and potential as storytellers. Each style has a tale of its own to share with us, a unique connection to its family history within the solera. Also, they magnificently showcase a path of endless diversity: multiple aromas, colors, and flavors."

—*Sergio Martínez Verdugo, cellar master and winemaker,*
House of Lustau

"As a winemaker, few wines have aroused as much passion as the wines of Jerez, as much for their variety as for their particular methods of production. Working with Palomino grapes is amazing, given that from this single variety it's possible to produce different wines, each very special: Manzanilla, Fino, Amontillado, Palo Cortado, Oloroso, and all of them adapt for all occasions! Sherry is excellent as an aperitif but also when paired with any type of dish. There isn't a meal you can't enjoy it with."

—*Paola Medina, technical director and winemaker,*
Bodegas Williams & Humbert

LEFT Sherry barrel repair at Bodegas Lustau

SOAVE

(SWAH-vay)

IN THE GLASS

SMALL BORDEAUX GLASS, PALE STRAW TO MEDIUM STRAW IN COLOR

TASTING PROFILE

ACIDITY

BODY

SWEETNESS

LOW   MEDIUM   HIGH

TASTING NOTES

MELON   PEACH   SALT

Young Soaves have fruity aromas of cantaloupe, white peach, and dried Mediterranean herbs. Flavors include melon, citrus, and a touch of wet river rock and salinity. Aged Soaves can have notes of jammy fruit, including orange marmalade, candied lemon peel, and fennel bulb.

YOU SHOULD KNOW

Veterans returning from the Italian theater of World War II helped popularize this wine made mostly from the Garganega variety. In the 1970s, Soave was the best-selling Italian DOC wine in the American market. Frank Sinatra reportedly loved it, which undoubtedly added to its allure. In the USA, Soave's momentum continued until the 1990s, when sales of Italian Pinot Grigio overtook it.

FOOD PAIRINGS

CLAMS

SUSHI

PORK

Enjoy young Soave with briny seafood dishes containing shrimp and clams. It also pairs perfectly with sushi, sashimi, and pasta with a light seafood marinara or cream sauce. Aged Soave matches nicely with oven-roasted white meats, such as veal or pork, with braised vegetables on the side. Open a bottle with a cremini mushroom or white truffle risotto.

RECOMMENDED WINES: SOAVE

BARGAIN
Bertani Sereole Soave
Fattori Danieli Soave
Inama Vin Soave
Pieropan Soave Classico →
Rocca Sveva Soave Classico
Suavia Soave Classico

VALUE
Bertani Soave Vintage Edition
Cantine Pra Cru Monte Grande Soave Classico
Fasoli Gino San Zeno Soave
Fattori Motto Piane Soave
Inama Carbonare Soave Classico
Pieropan La Rocca Soave Classico

RIGHT Pieropan winery in Soave

I N THE VENETO, the Soave region lies between Verona and Venice. By 300 BCE, the Roman Republic controlled the area, deeming it a colony in 89 BCE and a city in 49 BCE. Romans here drank *vino retico*, made with raisinated grapes. Emperor Augustus reportedly loved the style, as did imperial poet Virgil. St. Zeno, eighth bishop of Verona, often appears depicted with grapevines surrounding him. Some historians hypothesize that the name Soave comes from the Svevi, a Germanic tribe that lived in the hills of northern Italy. Other researchers attribute the name to Dante Alighieri, author of the *Divine Comedy*, in the early 1300s.

Whatever its source, Soave had the distinction, in 1931, of becoming the first wine in the kingdom of Italy recognized as a "prestigious fine wine" by royal decree. The government of King Victor Emmanuel III set the area's boundaries, and in 1968, the region received DOC status. The DOC consists of 17,000 acres tended by more than 3,000 winegrowers, many of them managing fewer than five acres of vines. Recent research has delineated 33 Additional Geographical Units (UGAs), which produce exceptional wine, much like France's Cru system.

The Soave Consortium has created three classifications for the wines. They all must come from at least 70 percent Garganega, with the balance consisting of Chardonnay, Trebbiano di Soave (Verdicchio), and fewer than 5 percent of other local varieties. Most of the best Soave wines exclusively contain Garganega. Soave DOC wines come from grapes grown on the region's flat plains. Those for Soave Classico grow on the hills between the towns of Soave and Monteforte d'Alpone. The grapes used for Soave Colli Scaligeri DOC grow on the horseshoe-shaped hills surrounding Soave Classico area. Recent changes allow the production of Soave Spumante, a sparkling wine, and Recioto di Soave, a sweet one. Around 80 percent of production today goes to more than 70 countries, making it one of Italy's most exported still white wines.

While taking in the medieval villages, churches, and castles, visitors to the area should partake in the local cuisine and of course the wine. The Italian tourism agency just established a new Volcanic Wine Park between Verona and Vicenza provinces. Don't expect a theme park, though. The beautiful park embraces the best of experiential tourism centered on food, wine, and culture, including horseback riding and hiking. If you time your trip just right, you can participate in the harvest and pick grapes with locals.

LEFT Tractor between the rows at Pieropan
BELOW Large wooden tanks at Bertani in Soave

WINEMAKER WISDOM

"The best Garganega wines often reflect its unique terroir (mostly volcanic), controlled yields in the vineyard, and a deft hand in cellar, balancing the sometimes-subtle blossom and peach aromas of the variety with oak, lees, and stirring. The best Soaves show moderate acidity, moderate palate weight, and wonderful perfume and notes of flintiness."

—*Andrea Lonardi, COO, Bertani*

"My family has been producing Soave wine since the early 1900s. We were one of the first wineries to label a wine Soave and the first in Soave to convert to organic farming. Our Soave is expressive of place and reflects the heritage of my family."

—*Dario Pieropan, winemaker, Pieropan*

TOKAJI

(toh-KAI)

IN THE GLASS

AROMATIC GLASS, GOLDEN TO AMBER IN COLOR

TASTING PROFILE

ACIDITY		
BODY		
SWEETNESS		
LOW	MEDIUM	HIGH

TASTING NOTES

PEACH   APRICOT   PINEAPPLE

Tokaji wines have a reputation for sweetness, but they also must have high acidity. Tokaji Aszú wines have aromas of honeysuckle, jasmine, beeswax, and yellow peach. Flavors include canned apricots, caramelized pineapple, tropical fruits, and white flowers. They have a silky-smooth mouthfeel and a pleasant burst of acidity in the finish.

YOU SHOULD KNOW

At the confluence of the Bodrog and Tisza rivers, Tokaj experiences heavy fog that blankets the vines in the mornings during the growing season. This high humidity fosters the *Botrytis cinerea*, or noble rot, required to make highly prized Tokaji Aszú wines. The region is Tokaj, and the wines are Tokaji (formerly spelled "Tokay" in English).

RIGHT The stages of botrytized grapes at Tokaj-Oremus

FOOD PAIRINGS

CHEESE   PASTA   SQUASH

Sweet Tokaji Aszú pairs perfectly with pungent cheeses, including Stilton, Éppoises, and aged Brie. Enjoy it with pasta in a Gorgonzola cheese sauce and dishes made from pumpkin or butternut squash. For the ultimate pairing, have it with roasted pumpkin gnocchi or butternut squash risotto in a blue cheese sauce.

RECOMMENDED WINES: TOKAJI

VALUE

Erzsébet Pince Édes Szamorodni

Tokaji-Hétszőlő Domain Imperial Édes Szamorodni

Tokaji-Hétszőlő Late Harvest

SPECIAL OCCASION

Béres Tokaji Aszú 5 Puttonyos

Château Dereszla Tokaji Aszú 5 Puttonyos

Disznókő Tokaji Aszú 5 Puttonyos

Oremus Tokaji Aszú 5 Puttonyos

Royal Tokaji Aszú Red Label 5 Puttonyos

Samuel Tinon Tokaji Aszú 5 Puttonyos

Tokaji-Hétzőlő Aszú 5 Puttonyos

SPLURGE

Disznókő Eszencia

Dobogó Tokaji Aszú 6 Puttonyos

Oremus Eszencia

Patricius Tokaji Aszú Bendecz Dúló 6 Puttonyos

Royal Tokaji Eszencia

Royal Tokaji Szt Tamás First Growth Single Vineyard 6 Puttonyos

Sauska Essencia

THE TOKAJ WINE REGION in Hungary famous produces Tokaji Aszú, made from the botrytized fruit of six varieties: Furmint, Hárslevelű, Kabar (Hárslevelű + Bouvier), Kövérszőlő, Muscat Blanc, Zéta (Furmint + Bouvier). Producers also use these grapes to make dry wines—Furmint, for example (page 64)—which have gained popularity in today's lower-carb, lower-sugar culture. For this chapter, we'll concentrate just on the sweet, ethereal, otherworldly Tokaji Aszu wines.

For centuries, aristocrats, poets, artists, and commoners have favored this delectable, sweet wine. King Louis XIV of France legendarily called it "the king of wines, the wine of kings." Voltaire waxed poetically about it, and Empress Maria Theresa of the Holy Roman Empire gifted it to Pope Benedict XIV, prompting him to declare: "Blessed be the land that has produced you. Blessed be the woman that sent you. Blessed be I who drink you." With that kind of pedigree, you *know* Tokaji Aszú wines taste heavenly.

During Communist rule in Hungary, winemakers couldn't produce Tokaji Aszú wines—except perhaps for high-ranking party leaders—because the labor-intensive process requires many steps. Simple dry wines made from hearty grapes fit the Communist work ethic better. But thankfully the skillset of making Tokaji Aszú survived.

In September, winemakers picked healthy grapes for the base wine, allowing other grapes to stay on the vine to develop botrytis. After they shriveled and the sugars concentrated, growers undertook the second picking in late October or November. They harvested them into large baskets, called *puttonyos*, and added them to the base wine. The number of baskets of sweet, infected grapes determined the sweetness level of the finished wine, with six puttonyos the upper limit.

Today the process looks exactly the same, but vintners make only late-harvest Szamorodni (around 100 grams of sugar per liter, comparatively dry for the style), five puttonyos Tokaji Aszú (120+ g/L), six puttonyos Tokaji Aszú (150+ g/L), and Eszencia. The last of these contains wine (up to a whopping 450 g/L) from only botrytized grapes, making it very rare and expensive liquid. Szamorodni, made from whole bunches of healthy and botrytized grapes, must age at least 12 months, 6 months in oak barrels. They generally cost less than their five or six puttonyos siblings, making them an excellent introduction to the style. Tokaji Aszu must age for at least 24 months, 18 in barrels. Some producers age their wines much longer.

Tokaji Aszú wines drinks deliciously sweet, but good winemakers know that high acidity must balance the sweetness to avoid a finished wine that tastes cloying or syrupy. Tokaji Aszú wine pair amazingly with lots of foods, so don't relegate them to the dessert category. They do complement ice cream, crème caramel, crème brûlée, and cakes, true, but they also go beautifully with savory foods, such as duck, goose, and wild boar pâté. Many chefs are pairing them with spicy foods, including Thai curries and Peking duck.

WINEMAKER WISDOM

"Six different grape varieties grow in the Tokaj wine region, and each gives different flavors to the final blends. Let's consider the three most important grapes in Tokaji. Furmint, which has the largest planted area, is always the 'spine' that adds structure; aromatic Muscat gives the perfume; and Hárslevelű provides a great honeyed elegance."

—*Zoltán Kovács, winery director, Royal Tokaji*

BELOW Candlelit cellars at Royal Tokaji
RIGHT Resting bottles at Royal Tokaji

VINHO VERDE

(VEEN-yo VEHR-day)

IN THE GLASS

SMALL BORDEAUX GLASS, PALE STRAW TO MEDIUM STRAW IN COLOR

TASTING PROFILE

ACIDITY

BODY

SWEETNESS

LOW   MEDIUM   HIGH

TASTING NOTES

CITRUS   PEACH   APRICOT

Vinhos Verdes vary, based on the blend, but they all share a common lightness and freshness with a strong mineral backbone. Alvarinho versions feature citrus, white peach, and apricot flavors, while blends including Arinto and Trajadura have aromas of white flowers and flavors of tropical fruits.

YOU SHOULD KNOW

Some Vinho Verde wines drink a little fizzy. Many wine experts consider this additional carbon dioxide a fault, but winemakers embrace this characteristic. Some even add a bit of CO_2 to their bottles. Vinhos Verdes don't qualify as sparkling or semisparkling, though, because the carbon dioxide generally gives them less than one bar of pressure.

FOOD PAIRINGS

SUSHI   SALAD   CHEESE

Vinho Verde wines pair wonderfully with seafood of all types, whether raw, steamed, grilled, or baked. They also taste great with fresh vegetables and salads. Oak-aged versions go well with dishes made with cream sauces, including oven-baked fish or meats. For a decadent treat, have it with lobster macaroni and cheese.

RECOMMENDED WINES

BARGAIN

Anselmo Mendes Contacto Alvarinho

João Portugal Ramos Vinho Alvarinho

João Portugal Ramos Vinho Loureiro

Quinta da Lixa Reserva Alvarinho

Quinta de Santiago Alvarinho

Valados de Melgaço Alvarinho

VALUE

Adega de Monção Alvarinho Deu La Deu Reserva

Anselmo Mendes Curtimenta Alvarinho

Quinta de Santiago e Miro Sou Alvarinho

Quinta de Soalheiro Alvarinho Granit

Quinta de Soalheiro Primeiras Vinhas Alvarinho

Vale do Ares Vinha da Coutada

SPECIAL OCCASION

Anselmo Mendes Parcela Unica Alvarinho

RIGHT Harvest at Quinta da Lixa

CULTIVATION OF WINE GRAPES in what is now Portugal dates to the Roman era, and our old friend Pliny the Elder may have written the first surviving mention of Vinho Verde some 2,000 years ago. Over the centuries, religious orders made wine for sacramental purposes and local consumption. The name of the region derives from its dense green (*verde*) foliage, not the color of the wine (*vinho* in Portuguese). One of Europe's oldest wine regions, it received official recognition in 1908 as Entre-Douro-e-Minho, meaning between the Douro and Minho rivers, two of its natural borders. The Vinho Verde DOC formed in 1984.

One of the greenest parts of Portugal, Vinho Verde receives more than 120 inches of rain per year. That dampness challenges growers and winemakers alike, who constantly must ward off fungus, molds, and mildews. To counteract these problems, growers use a high pergola system to trellis their vines, minimizing grape contact with the wet ground and allowing ample air circulation to keep the grapes dry and free of disease.

The area has nine subregions: Amarante, Ave, Baião, Basto, Cávado, Lima, Monção and Malgaço, Paiva, and Sousa. Allowed grapes includ: Alvarinho, Arinto, Avesso, Azal, Loureiro, and Trajadura. Monção and Malgaço grow significant amounts of Alvarinho. Ave, Cavado, and Lima specialize in Loureiro. The Avesso grape grows primarily in Amarante and Baiao. Often bottled as a single-varietal, Alvarinho gives aromas and flavors of lychee, kumquat, orange, purple flowers, and roasted nuts. When blended, Arinto adds more citrus characteristics, while Azal adds stone-fruit flavors. Loureiro adds secondary notes, such as eucalyptus and mint, and Trajadura imparts pear and peach aromas and flavors. Another 13 grape varieties can go into a Vinho Verde blend, but most producers use only the well-established grapes noted earlier.

Most Vinhos Verdes ferment and age in stainless steel, but some winemakers use oak barrels to add complexity to their wines, which have fuller body and aromas of vanilla and toasted nuts from the barrels. Portuguese chefs love pairing Vinho Verde wines made in this style with the complex flavors of their food.

WINEMAKER WISDOM

"I love their complexity, versatility, and capacity for aging. I've tried some from Rías Baixas in Spain, some from Australia and California. Portuguese Alvarinhos have great acidity and freshness, great fruit expression, and enormous minerality."

—*Carlos Teixeira, chief winemaker and export manager, Quinta da Lixa*

"I love the expression of the grape variety: full-bodied, complex, and persistent in the mouth; balanced and harmonious. Monção and Melgaço bottles have a higher alcohol content, higher natural acidity, and more minerality."

—*José Gonçalves, winemaker, Valados de Melgaço*

"It's a very versatile wine with subtle aromas and intense flavor, elegant and fresh. It has a high capacity to evolve both in vat and bottle. In young wines, the aromas of white flowers, tropical fruits, stone fruits, and citrus dominate. In wines with some age, minerality, roasted nuts, and honeycomb aromas dominate. It can serve as an aperitif, enjoyed with friends or colleagues after a hard day at work, or it can accompany a main course or dessert."

—*Fernando Moura, winemaker, Adega de Monção*

ABOVE Tank room at Adega de Monção
RIGHT Alvarinho vineyard at Soalheiro in Portugal

ACKNOWLEDGMENTS

It's been said that "it takes a village," and putting a book together is no exception. Once we came up with the idea for *White Wine*, we had to find an editor to champion the book at a worthy publisher. That done, we settled on our grapes and styles, requested samples, tasted wines, and chose what we wanted to include in the book. After all that, we had to sit down and write it, which ultimately was the easy part. Once we delivered the manuscript, it became the work of the "village," which encompasses the wonderful team at W. W. Norton & Company, Inc. That's where the magic happens: sculpting our words, editing the text, choosing the photographs, laying out the book, and getting the final product to the printer, all on deadline the whole time.

For *all* the above-mentioned steps, we thank the following people for their help in putting together the book that you're holding in your hands: James Jayo, Ann Treistman, Maya Goldfarb, Danita Mapes, Jess Murphy, Iris Bass, Roxanne Palmer, Krister Swartz, Allison Chi, Chrissy Kurpeski, Ken Hansen, Devon Zahn, Devorah Backman, and Rhina Garcia.

We also thank, in no particular order: Christina

Historic cellar at Bisol Prosecco

An, Catherine Cutier, Caroline Shook McDaniel, Alison Hahn, Bethany Burke, Lydia Richards, Joe Janish, Elizabeth Gillespie, Jennica Ossi, Jillian Lepore, Jack Horn, Marilyn Krieger, Rosyln Russel, Anna Miranda, Jean-Charles Boisset, Rob Mondavi Jr., Rebecca Hopkins, Sydnie Hamby, Kimberly Utterback, Suzie Kukaj, Jane Shapiro, Gino Colangelo, Juliana Colangelo, Stefan Sigurdsson, Amanda Torres, Erin Healy, Leah Isenberg, Michelle Erland, Rebecca Johnson, Katie Canfield, Ella Winje, David Greenberg, Nicole Drummer, Kristen Reitzell, Erin Inman, Janet Mick, Taylor Camp, Claire Gibbs, Jayleen Murray, Cathy Lischak, Katie Calhoun, Michelle Keene, Tinka Bush, Katherine Jarvis, Kiernan Spencer, Monique Belden, Anika Crone, Madison Gann, Sam Vicklund, Laine Boswell, Nora Feeley, Alexandra O'Gorman, Julie Ann Kodmur, Morgan Perry, Victor Ordóñez, Ernest Tolj, Ivana Tolj, Mirena Bagur, Ana Vieira-Soares, Dominique Rizzi, Angela Slade, and, last but certainly not least, Karen Brennan.

We *think* that we included everyone, but if you don't see your name here, please know that we couldn't have done this without your contribution.

Thank you, all, from the bottom of our hearts and the bottom of our wine glasses!

CREDITS

Adega Cooperativa e Regional de Monção, CRL: xii, 250 (top, bottom right)

Albert Bichot USA: 182, 198

Amavi Cellars: 159, 161 (top left)

Azienda Agricola Pelilia: 84, 85 (top)

BODEGAS GODELIA S.L.: 77

BODEGAS GODEVAL: 76

Bodegas Marqués de Cáceres: 4, 156 (middle left), 228

Bodegas Muga S.L.: 231

Bodegas Naia: 171 (bottom)

Boisset Collection: 23 (bottom left), 25, 26 (top left, top right), 43 (top right, bottom left), 152 (right), 192, 199 (right)

Calabria Family Wine Group: 109 (bottom left)

Cantina Valle Isarco for Alto Adige Wines: 92

Castello di Monsanto: 33, 34

Caves Du Paradis Olivier Roten SA: 51

Cool Hand Vineyards LLC dba Jonata, The Hilt, The Paring: 151 (bottom left)

COPPO SRL: 109 (top left, top right), 203 (top)

Craggy Range Vineyards Ltd.: 36, 267

Domaine J. de Villebois: 145

Domaine Keyser Kohll: 15

Domaine Thibault Liger-Belair: 7 (bottom)

Domaine Zind-Humbrecht: 69, 70, 71 (left), 134 (left)

Donnafugata Srl Società Agricola: 18, 19, 88, 89

Dr. Konstantin Frank Winery: 42, 137 (right)

Dreyfus Ashby & Co.: 2, 21, 24, 27, 28, 46, 48, 49, 50, 51, 156 (bottom left)

Dusted Valley: 124 (top right)

E & J Gallo Winery: 121 (top left, top right), 123, 148, 240, 241, 242, 243 (middle right)

El Enemigo: 160, 161 (bottom left)

Elena Walch for Alto Adige Wines: 93 (bottom), 112, 114

Emilio Lustau S.A.: 238, 239 (bottom left)

Estate Argyros: 11, 12, 13

Europvin USA: 65, 66, 67, 245, 247

FAKINWINES: 100 (top), 101 (top)

Far Niente Family of Wineries and Vineyards: 41 (bottom left)

Folio Fine Wine Partners for Oberon Wines: 40, 41

Gerard van Honthorst: *The happy Violinist*, 1624 © Museo Nacional Thyssen-Bornemisza, Madrid: x

González Byass USA: 237, 239 (top left)

Hamilton Russell: 37 (top)

Hermann J. Wiemer Vineyard: 74

Henri Champliau: 199 (left)

iStock/AnnWorthy: 173 (bottom left)

iStock/barmalini: 213, 271

iStock/Cesare Ferrari: 261

iStock/darioracane: 207 (top)

iStock/Digoarpi: 80

iStock/georgeclerk: 254

iStock/inkoly (maps): 3, 7, 9, 11, 15, 17, 19, 21, 53, 59, 63, 65, 69, 77, 79, 83, 87, 91, 93, 95, 99, 103, 105, 111, 117, 127, 129, 143, 159, 163, 167, 171, 173, 175, 179, 185, 187, 193, 203, 207, 211, 215, 219, 229, 233, 237, 241, 245, 249

iStock/JimmyLung: 79

iStock/Marco_de_Benedictis: 215 (bottom)

iStock/MarkSwallow: 162

iStock/pacaypalla: 212

iStock/petrenkod: 258

iStock/Silberkorn: T-Title

iStock/13threephotography: 81

Jackson Family Wines: 31 (bottom left), 37 (bottom), 39 (top), 41 (top right), 44, 45, 46 (top right, bottom left), 141 (top left), 151 (top right), 180

Jorge Ordoñez Málaga, S.L.: 105, 107, 108

Joseph Drouhin: 21, 24, 27, 28, 46 (top left)

Kobrand Corporation: 9, 23 (top left, bottom right), 30 (top right), 40, 43 (top left), 100 (middle), 164 (top right, bottom right), 194, 195, 201, 202

Lakewood Vineyards, Inc.: 124 (bottom right), 125

Lapostolle: viii, 155 (bottom), 157 (top left)

Laurenz Five Fine Wine GMBH: 91 (top)

Lieb Cellars: 111, 113, 115 (top left)

Livio Felluga SRL: 63, 121 (middle left)

Loimer: 91 (bottom)

Long Shadows Vintners: 138, 139

Luigi Bosca: 156 (top right)

Macari Vineyards: 150, 153 (top left)

WHITE WINE CHECKLIST

- ❏ Albariño
- ❏ Aligoté
- ❏ Arneis
- ❏ Assyrtiko
- ❏ Auxerrois Blanc
- ❏ Bordeaux
- ❏ Carricante
- ❏ Catarratto
- ❏ Cava
- ❏ Champagne
- ❏ Chardonnay
- ❏ Chasselas
- ❏ Chenin Blanc
- ❏ Crémant d'Alsace
- ❏ Crémant de Bourgogne
- ❏ Crémant de Limoux
- ❏ Crémant de Loire
- ❏ Fiano
- ❏ Franciacorta
- ❏ Friulano
- ❏ Furmint
- ❏ Gavi
- ❏ Gewürztraminer
- ❏ Godello
- ❏ Graševina
- ❏ Greco
- ❏ Grillo
- ❏ Grüner Veltliner

- ❏ Kerner
- ❏ Macabeo
- ❏ Madeira
- ❏ Malvasia
- ❏ Marsala
- ❏ Müller-Thurgau
- ❏ Muscat
- ❏ Pinot Blanc
- ❏ Pinot Grigio
- ❏ Pošip
- ❏ Prosecco
- ❏ Rhône Valley
- ❏ Riesling
- ❏ Rioja
- ❏ Sauternes
- ❏ Sauvignon Blanc
- ❏ Sémillon
- ❏ Sherry
- ❏ Soave
- ❏ Tokaji
- ❏ Torrontés
- ❏ Trebbiano
- ❏ Trentodoc
- ❏ Verdejo
- ❏ Verdicchio
- ❏ Vermentino
- ❏ Vinho Verde
- ❏ Viognier

FOOD PAIRING INDEX

ALMONDS: Marsala, 210; Sherry, 236

APPLE PIE: Malvasia, 98; Madeira, 98; Sauternes, 232; Sherry, 236

ASPARAGUS: Aligoté, 7; Friulano, 62; Grüner Veltliner, 90; Rioja, 228; Verdejo, 170; Viognier, 179

AVOCADO: Cava, 188; Verdejo, 170

BEEF: Arneis, 8; Torrontés, 164

BOUILLABAISSE: Catarratto, 18

CHEESE: Arneis, 8; Auxerrois Blanc, 14; Bordeaux, 184; Chardonnay, 31, 32, 47; Chasselas, 48; Chenin Blanc, 52; Fendant, 51; Furmint, 64; Greco, 82; Grillo, 86; Grüner Veltliner, 90; Kerner, 92; Madeira, 206; Malvasia, 98; Marsala, 210; Moscato d'Asti, 109; Muscat de Beaumes de Venise, 227; Pinot Blanc, 110; Pinot Grigio, 116; Pošip, 126; Quarts de Chaume, 54; Rioja, 229; Sauternes, 232; Sauvignon Blanc, 142; Sémillon, 158; Sherry, 236; Tokaji, 244; Torrontés, 162; Trebbiano, 166; Verdejo, 170; Viognier, 178; Vinho Verde, 248

CHICKEN: Aligoté, 6; Cava, 188; Champagne, 192; Chardonnay, 41; Chenin Blanc, 52; Crémant, 192, 197; Fiano, 58; Furmint, 64, 67; Gewürztraminer, 68; Godello, 76; Graševina, 78; Grillo, 86; Grüner Veltliner, 90; Kerner, 92; Macabeo, 94, 96; Malvasia, 98; Pinot Blanc, 110, 115; Pinot Grigio, 116;

Prosecco, 214; Rhône Valley, 218; Sauternes, 213; Torrontés, 162

CHOCOLATE: Madeira, 206; Prosecco, 214; Sauternes, 232; Sherry, 236

CRAB: Aligoté, 6; Cava, 188; Macabeo, 94; Vermentino, 174

CURRY: Assyrtiko, 10; Furmint, 64; Gewürztraminer, 68; Macabeo, 94; Muscat, 104, 109; Riesling, 128; Torrontés, 162; Vermentino, 174; Viognier, 178

EGGS: Cava, 188; Chardonnay, 20, 33; Müller-Thurgau, 102; Pinot Blanc, 110; Rioja, 228

FISH: Albariño, 2; Aligoté, 6; Auxerrois Blanc, 14; Carricante, 16; Catarratto, 18; Champagne, 192; Chardonnay, 32, 33; Crémants, 192, 200; Fiano, 58; Greco, 82; Grillo, 87; Kerner, 93; Macabeo, 94; Malvasia, 98; Müller-Thurgau, 102; Pinot Blanc, 115; Prosecco, 214; Torrontés, 162, 164; Trebbiano, 166; Vermentino, 174; Vinho Verde, 248

FRENCH FRIES: Aligoté, 6

HAM: Friulano, 62; Gewürztraminer, 68; Moscato d'Asti, 109; Rioja, 228

ICE CREAM: Bonnezeaux, 54; Graševina, 78; Muscat, 104; Sémillon, 158; Sherry, 236; Tokaji, 246

LOBSTER: Alsace, 71; Verdicchio, 172; Vinho Verde, 248

OCTOPUS: Albariño, 2; Auxerrois Blanc, 14; Carricante, 16; Pošip, 126

OLIVES: Friulano, 62; Madeira, 206; Sherry, 236

OYSTERS: Albariño, 2; Aligoté, 6; Assyrtiko, 10; Cava, 188; Champagne, 192; Chardonnay, 20; Crémant, 192; Godello, 76; Macabeo, 94, 95; Moscato d'Asti, 109; Pinot Blanc, 113; Pošip, 126; Prosecco, 214; Rieslings, 132; Verdicchio, 172

PAD THAI: Catarratto, 18; Furmint, 64

PAELLA: Albariño, 2; Cava, 188; Chardonnay, 32; Pošip, 126

PASTA: Albariño, 2; Chardonnay, 20, 33; Fiano, 58; Gavi, 202; Greco, 82; Grillo, 88; Kerner, 92; Pinot Grigio, 116; Sauternes, 232; Sémillon, 158; Soave, 240; Tokaji, 244; Trebbiano, 166

POPCORN: Champagne, 192; Crémant, 192

PORK: Bonnezeaux, 54; Cava, 188; Chenin Blanc, 52; Furmint, 64, 67; Gewürztraminer, 68; Godello, 76; Graševina, 78; Macabeo, 94, 96; Marsala, 210; Prosecco, 214; Rhône Valley, 218; Riesling, 128; Soave, 240

SALAD: Auxerrois Blanc, 15; Bordeaux, 184; Chasselas, 48; Fiano, 58; Gavi, 202; Greco, 82; Grillo, 86, 87; Macabeo, 94; Müller-Thurgau, 102; Muscat, 104; Pinot Blanc, 113; Pošip, 126; Rhône Valley, 218; Riesling, 128; Sauvignon Blanc, 142;

SALAD (*CONTINUED*): Torrontés, 162; Verdejo, 170; Verdicchio, 172; Vinho Verde, 248

SALAMI: Arneis, 8

SAUSAGE: Gavi, 202; Viognier, 178

SHRIMP: Aligoté, 6; Chardonnay, 31; Chasselas, 48; Fiano, 58; Furmint, 64; Godello, 76; Graševina, 78; Grillo, 86; Müller-Thurgau, 102; Pinot Grigio, 116; Rhône Valley, 218; Rioja, 228; Sauvignon Blanc, 142; Sherry, 236; Soave, 240; Verdicchio, 172

SQUASH: Sauternes, 232; Tokaji, 240

SUSHI: Albariño, 2; Assyrtiko, 10; Bordeaux, 184; Carricante, 16; Cava, 188; Champagne, 192; Crémants, 192, 197; Gavi, 202; Godello, 76; Greco, 82; Macabeo, 94; Madeira, 206; Müller-Thurgau, 103; Pinot Grigio, 116; Prosecco, 214; Riesling, 128; Sauvignon Blanc, 142; Soave, 240; Torrontés, 164; Verdicchio, 172; Vinho Verde, 248

VEAL: Arneis, 8; Bordeaux, 184; Chasselas, 48; Graševina, 78; Rhône Valley, 218; Soave, 240

RIGHT Planeta winery in Menfi, Sicily

GENERAL INDEX

Entrance to Quinta de Lixa in Portugal